# GLASGOW
## COLOUR ATLAS

Geographia, part of John Bartholomew & Son Ltd, was founded over 70 years ago. This Geographia street atlas is one of a new and up to the minute series of street atlases, each one of which has clear easy to read mapping and a full street index based on the National Grid.

The greatest care and attention is taken when we produce these atlases but, if you find any errors, we would be grateful to hear from you.

If you wish to send us information relating to this product, please contact:-

The Chief Cartographer,
Geographia Limited,
105/107 Bath Road,
Cheltenham,
Glos. GL53 7LE

Information Section © Geographia Ltd, 1989

Published by Geographia, an imprint of John Bartholomew & Son Ltd, Duncan Street,
Edinburgh EH9 1TA.

Great care has been taken through this book to be accurate but the publishers cannot accept responsibility for any errors which appear, or their consequences.

Printed in Great Britain by Bartholomew & Son Ltd.
RAN B/N2927

# Glasgow Colour Atlas
# Contents

# Legend

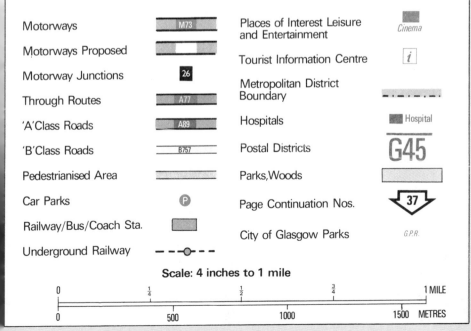

| | | | |
|---|---|---|---|
| Motorways | M73 | Places of Interest Leisure and Entertainment | Cinema |
| Motorways Proposed | | Tourist Information Centre | i |
| Motorway Junctions | 26 | Metropolitan District Boundary | |
| Through Routes | A77 | | |
| 'A'Class Roads | A89 | Hospitals | Hospital |
| 'B'Class Roads | B757 | Postal Districts | G45 |
| Pedestrianised Area | | Parks,Woods | |
| Car Parks | P | Page Continuation Nos. | 37 |
| Railway/Bus/Coach Sta. | | City of Glasgow Parks | G.P.R. |
| Underground Railway | --○-- | | |

**Scale: 4 inches to 1 mile**

| 0 | ¼ | ½ | ¾ | 1 MILE |
|---|---|---|---|---|
| 0 | 500 | 1000 | 1500 | METRES |

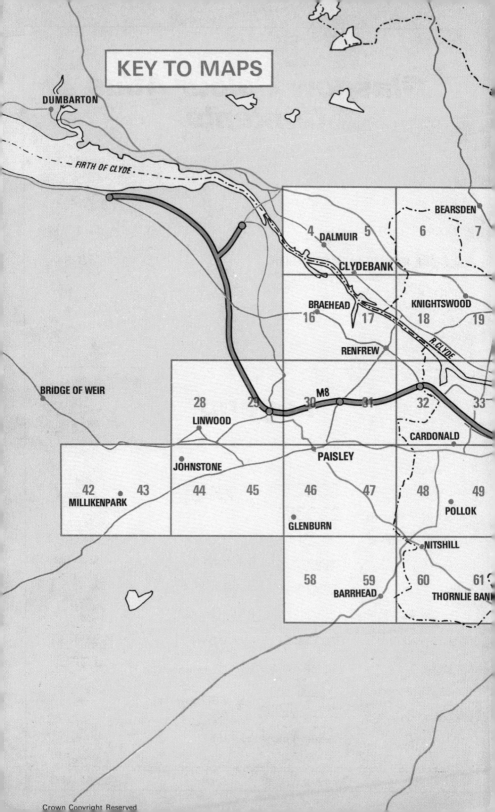

# KEY TO MAPS

DUMBARTON

FIRTH OF CLYDE

BEARSDEN

4 DALMUIR 5 6 7

CLYDEBANK

BRAEHEAD KNIGHTSWOOD
16 17 18 19

RENFREW R.CLYDE

BRIDGE OF WEIR

M8
28 29 30 31 32 33

LINWOOD CARDONALD

PAISLEY

JOHNSTONE

42 43 44 45 46 47 48 49
MILLIKENPARK POLLOK

GLENBURN

NITSHILL

58 59 60 61
BARRHEAD THORNLIE BAN

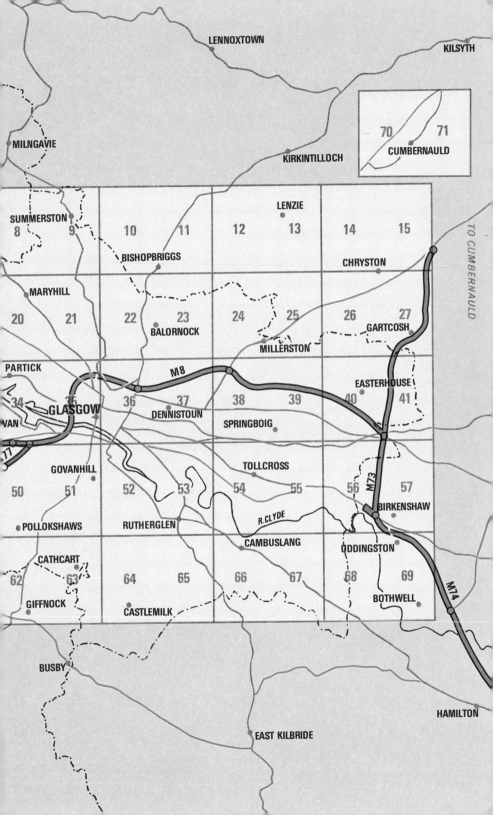

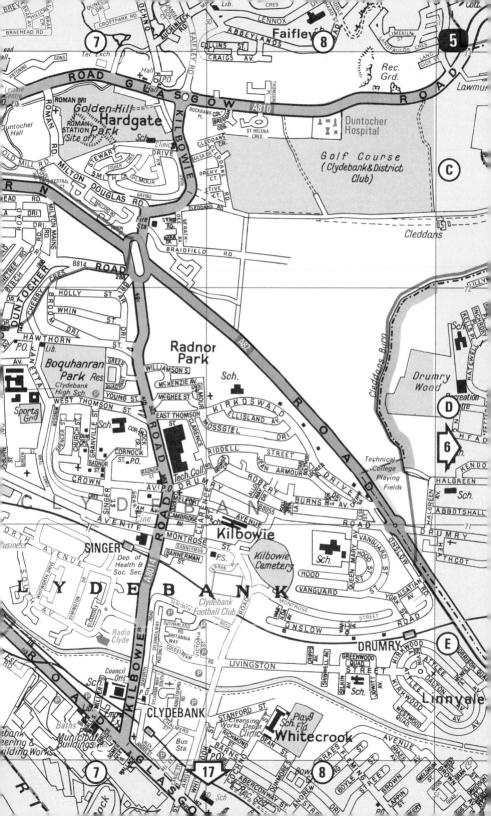

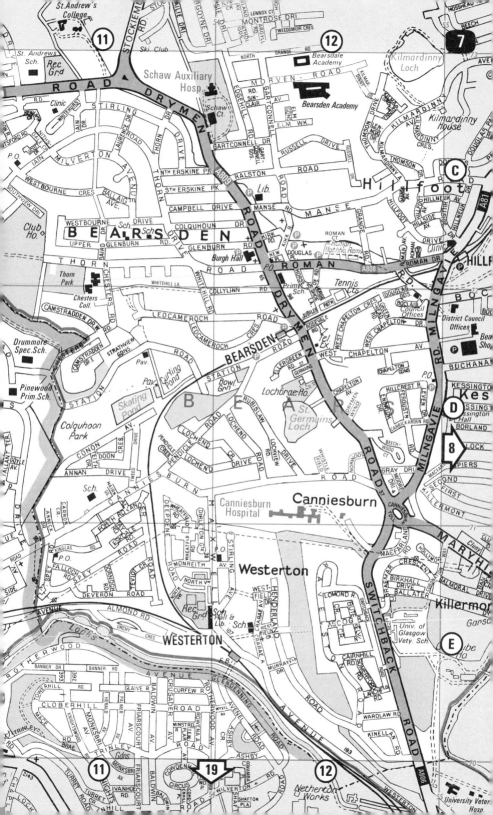

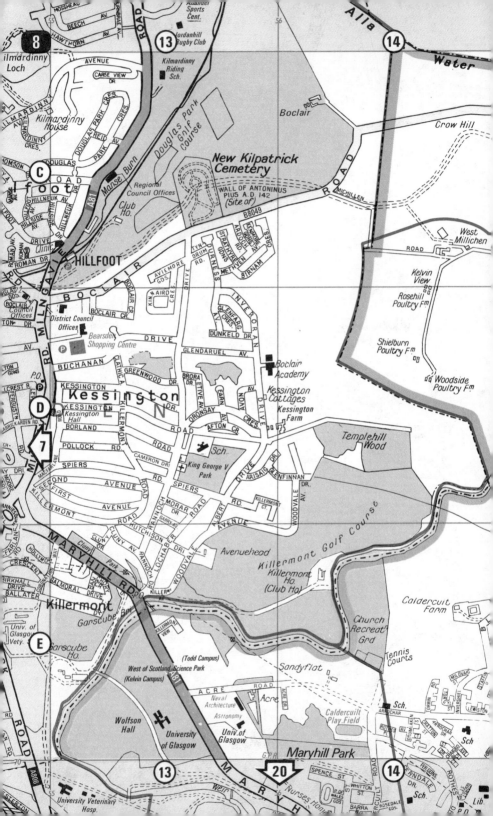

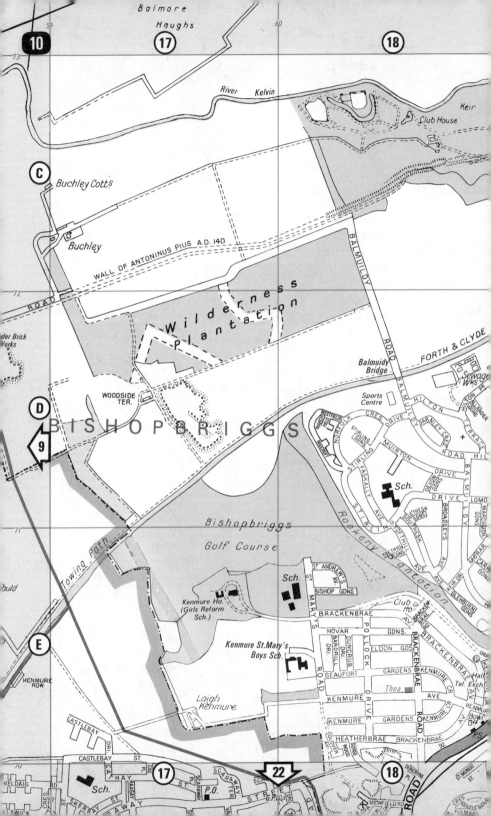

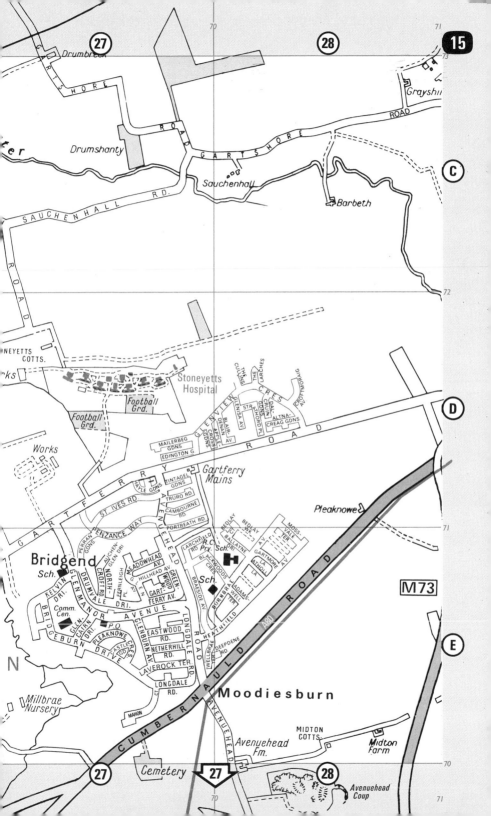

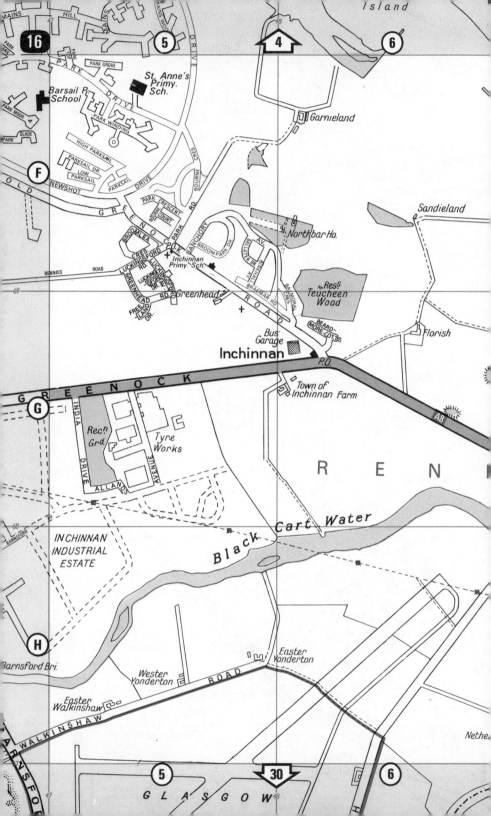

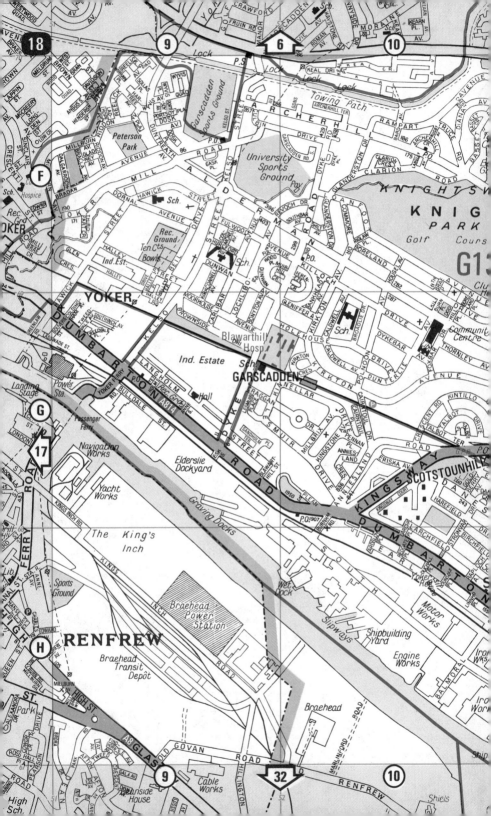

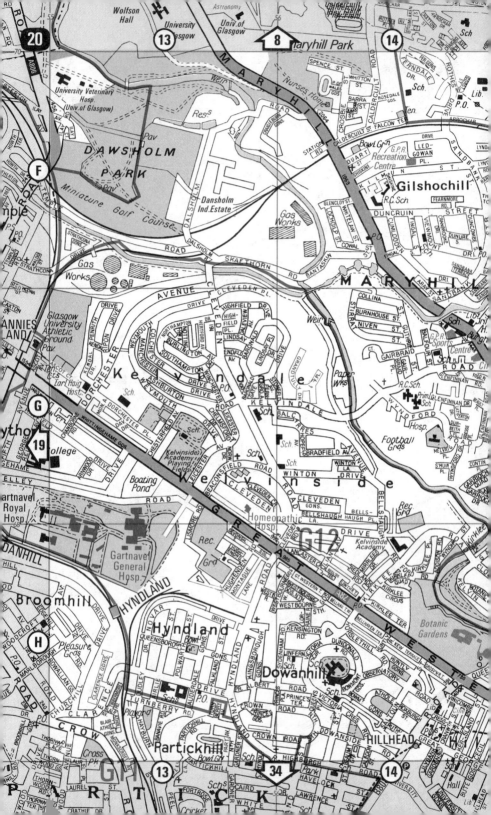

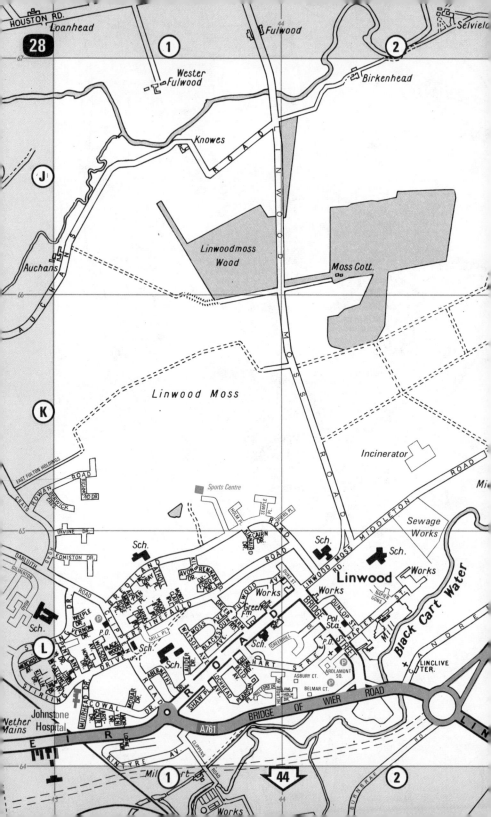

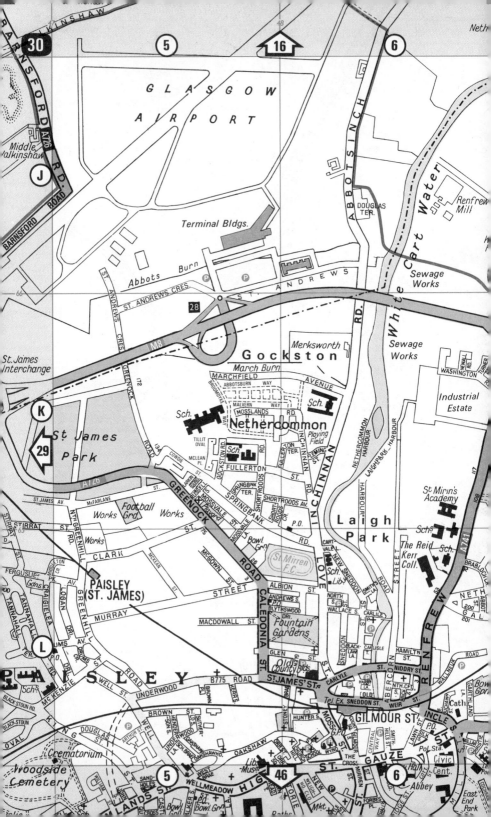

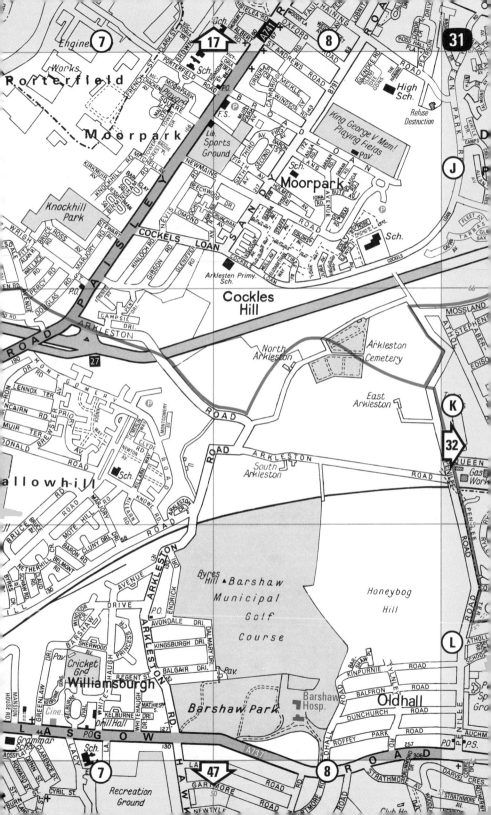

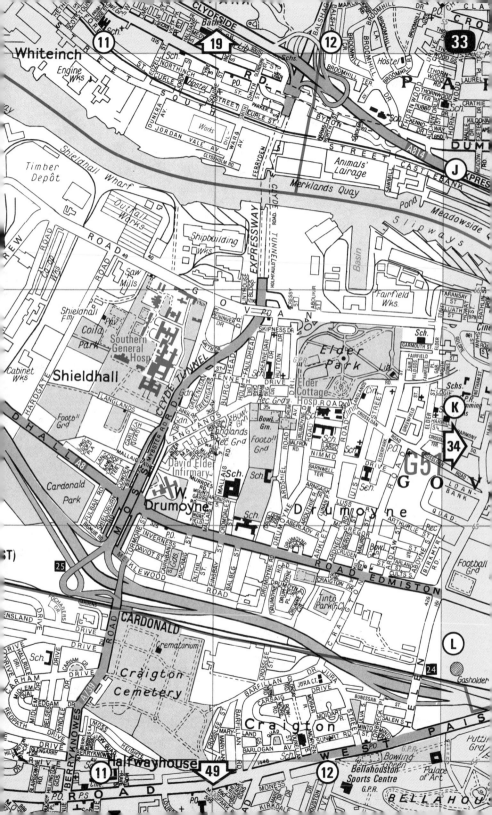

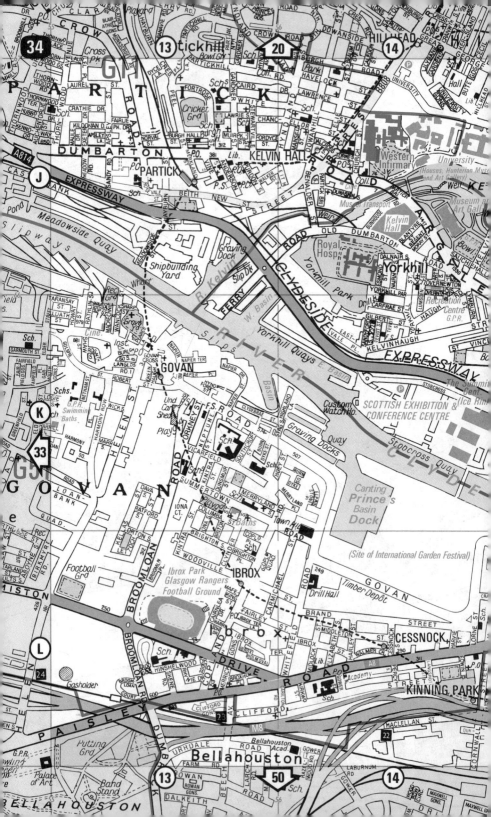

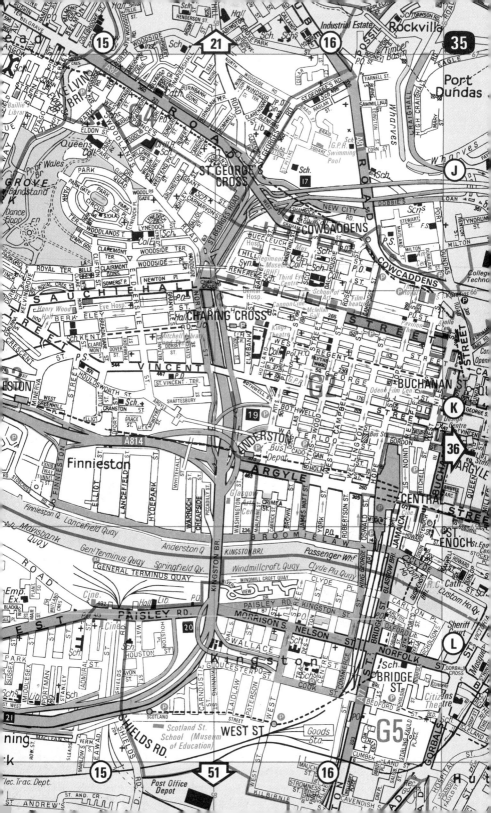

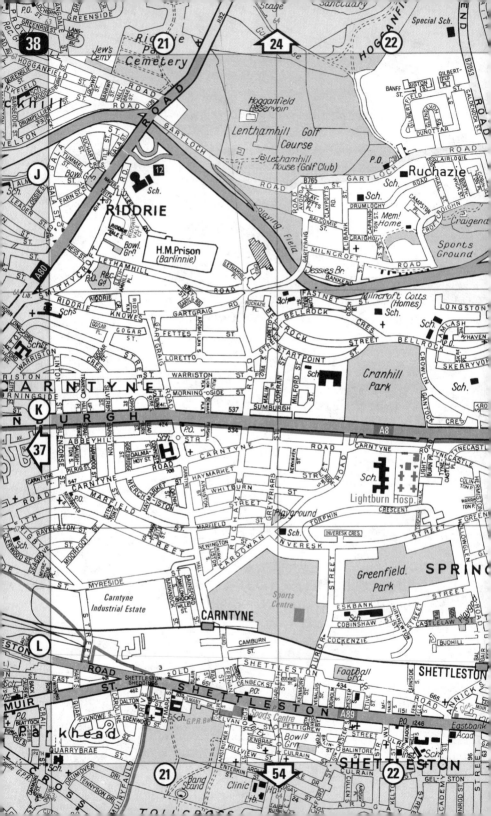

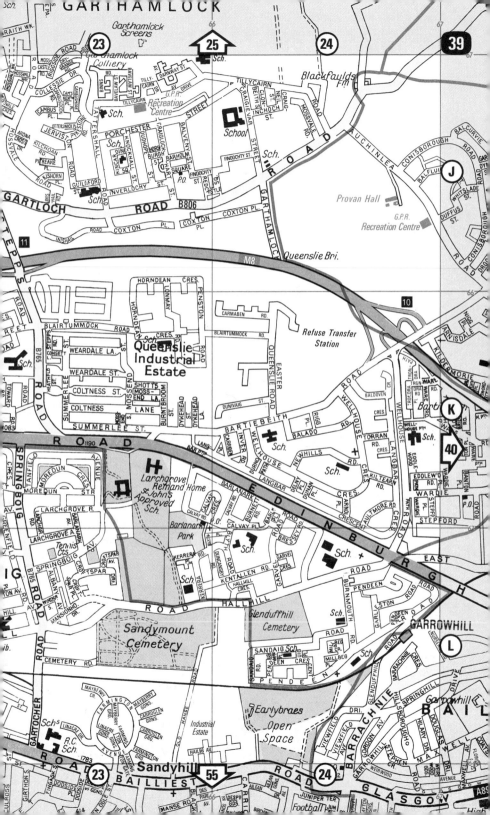

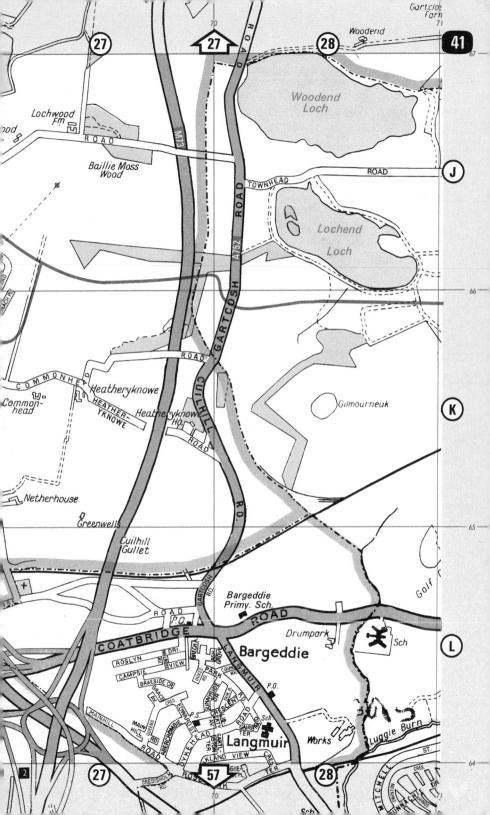

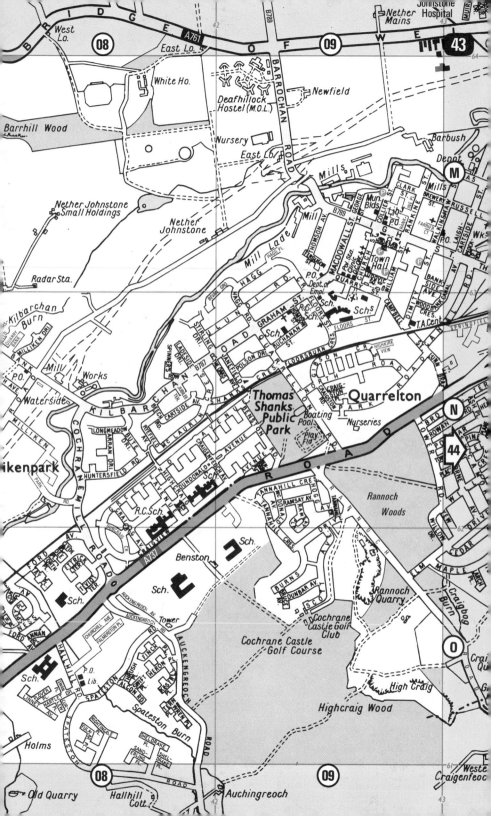

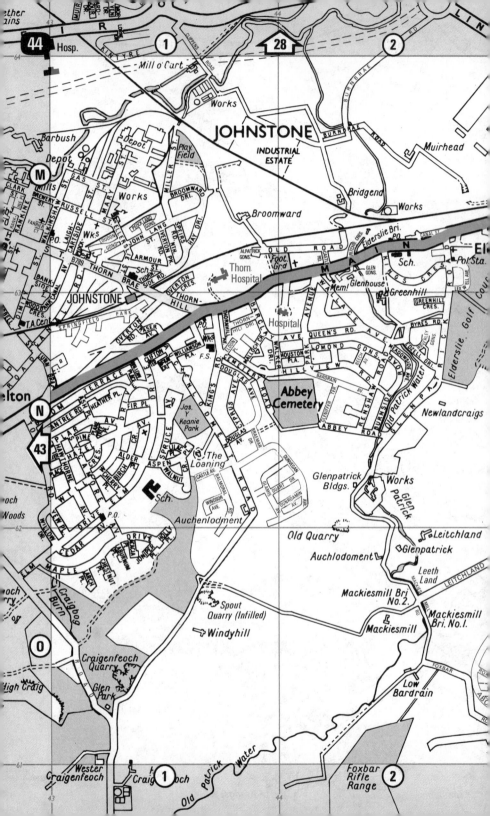

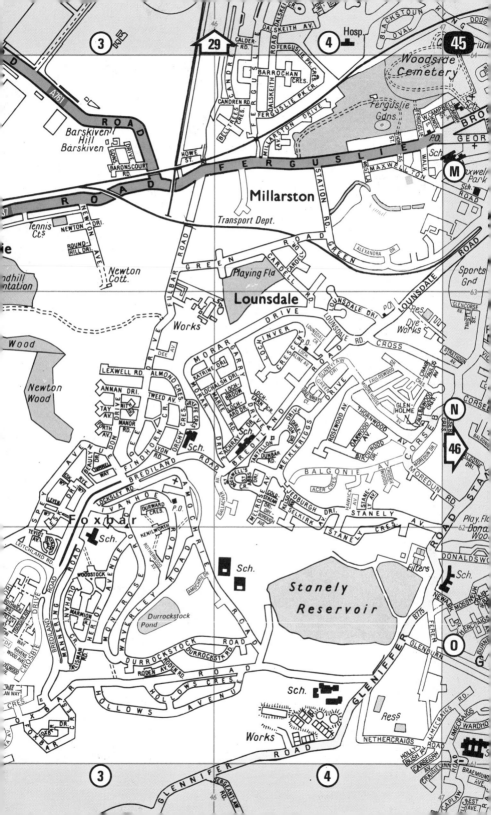

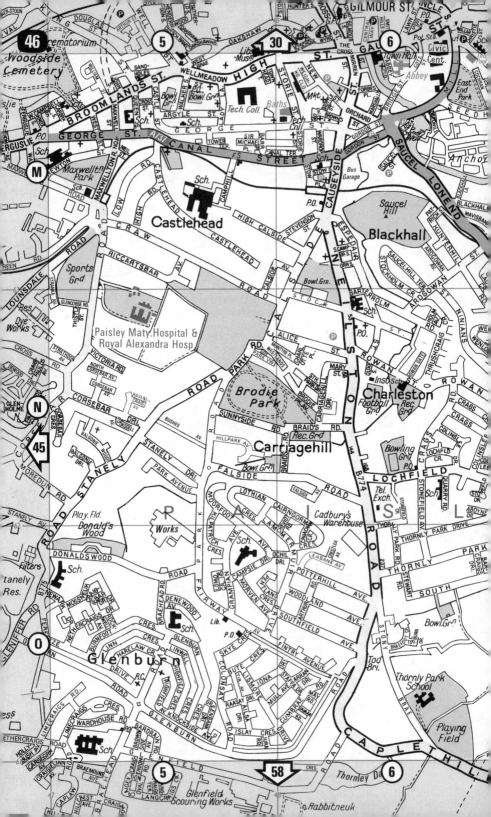

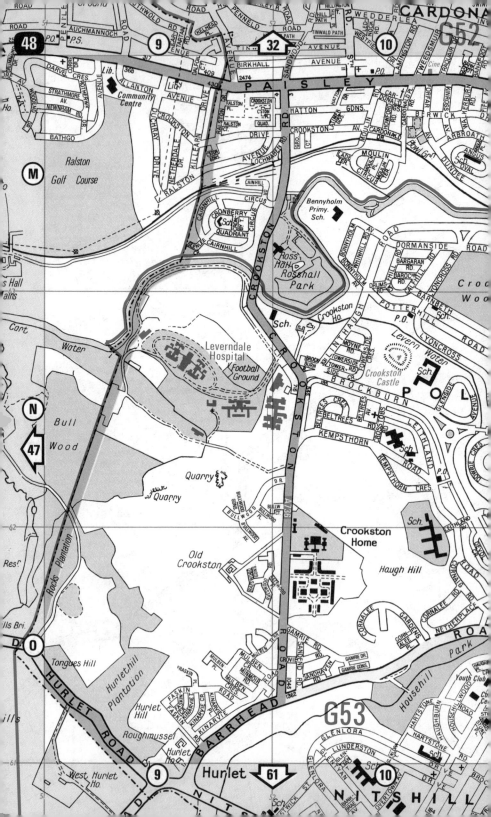

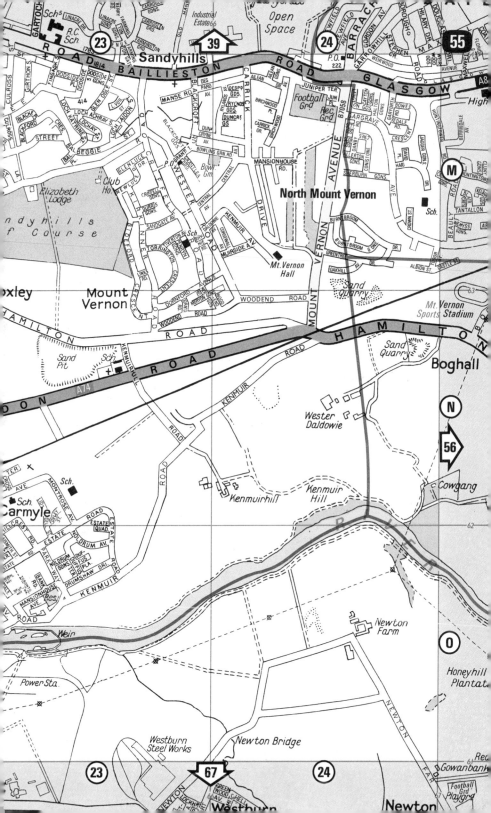

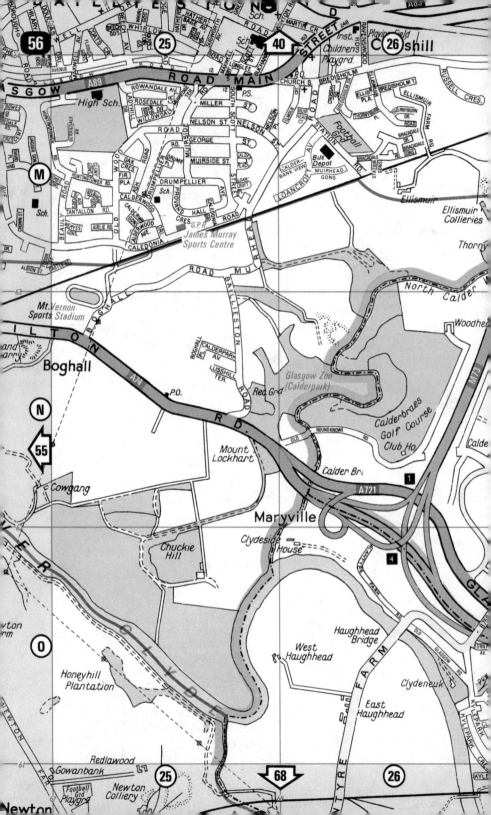

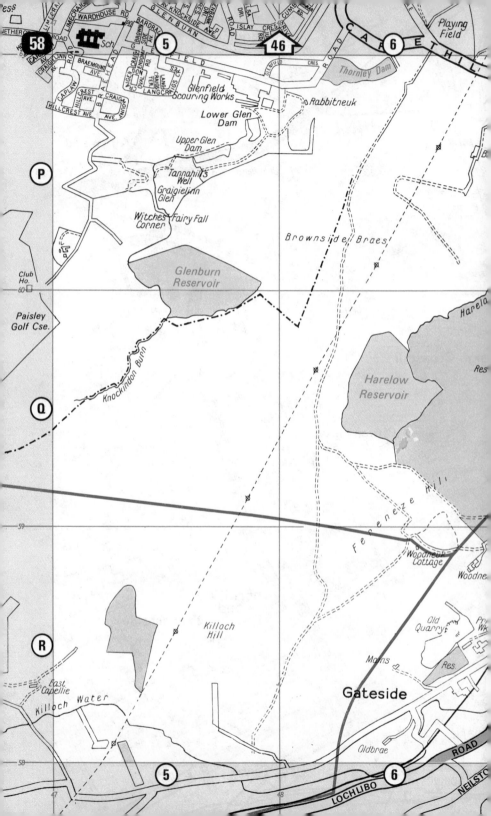

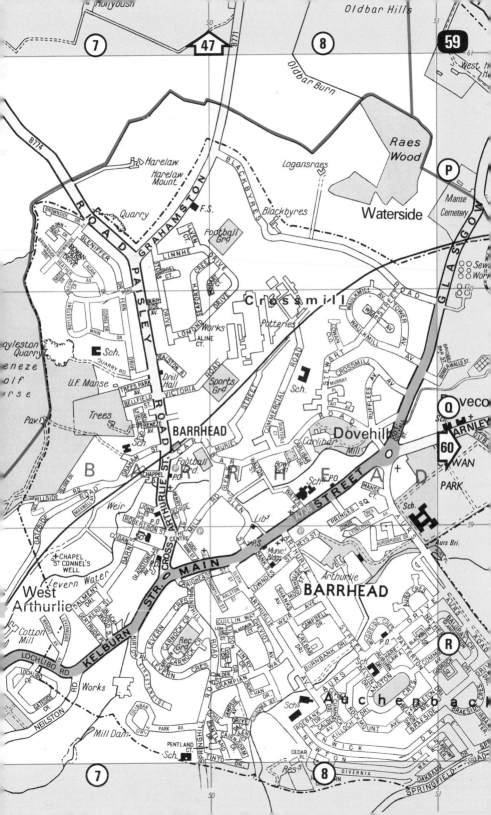

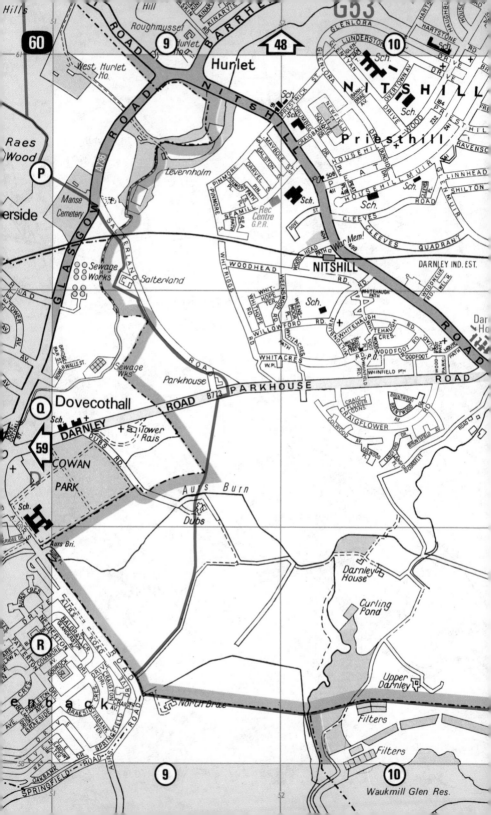

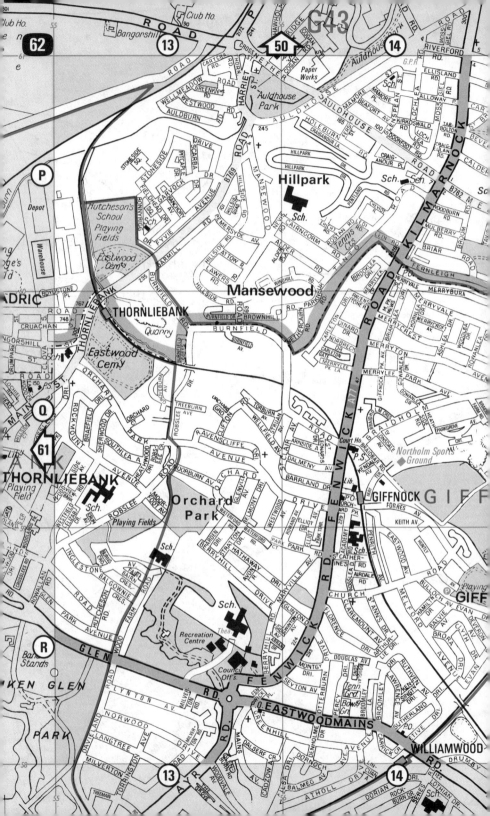

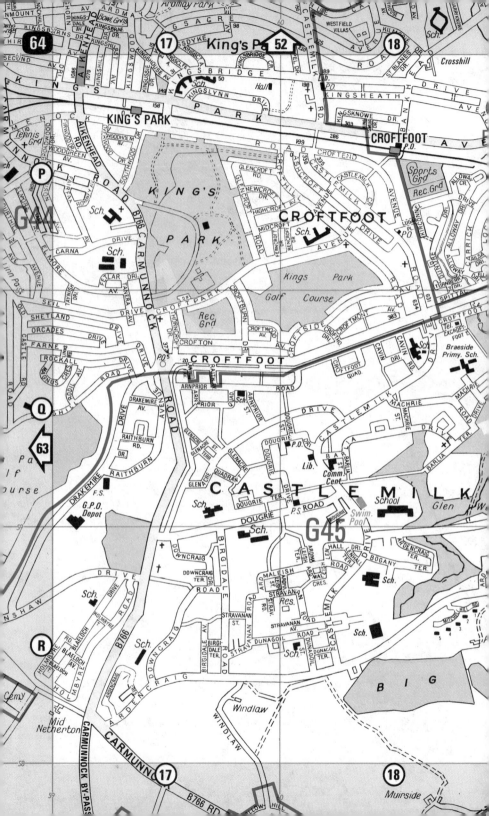

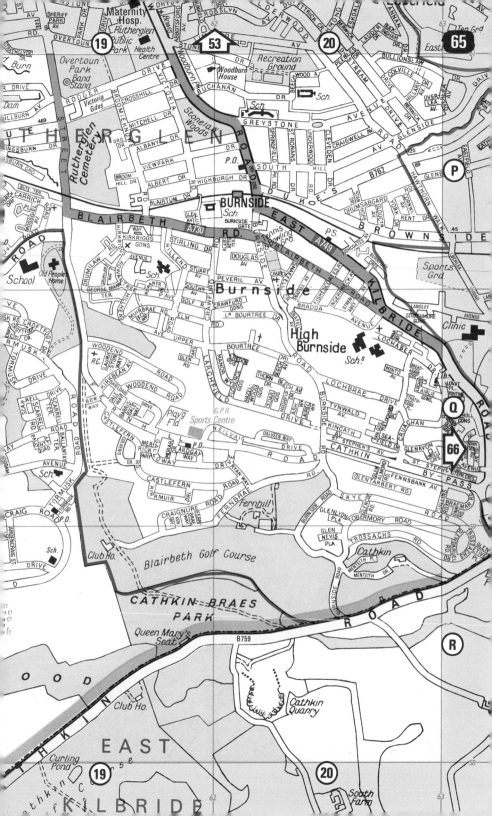

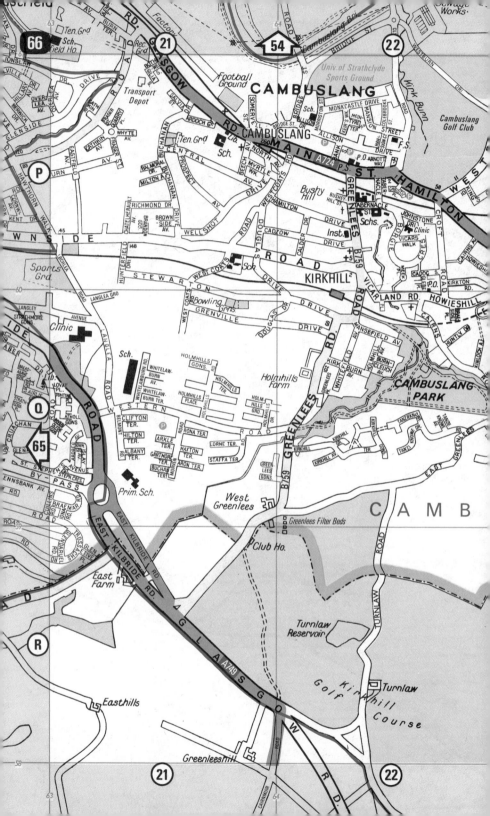

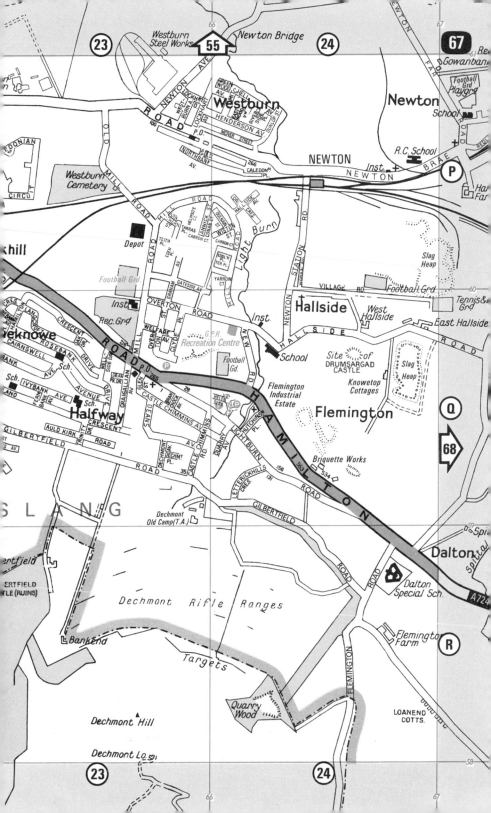

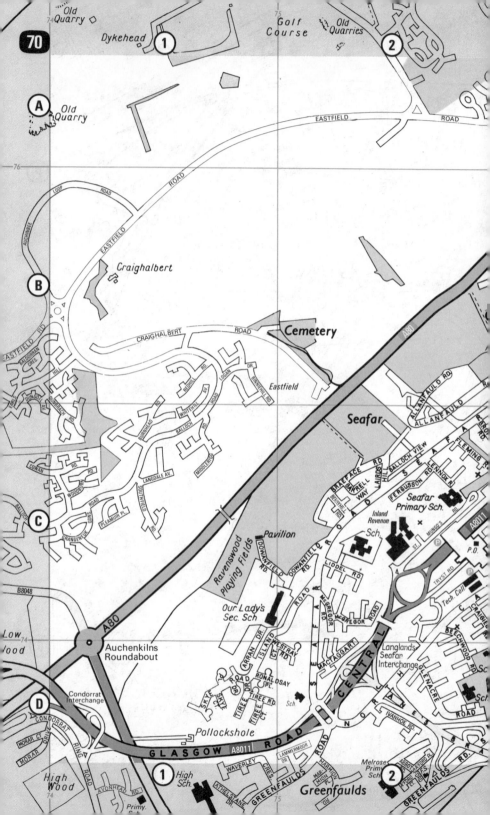

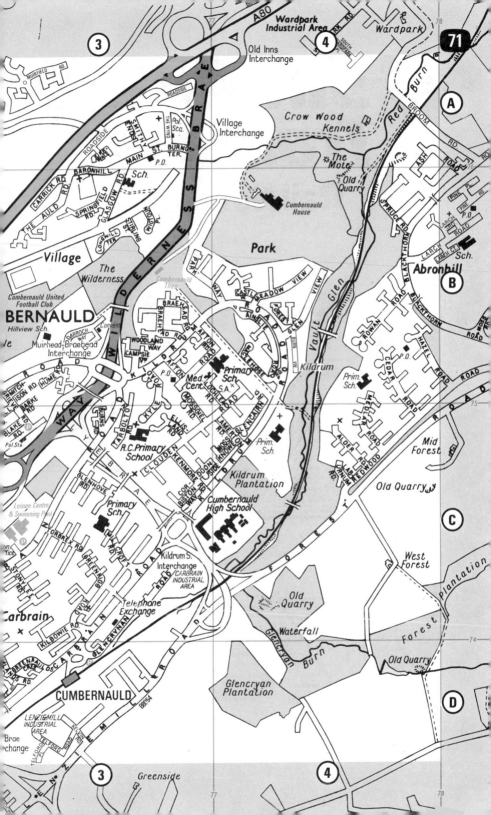

# Strathclyde Transport
## Rail Network

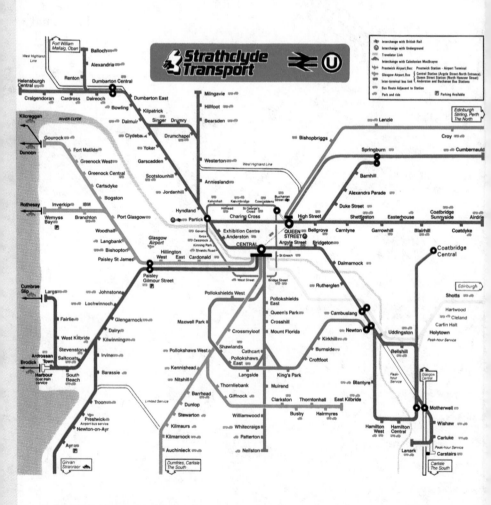

Reproduced by kind permission of Strathclyde Transport

# Glasgow

## Local Information Guide

# Contents

## Useful information

**Area of City** 76 sq. miles

**Population (Glasgow District)**
(1980 estimate) 781,694.

**Early Closing Days**
Tuesday with alternative of Saturday.
Most of the shops in the central area
operate six-day trading.

**Electricity** 240 volts A.C.

**Emergency Services**
Police, Fire and Ambulance. Dial 999
on any telephone.

**Licensing Hours**
Public Houses
Daily (except Sundays) 11 a.m. to
2.30 p.m. and 5 to 11 p.m. (many
open continuously 11 a.m. to
11 p.m.)
Sundays, 12.30 to 2.30 p.m. and 6.30
to 10.30 p.m.
Restaurants, Hotels and Public
Houses with catering facilities, same
as above but can be extended for
drinks with meals.

## Information Bureau

**Tourist Information Centres:**
35–39 St. Vincent Place
Glasgow. 041-227 4880

Town Hall, Abbey Close
Paisley. 041-889 0711

Glasgow Airport 041-848 4440

**Travel Information Centre**
St. Enoch Square
Open Monday–Saturday 9.30 a.m.
to 5.30 p.m. 041-226 4826 (Monday
to Saturday 7 a.m. to 12 midnight,
Sunday 9 a.m. to 9 p.m.) for City
services, ferry services, local airlines,
train and express services. Free
timetables are available.

## Help & Advice

**British Broadcasting Corporation**
Queen Margaret Drive, G12.
041-339 8844

**British Council**
6 Belmont Crescent, G12.
041-339 8651

**British Telecom Scotland**

**Glasgow Area**
Marland House, 40 George Street
Glasgow G1 1BA
All Enquiries 041-220 1234 or dial
100 and ask for FREEFONE BT
GLASGOW.

**Chamber of Commerce**
30 George Square, G2.
041-204 2121

**Citizens Advice Bureau**
212 Bath Street, Glasgow G2 4HW.
041-331 2345/6/7/8
119 Main Street, Glasgow G40 1HA.
041-554 0336

# gallery guide

1. Courtyard
2. Ancient Egypt
3. Ancient Greece and Rome
4. Hutton Rooms
5. Paintings
6. Chinese Art
7. Gothic Art
8. Islamic Art
9. 16th and 17th Century Room
10. Arms and Armour
11. Tapestry Galleries
12. Needlework Room
13. The Montron Arch
14. Stained Glass
15. Burrell the Man, Burrell the Building

The Burrell Collection comprises some 9,000 items. It was gifted to the city of Glasgow in 1944 by Sir William Burrell and his wife Constance. The museum opened its doors to the public in October 1983, and is one of 12 museums and galleries run by Glasgow City Council, Cultural and Leisure Services. For more information visit www.glasgowmuseums.com.

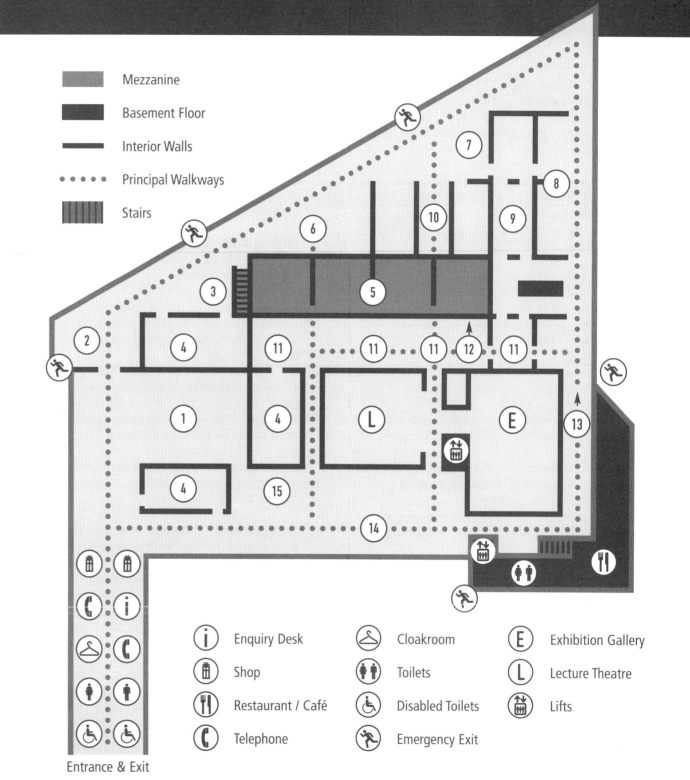

Mezzanine

Basement Floor

Interior Walls

Principal Walkways

Stairs

(i) Enquiry Desk

(gift) Shop

(fork/knife) Restaurant / Café

(phone) Telephone

(hanger) Cloakroom

(toilets) Toilets

(disabled) Disabled Toilets

(E) Exhibition Gallery

(L) Lecture Theatre

(lift) Lifts

(emergency) Emergency Exit

Entrance & Exit

**1. Courtyard**   The famous Warwick Vase, dating from the 2nd century AD and found in the ruins of the Emperor Hadrian's Villa at Tivoli, dominates the central courtyard. In this area, too, you can see bronze sculptures by the French artist Auguste Rodin.

**2. Ancient Egypt**   Stone sculptures, reliefs and vessels predominate in this gallery, but you can also see exquisite works in bronze, glass and faience. Exhibits date from the Archaic Period (about 3,000 BC) to the Ptolemaic Period (332–30 BC).

**3. Ancient Greece and Rome**   The art of the ancient world is well represented in this gallery – the vases, sculptures and jewellery are particularly fine. A small selection of Etruscan and Assyrian items and some Luristan bronzes are also on display in this area.

**4. Hutton Rooms**   The Drawing Room, Dining Room and Hall which surround the courtyard are accurate reconstructions of rooms from Sir William Burrell's last home, Hutton Castle. Items from the collection were used to furnish and decorate these rooms in the Gothic style.

**5. Paintings**   On the mezzanine floor (accessible by the staircase in the Ancient Greece & Rome area) you will find examples of important paintings from Sir William Burrell's collection. These generally include works by the French 19th-century artists Degas, Cézanne and Boudin.

**6. Chinese Art**   Ceramics to be found in this area include Neolithic burial urns, T'ang Dynasty earthenware figures and a broad selection of delicate porcelain items. Here too are bronze ritual vessels, carved jades and deceptively modern-looking antique Chinese furniture.

**7. Gothic Art**   A stunning collection of religious art from medieval times fills this and adjacent galleries. Wood and stone sculptures, precious metalwork and fine ivories complement wooden church furnishings and historic architectural details in this area of the building.

**8. Islamic Art**   In this gallery you can see an important collection of carpets and rugs from the Muslim world as well as early Islamic ceramics and metalwork. The artefacts came from areas stretching from modern Turkey to India and date from the 9th to the 19th centuries.

**9. 16th and 17th Century Room**   A luxurious display of paintings together with associated embroidered furnishings and textiles in a period setting.

**10. Arms and Armour**   The collection includes high - quality European armour and weapons dating from the 13th to the 17th century.

**11. Tapestry Galleries**   One of the glories of the collection, a selection of tapestries – large and small – is displayed in four consecutive galleries, together with furniture of the period.

**12. Needlework Room**   Selected items from Sir William Burrell's collection of embroidered textiles and lace can be seen in this small internal gallery. Light levels are kept low to protect the vulnerable materials.

**13. The Montron Arch**   This late 12th-century stone portal from a ruined church in Montron, France, leads to the floor above the restaurant.

**14. Stained Glass**   A display of some of the best stained and painted glass from the collection lines the corridor route leading directly from the entrance area to the restaurant. More stained glass can be seen in a small internal room leading off the largest tapestry gallery.

**15. Burrell the Man, Burrell the Building**   These two linked displays provide a background to 'The Burrell Experience'. Here are exhibits relating to Sir William Burrell and to the prize-winning building in which his collection is now housed.

© text and images Glasgow City Council (Museums), 2004.

Glasgow
CITY COUNCIL

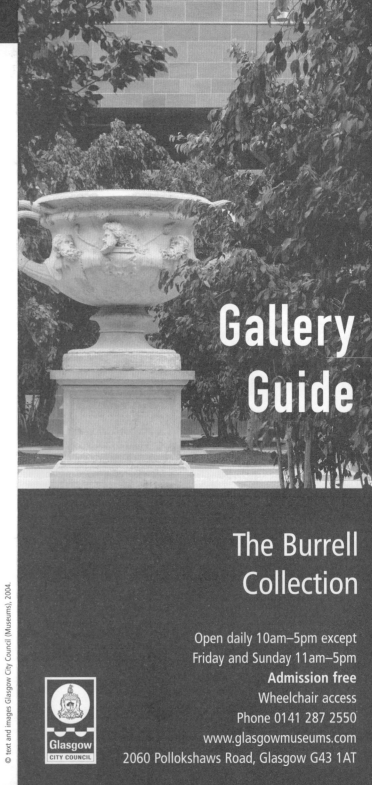

# Gallery Guide

# The Burrell Collection

Open daily 10am–5pm except Friday and Sunday 11am–5pm
**Admission free**
Wheelchair access
Phone 0141 287 2550
www.glasgowmuseums.com
2060 Pollokshaws Road, Glasgow G43 1AT

27 Dougrie Drive, Castlemilk,
Glasgow G45 9AD 041-634 0338
139 Main Street (Town Hall)
Rutherglen G73 4HG 041-647 5100
66 Main Street, Barrhead
041-881 2032/880 7686
Civic Centre, East Kilbride
East Kilbride 21295
1143 Maryhill Road, Glasgow G20
041-946 6373/4
46 Township Centre, Easterhouse,
Glasgow G34 9DS 041-771 2328

**Consumer Advice Centre**
St. Enoch House, 1 St. Enoch Square
Glasgow G1 4BH. 041-204 0262

**Customs and Excise**
21 India Street, G2.
041-221 3828

**H.M. Immigration Office**
Admin Block D, Argyll Avenue
Glasgow Airport
Tel. 041-887 4115

**Housing Aid and Advice**
Shelter, 53 St. Vincent Crescent
Glasgow G3 8NQ. 041-221 8995/6

**Legal Aid and Advice**
Castlemilk Advice & Law Centre
27 Dougrie Drive, Glasgow G45.
041-634 0338

**Law Centre**
30 Dougrie Drive
041-634 0313

**Lost Property**
Strathclyde Passenger Transport
Executive
St. Enoch Underground Station
Tel. 041-248 6950 (City Buses)
12 West George Street G32
041-332 6811. (Underground)
Other Buses–Office of Bus Company.
Trains–Station of arrival.
Elsewhere in City–Strathclyde Police
Lost Property Department,
173 Pitt Street, G2
041-204 2626

**Passport Office**
Northgate 96 Milton Street
Glasgow G4. Tel. 041-332 0271

**Registrar of Births, Deaths and Marriages**
1 Martha Street, G1. 041-227 6343
Hours – Monday to Friday 9.15 a.m.
to 4.15 p.m., Friday evenings
5.30 p.m. to 7.15 p.m.
Births must be registered within
twenty-one days, deaths within eight
days, and marriages within three
days. The Registrar should be
consulted at least one month before
intended date of marriage.

**Royal Scottish Society for the Prevention of Cruelty to Children**
15 Annfield Place, G31.
041-556 1156

**RNID–**
**Royal National Institute for the Deaf**
9a Clairmont Gardens, Glasgow
G3 7LW. 041-332 0343

**Samaritans**
218 West Regent Street, Glasgow
G2 4DQ. 041-248 4488

**Scottish Society for the Mentally Handicapped**
13 Elmbank Street, Glasgow G2.
041-226 4541

**Scottish Television**
Cowcaddens. G2. 041-332 9999

**Society for the Prevention of Cruelty to Animals**
15 Royal Terrace, G3.
(Business Hours)          041-332 0716
(After Hours)               041-204 2626

# Newspapers

*Morning Daily*
**Daily Record**
Anderston Quay, G3.    041-248 7000

**Glasgow Herald**
195 Albion Street, G1.    041-552 6255

**Scottish Daily Express**
Park Circus Place, G3. 041-332 9600

**The Scotsman**
78 Queen Street, G1.    041-221 6485

*Evening Daily*
**Evening Times**
195 Albion Street, G1.    041-552 6255

*Weekly*
**Scottish Sunday Express**
Park Circus Place, G3. 041-552 3550

**Sunday Mail**
Anderston Quay, G3.    041-248 7000

**Sunday Post**
144 Port Dundas Road, G4.
041-332 9933

## Parking

Car parking in the central area of Glasgow is controlled. Parking meters are used extensively and signs indicating restrictions are displayed at kerbsides and on entry to the central area. Traffic Wardens are on duty.

**British Rail Car Parks**
(Open 24 hours)
Central Station
Queen Street Station

**Multi-Storey Car Parks**
(Open 24 hours)
Anderston Cross: Cambridge Street: George Street: Mitchell Street: Port Dundas Road: Waterloo Street.

(Limited Opening)
Charing Cross
Sauchiehall Street Centre

**Surface Car Parks**
Carrick Street: Holland Street: Ingram Street: McAlpine Street: North Frederick Street: Albion Street: Oswald Street: St. Enoch: Shuttle Street: Wemyss Street.

## Post Offices

**Head Post Office**
George Square, G2.          041-248 2882
Open Monday to Friday 9 a.m. to 5.30 p.m. Saturdays 9 a.m. to 12.30 p.m. Closed Sunday.

**Branch Offices**
85–91 Bothwell Street, G2.
4 Dixon Street, G1.

216 Hope Street, G2.
533 Sauchiehall Street, G3.

**Cables** can be handed in to any Post Office doing telegraph business.

## Taxis

**Fares by Distance**
For one person of 14 years of age or over for a distance not exceeding 1 mile — 80p
sixth of a mile or part thereof 10p.
Minimum fare — 80p

**Waiting Time**
for each completed period of two minutes — 10p. Hires beginning or ending between 12 midnight and 6.00 a.m. — surcharge 20p.
Where there is more than 1 person of 14 years of age or over an extra charge of 5p per person for the whole journey is made. The maximum number of persons to be carried at any time not to exceed 5. Under no circumstances will passengers be charged separate fares. An additional charge is made for luggage exceeding 56 lb. (25½ kilos), prams and bicycles.

**Complaints**
Any complaints about taxis should be taken up with the Town Clerk's Office, Licensing Department, City Chambers, Glasgow.
Tel.041 227 4535 or any Police Station

**Note**
*Fares and conditions apply to meter taxis within the boundary of the City of Glasgow. A surcharge of ⅓ of the meter fare is added if the taxi is hired to travel to a place beyond the boundary and within a distance of 8 miles from the Head Post Office, George Square. Persons wishing to travel beyond the 8 miles should obtain an estimate.*

# Local Government

Strathclyde Regional Council
Strathclyde House, 20 India Street
Glasgow G2 4PF
041-204 2900

## District Councils:

**Argyll & Bute**
District Council Headquarters
Kilmory, Lochgilphead PA31 8RT
0546 2127

**Bearsden & Milngavie**
Municipal Building, Boclair
Bearsden G61 2TQ
041-942 2262

**Clydebank**
Council Offices, Rosebery Place
Clydebank G81 1TG
041-941 1331

**Clydesdale**
Clydesdale District Offices
Lanark ML11 7JT
0555 61331

**Cumbernauld & Kilsyth**
Council Offices, Bron Way
Cumbernauld G67 1DZ
02367 22131

**Cummock & Doon Valley**
Council Offices, Lugar
Cumnock KA18 3JQ
0290 22111

**Cunninghame**
Cunninghame House
Irvine KA12 8EE
0294 74166

**Dumbarton**
Crosslet House
Dumbarton G82 3NS
0389 65100

**East Kilbride**
Civic Centre
East Kilbride G74 1AB
035-52 28777

**Eastwood**
Council Offices
Eastwood Park, Rouken Glen Road
Rouken Glen, Giffnock
Glasgow G46 6UG
041-638 6511
041-638 1101

**Glasgow City**
City Chambers
Glasgow G2 1DU
041-221 9600

**Hamilton**
Town House
102 Cadzow Street
Hamilton ML3 6HH
0698 282323

**Inverclyde**
Municipal Buildings
Greenock PA15 1LY
0475 24400

**Kilmarnock & Loudoun**
Civic Centre
Kilmarnock KA1 1BY
0563 21140

**Kyle & Carrick**
Burns House
Burns Statue Square
Ayr KA7 1UT
0292 281511

**Monklands**
Municipal Buildings
Dunbeth Road
Coatbridge ML5 3LF
0236 24941

**Motherwell**
PO Box 14
Civic Centre
Motherwell ML1 1TW
0698 66166

**Renfrew**
Municipal Buildings
Cotton Street
Paisley PA1 1BU
041-889 5400

**Strathkelvin**
PO Box 4
Council Chambers
Kirkintilloch
Glasgow G66 1PW
041-776 7171

# Explore the History and Clans of

# SCOTLAND

## with these Full Colour Pictorial Maps from GEOGRAPHIA

### with an introduction by Nigel Tranter

THE CLANS OF SCOTLAND

A Full Colour, Pictorial Map depicting the Clan's & Ancient Families of Scotland

with an introduction by Nigel Tranter

HISTORIC SCOTLAND

A Full Colour, Pictorial Map depicting the Characters & Events of Scotland's Stirring Past.

with an introduction by Nigel Tranter

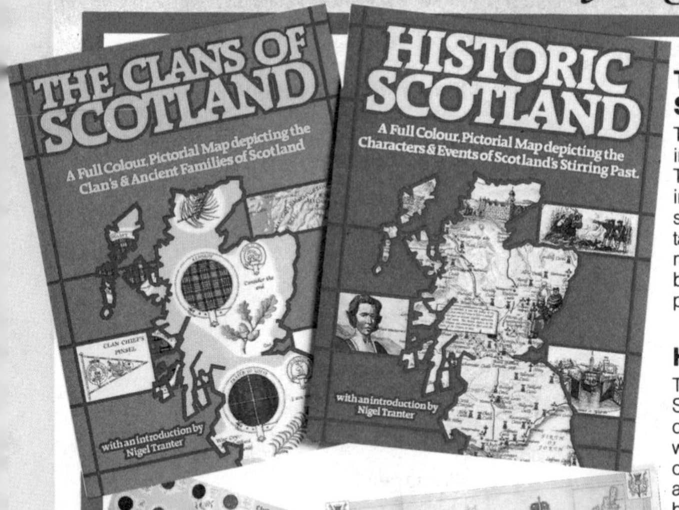

## THE CLANS OF SCOTLAND

The Clans of Scotland are of infinite variety and fascination. This map illustrates the areas in which they were prominent, shows names with their related tartans and where relevant the mottoes, war cries and plant badges which are so much a part of their tradition.

## HISTORIC SCOTLAND

There is scarcely a yard of Scotland without a story to tell, of heroism and treachery, of warfare or worship, of flourish or folly or heartbreak. There are more castles, abbeys, battlefields, graveyards, monuments and ancient relics than any land of its size.

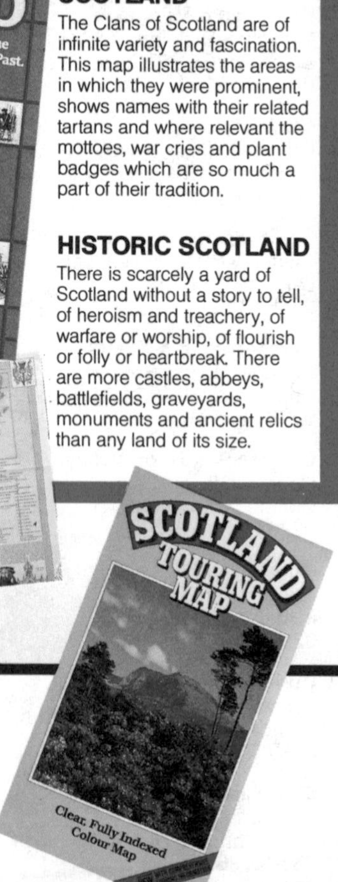

SCOTLAND TOURING MAP

Clear, Fully Indexed Colour Map

## SCOTLAND TOURING MAP
## New Fully Indexed Colour Map

More than twenty different classifications of tourist information, including Castles, Historic Houses, Forest Parks, Golf Courses, Skiing, Picnic Sites, Camping/Caravan Sites and Beaches.

# History & Development

The City of Glasgow began life as a makeshift hamlet of huts huddled round a 6thC church, built by St Mungo on the banks of a little salmon river — the Clyde. It was called Gleschow, meaning 'beloved green place' in Celtic. The cathedral was founded in 1136; the university, the second oldest in Scotland, was established in the 15thC; and in 1454 the flourishing mediaeval city wedged between the cathedral and the river was made a Royal burgh. The city's commercial prosperity dates from the 17thC when the lucrative tobacco, sugar and cotton trade with the New World flourished. The River Clyde, Glasgow's gateway to the Americas, was dredged, deepened and widened in the 18thC to make it navigable to the city's heart.

By the 19thC, Glasgow was the greatest shipbuilding centre in the world. From the 1820s onwards, it grew in leaps and bounds westwards along a steep ridge of land running parallel with the river. The hillside became encased in an undulating grid of streets and squares. Gradually the individualism, expressed in one-off set pieces characteristic of the 18thC and early 19thC, gave way to a remarkable coherent series of terraced squares and crescents of epic proportions — making Glasgow one of the finest of Victorian cities. But the price paid for such rapid industrialisation, the tremendous social problems manifest in the squalor of some of the worst of 19thC slums, was high. Today the city is still the commercial and industrial capital of the West of Scotland. The most notorious of the slums have been cleared but the new buildings lack that sparkling clench-fisted Glaswegian character of the 19thC. Ironically, this character was partially destroyed when the slums were cleared for it wasn't the architecture that had failed, only the bureaucrats, who designated such areas as working class ghettos.

## Districts

Little remains of mediaeval Glasgow, which stood on the wedge of land squeezed between the cathedral and the River Clyde. Its business centre was The Cross, a space formed by the junction of several streets — the tall, square Tolbooth Steeple, 1626, in the middle. Opposite is Trongate, an arch astride a footpath, complete with tower and steeple salvaged from 17thC St Mary's Church — destroyed by fire in 1793. The centre of 20thC Glasgow is George Square, a tree-lined piazza planned in 1781 and pinned down by more than a dozen statues including an 80-foot-high Doric column built in 1837 to carry a statue of Sir Walter Scott. Buildings of interest: the monumental neo-Baroque City Chambers 1883-88 which take up the east side and the Merchants' House 1874, on the west. To the south of the square, in a huddle of narrow streets, is the old Merchant City. Of interest here is the elegant Trades House, 85 Glassford Street, built by Robert Adam in 1794. An elegant Ionic portico stands on a rusticated ground storey flanked by domed towers. Hutcheson's Hospital, 158 Ingram Street, is a handsome Italianate building designed by David Hamilton in 1805. Nearby is Stirling's Library, originally an 18thC private residence, it became the Royal Exchange in 1827 when the Corinthian portico was added. To the north west is Kelvingrove, Victorian Glasgow at its best. Built around a steep saddle of land, landscaped by Paxton in 1850 and lined along its edge with handsome terraces.

Last but not least are the banks of the River Clyde. From Clyde Walkway on the north bank you can see: the Suspension Bridge of 1871 with its pylons in the form of triumphal arches; the old clipper ship, C. V. Carrick, a contemporary of the Cutty Sark, moored by Victoria bridge; 17thC Merchants' Steeple; the Gothic Revival St Andrew's R.C. Cathedral of 1816; the church, built 1739, in nearby St Andrew's Square is a typical copy of London's St Martin-in-the-Fields.

## Interesting buildings

Victorian Glasgow was extremely eclectic architecturally. Good examples of the Greek Revival style are Royal College of Physicians 1845, by W. H. Playfair and the Custom House 1840, by G. L. Taylor. The Queen's Room 1857, by Charles Wilson, is a handsome temple used now as a Christian Science church. The Gothic style is seen at its most exotic in the Stock Exchange 1877, by J. Burnet. The new Victorian materials and techniques with glass, wrought and cast iron were also ably demonstrated in the buildings of the time. Typical are: Gardener's Stores 1856, by J. Baird; the Buck's Head, Argyle Street, an amalgam of glass and cast iron; and the Egyptian Halls of 1873, in Union Street, which has a masonry framework. Both are by Alexander Thomson. The Templeton Carpet Factory 1889, Glasgow Green, by William Leiper, is a Venetian Gothic building complete with battlemented parapet.

Glasgow University

The great genius of Scottish architecture is Charles Rennie Mackintosh whose major buildings are in Glasgow. In the Scotland Street School 1904-6, he punctuated a 3-storey central block with flanking staircase towers in projecting glazed bays. His most famous building — Glasgow School of Art 1897-9 — is a magnificent Art Nouveau building of taut stone and glass; the handsome library, with its gabled facade, was added later in 1907-9.

Stirling's Library

## Galleries & museums

Scotland's largest tourist attraction, The Burrell Collection, is situated in Pollok Country Park, Haggs Road and has more than 8,000 objects, housed in an award-winning gallery. The Art Gallery and Museum, Kelvingrove Park, Argyle Street, a palatial sandstone building with glazed central court, has one of the best municipal collections in Britain; superb Flemish, Dutch and French paintings, drawings, prints, also ceramics, silver, costumes and armour, as well as a natural history section. Provand's Lordship c1471, in Castle Street, is Glasgow's oldest house and now a museum of 17th-18thC furniture and household articles. Pollok House, Pollok Country Park, a handsome house designed by William Adam in 1752, has paintings by William Blake and a notable collection of Spanish paintings, including works by El Greco. The Museum of Transport, housed in Kelvin Hall, Bunhouse Road, has a magnificent collection of trams, cars, ships models, bicycles, horse-drawn carriages and 7 steam locos. The People's Palace, The Green, built 1898 with a huge glazed Winter Garden, has a lively illustrated history of the city. But the oldest museum in Glasgow is the Hunterian Museum, University of Glasgow, University Avenue, opened in 1807, it has a fascinating collection of manuscripts, early printed books, as well as some fine archaeological and geological exhibits. 400-year-old Haggs Castle, St Andrew's Drive, is now a children's museum with practical demonstrations and exhibits showing how everyday life has changed over the centuries.

## Streets & shopping

The Oxford Street of Glasgow is Sauchiehall (meaning 'willow meadow') Street. This with Buchanan Street and Argyle Street is the main shopping centre. Here you will find the department stores, boutiques and general shops. All three streets are

*Sheriff Court*

partly pedestrianised, but the most exhilarating is undoubtedly Buchanan Street. Of particular interest is the spatially elegant Argyll Arcade 1828, the Venetian Gothic-style Stock Exchange 1877, and the picturesque Dutch gabled Buchanan Street Bank building 1896. In Glasgow Green is The Barrows, the city's famous street market, formed by the junction of London Road and Kent Street. The Market is *open weekends*. Some parts of the city have *EC Tue*.

*Art Gallery & Museum Kelvingrove*

# Cathedrals & Churches

Glasgow Cathedral is a perfect example of pre-Reformation Gothic architecture. Begun in 1238, it has a magnificent choir and handsome nave with shallow projecting transepts. On a windy hill to the east is the Necropolis, a cemetery with a spiky skyline of Victoriana consisting of pillars, temples and obelisks, dominated by an 1825 Doric column carrying the statue of John Knox. Other churches of interest: Lansdowne Church built by J. Honeyman in 1863; St George's Tron Church by William Stark 1807; Caledonian Road Church, a temple and tower atop a storey-high base, designed by Alexander Thomson in 1857; a similar design is to be found at the United Presbyterian Church, St Vincent Street, 1858, but on a more highly articulated ground storey; Queen's Cross Church 1897 is an amalgam of Art Nouveau and Gothic Revival by the brilliant Charles Rennie Mackintosh.

*Churches within the central area of Glasgow are:*

**Church of Scotland**
Glasgow Cathedral
Castle Street
Renfield St. Stephen's Church
262 Bath Street
St. George's Tron Church
165 Buchanan Street
St. Columba Church (Gaelic)
300 St. Vincent Street

**Baptist**
Adelaide Place Church
209 Bath Street

**Congregational**
Hillhead Centre
1 University Avenue

**Episcopal Church of Scotland**
Cathedral Church of St. Mary
300 Great Western Road, G4.

**First Church of Christ Scientist**
1 la Bell Place, Clifton Street, G3.
(off Sauchiehall Street)

**Free Church of Scotland**
265 St. Vincent Street

**German Speaking Congregation**
Services held at 7 Hughenden Terrace, G12.

**Greek Orthodox Cathedral**
St. Luke's, 27 Dundonald Road, G12.

**Jewish Orthodox Synagogue**
Garnethill, 29 Garnet Street

**Methodist**
Woodlands Church
229 Woodlands Road

**Roman Catholic**
St. Andrew's Cathedral
190 Clyde Street
St. Aloysius' Church
25 Rose Street

**Unitarian Church**
287 St. Vincent Street

**United Free**
Wynd Church,
427 Crown Street, G5.

*Glasgow Cathedral*

# Entertainment

As Scotland's commercial and industrial capital, Glasgow offers a good choice of leisure activities. The city now has 6 theatres where productions ranging from serious drama to pantomime, pop and musicals are performed. The Theatre Royal, Hope Street, is Scotland's only opera house and has been completely restored to its full Victorian splendour. The Scottish National Orchestra gives concerts at the City Hall, Candleriggs, every *Sat night in winter,* while the Kelvin Hall is the venue for the proms in *Jun.* Cinemas are still thriving in Glasgow, as are the many public houses, some of which provide meals and live entertainment. In the city centre and Byres Road, West End, there is a fair number of restaurants where traditional home cooking, as well as international cuisines, can be sampled. More night life can be found at the city's discos and dance halls — Tiffany's, Sauchiehall Street and the Plaza, Eglinton Toll. Outdoors, apart from the many parks and nature trails, there is Calderpark Zoological Gardens, situated 6 miles from the centre between Mount Vernon and Uddingston. Here you may see white rhinos, black panthers and iguanas among many species. Departing from Stobcross Quay, you can also cruise down the Clyde in 'P.S. Waverley' – the last sea-going paddle-steamer in the world.

## Cinemas

**Cannon Cinema,** 380 Clarkston Rd, G44.
041-637 2641
**Cannon Film Centre–**
326 Sauchiehall St, G2.    041-332 9513
(Admin Dept), 326 Sauchiehall St, G2
041-332 1592
326 Sauchiehall St, G2.    041-332 1593
Caledonian Associated Cinemas Ltd–
Regent House, 72 Renfield St, G2
041-332 0606
**Cannon Grand–**
18 Jamaica St, G1.    041-248 4620
**Glasgow Film Theatre–**
12 Rose St, G3. (Box Off)    041-332 6535

**Grosvenor Cinema–**
Ashton Lane, G12.    041-339 4298
**Kelburne Cinema–**
(Manager), Glasgow Rd, Paisley
041-889 3612
**Odeon Film Centre,** 56 Renfield St, G2.
041-332 8701
**Salon Cinema,** Vinicombe St, G12.
041-339 4256

## Halls

**City Hall,** Candleriggs, G1.
**Couper Institute**
86 Clarkston Road, G44.
**Dixon Halls,** 650 Cathcart Road, G42.
**Govan Hall,** Summertown Road, G51.
**Kelvin Hall,** Argyle Street, G3.
**Langside Hall,** 5 Langside Avenue, G41.
**McLellan Galleries**
270 Sauchiehall Street, G2.
**Partick Hall,** 9 Burgh Hall Street, G11.
**Pollokshaws Hall**
2025 Pollokshaws Road, G43.
**Woodside Hall,** Glenfarg Street, G20.

*(More information about the above G.D.C. halls and others from the Director, Halls and Theatres Department, Candleriggs, G1. 041-552 1201).*

## Theatres

**Citizens' Theatre**
Gorbals Street.    041-429 0022
**King's Theatre,** Bath Street.
**Mitchell Theatre and Moir Hall**
Granville Street.
**Pavilion Theatre**
Renfield Street.    041-332 1846
**Theatre Royal**
Hope Street.    041-331 1234
**Tron Theatre**
38 Parnie Street.    041-552 3748
**The Ticket Centre**
Glasgow's Central Box Office for King's Theatre, Mitchell Theatre, Kelvin Hall, Citizen's Theatre, Theatre Royal and City Hall at Candleriggs, G1.
Open Monday to Saturday 10.30 a.m. to 6.30 p.m.
041-227 5511

# Glasgow *(Abbotsinch)* Airport

Glasgow Airport is located eight miles West of Glasgow alongside the M8 motorway at Junction 28. It is linked by a bus service to Anderston Cross Bus Station, the journey time is 25 minutes and buses leave at 30 minute intervals. There is a frequent coach service linking the Airport with

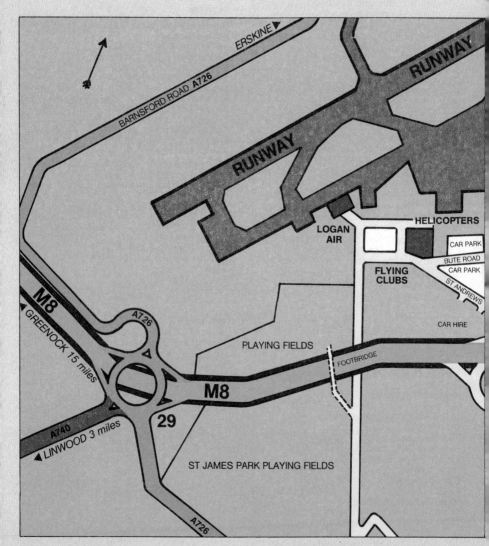

all major bus and rail terminals in the City and a Coach/Air link to and from Prestwick Airport.

The Airport Terminal has a restaurant, grill, buffet, three bars, lounges, shop, post office and banking facilities.

Car parking is available with a graduated scale of charges.

The Airport telephone no is 041-887 1111.

## Airlines

**(Domestic Routes)**
**British Airways**
66 Gordon Street
Glasgow G1
Reservations Tel: 041-332 9666
**British Caledonian Airways**
(contact British Airways)
**British Midland**
Glasgow Airport,
Paisley PAU PA3
Reservations Tel: 041-204 2436
**Loganair Ltd.**
Glasgow Airport (administration)
Tel: 041-889 3181.
Trident House, Renfrew Road, Paisley

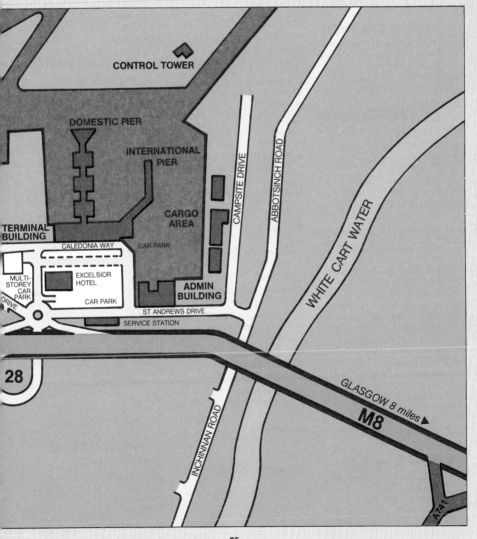

# Sport & Recreation

For both spectator and participant, football is Glasgow's favourite sport. Both Celtic and Rangers, Scotland's most famous rival teams, have their grounds within the City. Glasgow houses Scotland's national football stadium at Hampden Park.

## Badminton

Scottish Badminton Union's Cockburn Centre, Bogmoor Place, G51.
041-445 1218

## Bowling Greens

There are greens in all the main Parks. Information about clubs from the Scottish Bowling Association:
50 Wellington Street, G2.
041-221 8999.

## Cricket Grounds

**Cartha** Haggs Road, G41.
**Clydesdale** Beaton Road, G41.
**Huntershill** Crowhill Road, Bishopbriggs.
**Poloc** Shawholm 2060 Pollokshaws Road, G43.
**West of Scotland** Peel Street, G11.

## Football Grounds

**Celtic Park (Celtic F.C.)** 95 Kerrydale St. G40
**Firhill Park (Partick Thistle F.C. & Clyde F.C.)** Firhill Rd. G20
**Hampden Park (Queen's Park F.C.)** Somerville Dr., G42
**Ibrox Park (Rangers F.C.)** Edmiston Dr., G51
**Kilbowie Park (Clydebank F.C.)** Argyll Rd., Clydebank
**Mertland** Kirkintilloch
**St. Mirren Park (St. Mirren F.C.)** Love St., Paisley

## Golf Courses

**Glasgow District Council**
**9 holes**
Alexandra Park
King's Park.
Knightswood, Lincoln Avenue, G13.
Ruchill, Brassey Street, G20.
**18 holes**
Lethamhill, Cumbernauld Road, Littlehill, Auchinairn Road, G64.
Linn Park.

**(Charges displayed)**
Dougalston Golf Course Strathblane Road, Milngavie. (Five miles from Glasgow). Open to the public daily.
041-956 5750 for charges.

## Putting Greens

There are putting greens in all main Parks.

## Pitch & Putt

Courses at Alexandra Park, Bellahouston Park, Dawsholm, Queen's Park, Rouken Glen and several others.

## Rugby Grounds

**Balgray (Kelvinside Academicals)** Great Western Road, G12.
**Garscadden (Glasgow University)** Garscadden Road South, G15.
**Hughenden (Hillhead High School)** Hughenden Road, G12.
**New Anniesland (Glasgow Acad.)** Helensburgh Drive, G13.
**Old Anniesland (Glasgow High School F.P.)** Crow Road, G11.
**Westerlands (Glasgow University)** Ascot Avenue, G12.

## Sports Centres

**Bellahouston**
Bellahouston Drive, G52.
041-427 5454.

**Burnhill**
Toryglen Road, Rutherglen.
041-643 0327.

**James Murray**
Caledonia Road, Baillieston.
041-773 1656

**Springburn**
Millarbank Street, Springburn.
041-558 7358.

**Helenvale**
Outdoor Sports Complex Helenvale Street, G31.
041-554 4109.

## Swimming Baths

**Glasgow District Council**
Castlemilk, 137 Castlemilk Drive, G45.
Drumchapel, 199 Drumry Road East.
Easterhouse, Bogbain Road, G34.
Govan, Harhill Street, G51.
Govanhill, 99 Calder Street, G42.
North Woodside, Braid Square.
Pollokshaws (Dry-Land/Water Sports Complex) Ashtree Road, G43.
Rutherglen, 44 Greenhill Road, G73.
Shettleston, Elvan Street, G32.
Temple, Knightscliffe Avenue, G13.
Whitehill, Onslow Drive, G31.
Whiteinch, Medwyn Street, G14.
Whitevale, 81 Whitevale Street, G31.

**Hours**
Monday to Friday 9 a.m. to 9 p.m.
Saturday 9 a.m. to 1 p.m.
*Sunday 9 a.m. to 1 p.m.

**Charges**
Admission charges are minimal. OAPs free at certain times.

## Turkish Baths/ Sun Beds

available at:
Govanhill          041-423 0233
Pollokshaws     041-632 2200
Shettleston       041-778 1346

and Whiteinch,   041-959 2465
Men and women on separate days. Telephone direct to baths for more information.

**Hours**
(All the year round).
Monday to Friday 9 a.m. to 9 p.m.
Saturday 9 a.m. to 1 p.m.

**SAUNA at:**
Castlemilk,        041-634 8254
Drumchapel,        041-944 5812
Rutherglen,        041-647 4530
and Whitehill,     041-551 9969

# Tennis
There are courts in all the main parks. Information about clubs from the Secretary of the West of Scotland Lawn Tennis Association:
Mr.N.Floyd, 1 Bocleir Road
Bearsden        041-942 0162

# Weather

The City of Glasgow is on the same latitude as the City of Moscow, but because of its close proximity to the warm Atlantic Shores, and the prevailing westerly winds, it enjoys a more moderate climate. Summers are generally cool and winters mostly mild, this gives Glasgow fairly consistent summer and winter temperatures. Despite considerable cloud the City is sheltered by hills to the south-west and north and the average rainfall for Glasgow is usually less than 40 inches per year.

The following table shows the approximate average figures for sunshine, rainfall and temperatures to be expected in Glasgow throughout the year:

**Weather Forecasts**
For the Glasgow Area including Loch Lomond and the Clyde Coast:
Weatherline
041-246 8091 (Recording)
The Glasgow Weather Centre (Meteorological Office)
33 Bothwell Street,G2
041-248 3451.

| Month | Hours of Sunshine | Inches of Rainfall | Temperature °C | | |
|-------|-------------------|--------------------|---------------|---|---|
| | | | Ave. Max. | Ave. Min. | High/Low |
| Jan | 36 | 3.8 | 5.5 | 0.8 | −18 |
| Feb | 62 | 2.8 | 6.3 | 0.8 | −15 |
| Mar | 94 | 2.4 | 8.8 | 2.2 | 21 |
| Apr | 147 | 2.4 | 11.9 | 3.9 | 22 |
| May | 185 | 2.7 | 15.1 | 6.2 | 26 |
| June | 181 | 2.4 | 17.9 | 9.3 | 30 |
| July | 159 | 2.9 | 18.6 | 10.8 | 29 |
| Aug | 143 | 3.5 | 18.5 | 10.6 | 31 |
| Sept | 106 | 4.1 | 16.3 | 9.1 | −4 |
| Oct | 76 | 4.1 | 13.0 | 6.8 | −8 |
| Nov | 47 | 3.7 | 8.7 | 3.3 | −11 |
| Dec | 30 | 4.2 | 6.5 | 1.9 | −12 |

# Renfrew District

## A selection of leisure, recreational and cultural attractions in Renfrew District:

### Barrhead Sports' Centre

The Centre contains swimming-pools, sports halls, activity rooms and sauna suite. Bar and restaurant facilities add to the wide range of sporting and leisure activities available.

### Barshaw Park, Glasgow Road, Paisley

The park is extensive with formal and informal areas. It adjoins the public golf course and incorporates a boating-pond, playgrounds, model "ride-on" railway and a nature corner.

### Castle Semple Country Park, Lochwinnoch

Castle Semple Loch is a popular feature for sailing and fishing. Canoes, rowing boats and sailing boards for hire. Fishing permits available. Tel: Lochwinnoch 842882 or Bridge of Weir 614791.

### Coats Observatory

The Observatory has traditionally recorded astronomical and meteorological information since 1882. Now installed with a satellite picture receiver, it is one of the best equipped Observatories in the country. Monday—Friday 2—5pm. Saturday 10am—1pm and 2—5pm. Also first Thursday in October—31st October 7—9.30pm. Tel: 041-889 3151.

### Erskine Bridge

The bridge is an impressive high level structure opened by HRH Princess Anne in 1971 and provides a direct link from Renfrew District to Loch Lomond and the Trossachs. The bridge replaced the Erskine Ferry and affords extensive views up and down river to pedestrian users.

### Finlayston Estate

Off the A8 at Langbank. The Estate is now a garden centre with woodland walks. The house has connections with John Knox and Robert Burns and is open April to August on Sundays from 2.30—4.30pm. At other times groups by appointment. Tel: Langbank 285.

### Formakin Estate, By Bishopton

A group of buildings and landscaped grounds designed in the Arts and Crafts style at the turn of the century. Currently being restored, visitors can take a guided tour in small groups — only by appointment. Open Saturday and Sunday 11am—6pm. Tel: 0505 863400.

### Gleniffer Braes Country Park, Glenfield Road, Paisley

1,000 breathtaking acres including Glen Park nature trail, picnic and children's play areas. Open dawn till dusk, the park affords extensive walks and spectacular views from this elevated moorland area, and contains an area reserved for model aero flying.

### Houston Village

Houston was developed in the 18th century as an estate village. The traditional smiddy building, village pubs and terraced houses combine to create a quiet, sleepy atmosphere which has successfully survived the development of extensive modern housing on its periphery.

### Inchinnan Bridges

Early 19th century stone bridges over the White Cart and Black Cart rivers close to St Conval's stone, and the site of the Inchinnan Church which houses the graves of the Knights Templar, whose order was introduced to Scotland in 1153 by King David I.

### Johnstone Castle

The remnants of a 1700 building formerly a much larger structure but largely demolished in the 1950's. The castle has significant historical links with the Cochrane and Houston families, major landowners who were instrumental in the development of the Burgh of Johnstone.

### Kilbarchan Village

A good example of an 18th century weaving village with many original buildings still fronting the narrow streets. A focal point is the steeple building in the square, orignally a school and meal market and now used as public meeting rooms.

### Laigh Kirk, Paisley

Originally built in 1738, the Laigh Kirk is now being converted to an Arts Centre. A former minister later became Principal Witherspoon of Princetown University, the only clergyman to sign the American Declaration of Independence in 1776. Theatre, workshop, cafeteria and bar open daily 10am—11pm. For further information telephone 041-887 1010.

## Linwood Sports' Centre

A modern sports' complex with a wide range of dry, indoor activity areas currently being complemented by extensive external facilities to cater for bowling, golf, hockey, rugby, cricket and tennis.

## Lochwinnoch Village

An attractive rural village close to the Castle Semple Water Park, Muirshiel Country Park and the R.S.P.B. nature reserve, Lochwinnoch contains a small local museum with displays reflecting agricultural, social and industrial aspects of village life. Museum open Monday, Wednesday and Friday 10am–1pm, 2–5pm and 6–8pm. Tuesday and Saturday 10am–1pm and 2–5pm. Open most days throughout the year, visitors should telephone Lochwinnoch 842615.

## Muirshiel Country Park

Four miles north of Lochwinnoch, the park features trails of varying length radiating from the Information Centre. Open daily 9am–8pm. Tel: Lochwinnoch 842803.

## Paisley Town Trail

An easy-to-follow route taking in the town's historic and architecturally significant buildings. Visitors can spend an hour or two walking round the trail and referring to a printed guide and wall plaques on the main buildings.

## Paisley Leisure Complex

Ultra-modern complex with extensive "fun" pool featuring artificial wave machine and water slides. Unique within the area, the complex is easily reached by public transport and has ample car parking. Monday–Saturday 10am–9.15pm, Sunday 10am–4.15pm. Tel: 041-889 4000.

## Paisley Abbey

Birthplace of the Stewart Dynasty, the Abbey dates, in part, to the 12th century and features regimental flags, relics, the Barochan Cross and beautiful stained glass windows. Monday–Friday 10.30am–12.30pm, 1.30–3.30pm, Saturday 10am–12 noon, 1.30–3.30pm. Tel: 041-889 3630.

## Paisley Town Hall

A Renaissance style building by the River Cart in the heart of Paisley, it features a slim clock tower and houses a Tourist Information Centre. It accommodates many exhibitions during the year and is also available for conferences and functions. Monday–Saturday 9am–5pm. Tel: 041-887 1007.

## Paisley Museum and Art Gallery, High Street, Paisley

In addition to the world famous collection of Paisley shawls, the Museum traces the history of the Paisley pattern, the development of weaving techniques and houses collections of local and natural history, ceramics and paints. Monday–Saturday 10am–5pm. Tel: 041-889 3151.

## Renfrew Town Hall

The Town Hall has a "fairy-tale" style to its 105 feet high spire and was the administrative centre of the Royal Burgh of Renfrew. Originally the principal town in the area, Renfrew was strategically placed on the River Clyde, and a passenger ferry continues to operate daily.

## Robert Tannahill, Weaver Poet

The works of Tannahill ranks with those of Burns. Born 1774 he took his own life in 1810 and is buried in a nearby graveyard. Visitors can visit his early home, site of his death, and his grave, and read his works in Paisley Library.

## Royal Society for Protection of Birds, Lochwinnoch

An interesting visitor centre with observation tower, hides, displays and gift shop. Open daily 10am–5.15pm. Tel: Lochwinnoch 842663.

## Sma' Shot Cottages, Paisley

Fully restored and furnished artisan's house of the Victorian era; exhibition room displaying photographs plus artefacts of local interest. 18th century weaver's loomshop with combined living quarters. Open May–September, Wednesday and Saturday 1–5pm. Group visits arranged by appointment. Tel: 041-812 2513 or 041-889 0530.

## The Clyde Estuary

Visitors travelling along the rural route of the Old Greenock Road above Langbank village at the western end of the District are able to take advantage of extensive views of the upper and lower Clyde Estuary, the Gareloch and the mountains beyond.

## Thomas Coats Memorial Church

Open daily 2–4pm. Visitors should check in advance. Another gift from the Coats family to Paisley, the Church was built in 1894 and, constructed of red sandstone, is one of the finest Baptist Churches in the country. Tel: 041-889 9980.

## Wallace Monument, Elderslie

The monument was erected in 1912 and marks the birthplace of the Scottish Patriot, Sir William Wallace. It stands adjacent to the reconstructed foundation plan of the adjacent Wallace Buildings which dated from the 17th century.

## Weaver's Cottage, Kilbarchan

This cottage, built in 1723, houses the last of the village's 800 looms and demonstrations are still given. It contains displays of weaving and domestic utensils, with Cottage garden and refreshments. Open April 2–May 31 and September 1–October 31 on Tuesdays, Thursdays, Saturdays and Sundays 2–5pm, June 1–August 31 from 2–5pm daily.

# Public Transport

The City of Glasgow has one of the most advanced, fully integrated public transport systems in the whole of Europe. The Strathclyde Transport network consists of; the local British Rail network, the local bus services and the fully modernised Glasgow Underground, with links to Glasgow Airport and the Steamer and Car Ferry Services.
*Note:* Although the information in this section is correct at the time of printing it should be checked before use.

## Bus Services and Tours

**Long Distance Coach Service**
Scottish Citylink Coaches Ltd
041-332 9191

**Shorter Journeys**
Tel: 041-226 4836
(0700-2400 Mon-Sat; 0900-2100 Suns)
for City Services and buses to Airdrie, Clydebank, Cumbernauld, Dumbarton, East Kilbride, Erskine, Hamilton, Johnstone, Kirkintilloch, Paisley, Wishaw
Buses leave from Anderston Cross Bus Station 041-248 7432.
*for* Ardrossan, Ayr, Blantyre, East Kilbride (via Busby), Edinburgh, Glasgow Airport, Gourock, Hamilton, Kilmarnock, Lanark, Largs, Motherwell, Paisley, Prestwick, Renfrew, Wemyss Bay, etc.
Buses leave from Buchanan Bus Station 041-332 7133.
*for* Aberfoyle, Airdrie, Bearsden, Blantyre, Callander, Clydebank, Crieff, Cumbernauld, Dundee, Dunfermline, East Kilbride (via

Bridgeton), Edinburgh, Glasgow Airport, Glencoe, Leven, Milngavie, Motherwell, Perth, St. Andrews, Stirling, etc.
**Day and Half Day Tours**
Scottish City Link
Buchanan Bus Station.
041-332 8055

Haldane's of Cathcart, Delvin Road, G44. 041-637 2234.

Strathclyde Buses Ltd.
197 Victoria Road, G42 7AD
041-636 3190
(Glasgow City Bus Tour and Glimpses of Charles R. Mackintosh Architecture with C.R.M. Society) 041-636 3195

## British Rail

Passenger enquiries: 041-204 2844.
Sleeper reservations: 041-221 2305.

**Central Station**
Inter-City electric services for English destinations, including Carlisle, Preston, Liverpool, Manchester (3 hours 35 minutes), Leeds, Nottingham, Crewe, Birmingham (4 hours 20 minutes), London (Euston) (5 hours). Also connections for Wales and West of England.
Scottish destinations in South and West include Ayr (for Burns country), Kilmarnock, Dumfries, Stranraer (for Ireland via Larne), Ardrossan and Largs. Electric trains include Gourock and Wemyss Bay (for Clyde steamers).

**Queen Street Station**
Trains for scenic West Highland Line to Oban, Fort William and Mallaig. Steamer connections to the Islands. Inter-City expresses for Edinburgh, connecting with trains to England including Newcastle, York, London (King's Cross). Services for North and East Scotland, including Fife, Stirling, Perth, Dundee, Aberdeen, Inverness, Wick, Thurso, Kyle of Lochalsh.
Electric trains: Dumbarton, Balloch (for Loch Lomond), Helensburgh. City Rail Link Service bus connects Queen Street Station and Central Station.

# Parks & Gardens

There are over 70 public parks within the city. The most famous is Glasgow Green. Abutting the north bank of the River Clyde, it was acquired in 1662. Of interest are the Winter Gardens attached to the People's Palace. Kelvingrove Park is an 85-acre park laid out by Sir Joseph Paxton in 1852. On the south side of the city is the 148-acre Queen's Park, Victoria Road, established 1857-94. Also of interest: Rouken Glen, Thornliebank, with a spectacular waterfall, walled garden, nature trail and boating facilities; Victoria Park, Victoria Park Drive, with its famous Fossil Grove flower gardens and yachting pond. In Great Western Road are the Botanic Gardens. Founded in 1817, the gardens' 42 acres are crammed with natural attractions, including the celebrated Kibble Palace glasshouse with its fabulous tree ferns, exotic plants and white marble Victorian statues.

The main public parks in Glasgow are:

**Alexandra**
671 Alexandra Parade, G31.

**Bellahouston**
Paisley Road West, G52.

**Botanic Gardens**
730 Gt. Western Road, G12.

**Hogganfield Loch**
Cumbernauld Road, G33.

**Kelvingrove**
Sauchiehall Street, G3.

**King's**
325 Carmunnock Road, G44.

**Linn**
Clarkston Road at Netherlee Road, G44.

**Queen's**
Victoria Road, G42.

**Rouken Glen**
Rouken Glen Road, G46.

**Springburn**
Broomfield Road, G21.

**Tollcross**
461 Tollcross Road, G32.

**Victoria**
Victoria Park Drive North, G14.

*Kibble Palace*

# Strathclyde
# Further Education

**Anniesland College**
Hatfield Drive, Glasgow, G12 0YE.
041-357 3969

**Ayr College**
Dam Park, Ayr, KA8 0EU.
Ayr (0292) 265184

**Barmulloch College**
186 Rye Road, Glasgow, G21 3JY.
041-558 9071/4

**Bell College of Technology**
Almada Street, Hamilton,
Lanarkshire, ML3 0JB.
Hamilton (0698) 283100

**Cambuslang College**
Janebank, Glasgow Road,
Cambuslang, Glasgow, G72 7BS.
041-641 6197

**Cardonald College of Further
Education**
690 Mosspark Drive, Glasgow,
G52 3AY.
041-883 6151/4

**Central College of Commerce**
300 Cathedral Street, G1 2TA.
041-552 3941

**Clydebank College**
Kilbowie Road, Clydebank,
Dunbartonshire, G81 2AA.
041-952 7771/6

**Coatbridge College**
Kildonan Street, Coatbridge,
Lanarkshire, ML5 3LS.
Coatbridge (0236) 22316

**Cumberland College**
Town Centre, Cumbernauld,
Glasgow, G67 1HU.
Cumbernauld (0236) 731811

**Glasgow College of Building and
Printing**
60 North Hanover Street, Glasgow,
G1 2BP.
041-332 9969

**Glasgow College of Food
Technology**
230 Cathedral Street, Glasgow,
G1 2TG.
041-552 3751

**Glasgow College of Nautical
Studies**
21 Thistle Street, Glasgow, G5 9XB.
041-429 3201

**Glasgow College of Technology**
Cowcaddens Road, Glasgow,
G4 0BA.
041-332 7090

**James Watt College**
Finnart Street, Greenock,
Renfrewshire, PA16 8HF.
Greenock (0475) 24433

**Kilmarnock College**
Holehouse Road, Kilmarnock,
Ayrshire, KA3 7AT.
Kilmarnock (0563) 23501

**Langside College**
50 Prospecthill Road, Glasgow,
G42 9LB.
041-649 4991

**Motherwell College**
Dalzell Drive, Motherwell,
Lanarkshire, ML1 2DD.
Motherwell (0698) 59641

**Reid Kerr College, The**
Renfrew Road, Paisley, Renfrewshire,
PA3 4DR.
041-889 4225/7

**Springburn College**
110 Flemington Street, Glasgow,
G21 4BX.
041-558 9001

**Stow College**
43 Shamrock Street, Glasgow,
G4 9LD.
041-332 1786

**University of Glasgow**
University Avenue, Glasgow
041-339 8855

**University of Strathclyde,**
16 Richmond Street, Glasgow,
G11XQ
041 552 4400

# Hospitals

**Greater Glasgow Health Board
(Administration)
225 Bath Street, Glasgow G2 4JT
041-204 2755**

Acorn Street Psychiatric Day Hospital
23 Acorn Street, Bridgeton,
Glasgow G40 4AN
041-556 4789

Baillieston Health Centre
20 Muirside Road,
Glasgow G69 7AD
041-771 0871

Belvidere Hospital
London Road, Glasgow G31 4PG
041-554 1855

Birdston Hospital, Milton of Campsie
Glasgow G65 8BY
041-776 6114

Blawarthill Hospital
Knightswood, Glasgow G13 3TG
041-954 9547

Bridgeton Health Centre
201 Abercromby Street
Glasgow G40 2EA
041-554 1866

Broomhill & Lanfine Hospitals
Kirkintilloch, Glasgow G66 1RR
041-776 5141

Carsewell House (Psychiatric
Outpatient)
5 Oakley Terrace, Glasgow G31 2HX
041-554 6267

Canniesburn Hospital
Switchback Road, Bearsden,
Glasgow G61 1QL
041-942 2255

Charing Cross (Alcohol and Drug)
Day Hospital, 8 Woodside Crescent,
Glasgow G3 7UL
041-332 5463

Children's Home Hospital
Strathblane, Glasgow G63 9EP
0360 70203

Clydebank Health Centre
Kilbowie Road, Clydebank G81 2TQ
041-952 2080

Cowglen Hospital
Boydstone Road, Glasgow G53 7XJ
041-632 9106

Darnley Hospital
Nitshill, Glasgow G53 7RR
041-881 1005

David Elder Infirmary
503 Langlands Road, Glasgow G51 4DY
041-445 2466

Douglas Inch Centre for Forensic
Psychiatry, 2 Woodside Terrace,
Glasgow G3 7UY
041-332 3844

Drumchapel Hospital
129 Drumchapel Road,
Glasgow G15 6PX
041-944 2344

Duke Street Hospital
253 Duke Street, Glasgow G31 1HY
041-556 5222

Duntocher Hospital
Duntocher, Clydebank G81 5QU
Duntocher 74294

Easterhouse Health Centre
9 Auchinlea Road, Glasgow G34 9NT
041-771 0781

Elder Cottage Hospital
1A Drumoyne Drive, Govan
Glasgow G51 4AT
041-445 2466

Gartloch Hospital
Gartcosh, Glasgow G69 8EJ
041-771 0771

Gartnavel General Hospital
1053 Great Western Road,
Glasgow G12 07N
041-334 8122

Gartnavel Royal Hospital
1055 Great Western Road,
Glasgow G12 0XH
041-334 6241

Glasgow Dental Hospital and School
378 Sauchiehall Street
Glasgow G2 3JZ
041-332 7020

Glasgow Eye Infirmary
2 Sandyford Place, Glasgow G3 7NB
041-204 0721

Glasgow Homeopathic Hospital
1000 Great Western Road,
Glasgow G12 0AA
041-339 0382

Glasgow Royal Infirmary
84 Castle Street, Glasgow G4 0SF
041-552 3535

Glasgow Royal Maternity Hospital
Rottenrow, Glasgow G4 0NA
041-552 3400

Glasgow School of Chiropody
757 Crookston Road,
Glasgow G53 7UA
041-883 0418

Glasgow School of Occupational
Therapy, 29 Sherbrooke Avenue,
Glasgow G41 4ER
041-427 3032

Gorbals Health Centre
45 Pine Place, Glasgow G5 0BQ
041-429 6291

Govan Health Centre
295 Langlands Road
Glasgow G51 4BJ
041-440 1212

Govanhill Health Centre
223 Calder Street
Glasgow G42 7DK
041-424 3003

Knightswood Hospital
125 Knightswood Road,
Glasgow G13 2XG
041-954 9641

Lennox Castle Hospital
Lennoxtown, Glasgow G65 7LB
Lennoxtown 313000

Lenzie Hospital
Lenzie, Kirkintilloch
Glasgow G66 5DE
041-776 1208

Leverndale Hospital
510 Crookston Road
Glasgow G53 7TU
041-882 6255

Lightburn Hospital
Carntyne Road, Glasgow G32 6ND
041-774 5102

Maryhill Health Centre
41 Shawpark Street,
Glasgow G20 9DR
041-946 7151

Mearnskirk Hospital
Newton Mearns, Glasgow G77 5RZ
041-639 2251

Parkhead Health Centre
101 Salamanca Street,
Glasgow G31 5ES
041-556 5232

Philipshill Hospital
East Kilbride Road, Busby,
Glasgow G76 9HW
041-644 1144

Possilpark Health Centre
85 Denmark Street,
Glasgow G22 5EG
041-336 5311

Queen Mother's Hospital
Yorkhill, Glasgow G3 8SH
041-339 8888

Royal Beatson Memorial Hospital
132 Hill Street, Glasgow G3 6UD
041-332 0286

Royal Hospital for Sick Children
129 Drumchapel Road
Glasgow G15 6PX
041-944 2344

Royal Hospital for Sick Children
Yorkhill, Glasgow G3 8SJ
041-339 8888

Royal Samaritan Hospital for Women
69 Coplaw Street, Glasgow G42 7JF
041-423 3033

Ruchill Hospital
Bilsland Drive, Glasgow G20 9NB
041-946 7120

Rutherglen Health Centre
130 Stonelaw Road, Rutherglen,
Glasgow G73 2PQ
041-647 7171

Rutherglen Maternity Hospital
120 Stonelaw Road, Rutherglen,
Glasgow G73 2PG
041-647 0011

Shettleston Health Centre
420 Old Shettleston Road,
Glasgow G32 7LU
041-778 9191

Southern General Hospital
1345 Govan Road, Glasgow G51 4TF
041-445 2466

Springburn Health Centre
486 Springburn Road,
Glasgow G21 1TR
041-558 0101

Stobhill General Hospital
133 Balornock Road,
Glasgow G21 3UW
041-558 0111

Stoneyetts Hospital
Chryston, Glasgow G69 0JG
041-776 1026

Townhead Health Centre
16 Alexandra Parade
Glasgow G31 2ES
041-552 3477

Victoria Geriatric Unit
Mansionhouse Road,
Glasgow G41 3DX
041-649 4511

Victoria Infirmary
Langside, Glasgow G42 9TY
041-649 4545

Waverley Park Hospital
Kirkintilloch, Glasgow G66 2HE
041-776 2461

Western Infirmary
Dumbarton Road, Glasgow G11 6NT
041-339 8822

Woodilee Hospital
Lenzie, Glasgow G66 3UG
041-776 2451

Woodside Health Centre
Barr Street, Glasgow G20 7LR
041-332 9977

# INDEX TO STREETS

## General Abbreviations

## District Abbreviations

## NOTES

The figures and letters following a street name indicate the postal district and map
square where the name will be found.

A street name followed by the name of another street in italics does not appear on the
map, but will be found adjoining or near the latter.

Alcaig Rd. G52 N12 49
Alder Av., Lenz. C22 12
Alder Ct., Barr. R 8 59
Alder Pl. G43 P14 62
Alder Pl., John. N 1 44
Alder Rd. G43 P14 62
Alder Rd., Cumb. C 4 71
Alder Rd., Dalm. C 6 4
Alderman Pl. G13 G11 19
Alderman Rd. G13 F 9 18
Aldersdyke Pl., Blan. R26 68
Alderside Dr., Udd. O27 57
Alexander St., Clyde. E 7 5
Alexandra Av. G33 G23 25
Alexandra Av., Lenz. D23 13
Alexandra Cross G31 K19 37
  *Duke St.*
Alexandra Ct. G31 K19 37
  *Roebank St.*
Alexandra Dr., Pais. M 4 45
Alexandra Dr., Renf. H 8 17
Alexandra Gdns., Lenz. D23 13
Alexandra Par. G31 K19 37
Alexandra Park St. G31 K19 37
Alexandra Rd., Lenz. D23 13
Alford St. G21 H17 22
Alfred Ter. G52 H14 20
  *Great Western Rd.*
Algie St. G41 O15 51
Alice St. G5 M17 52
Alice St., Pais. N 6 46
Aline Ct., Barr. Q 7 59
Allan Av., Renf. J 9 32
Allan Pl. G40 M19 53
Allan St. G40 N19 53
Allander Gdns., Bish. D18 10
Allander Rd., Bear. D11 7
Allander St. G22 H17 22
Allands Av., Renf. G 5 16
Allanfauld Rd., Cumb. B 2 70
Allanton Av., Pais. M 9 48
Allanton Dr. G52 L10 32
Allerton Gdns., Bail. M24 55
Alleysbank G73 N19 53
Allison Dr. G72 P22 66
Allison Pl. G42 N16 51
  *Prince Edward St.*
Allison Pl. Gart. H27 27
Allison St. G42 N16 51
Allnach Pl. G34 K27 41
Alloway Cres. G73 P18 64
Alloway Dr. G73 P18 64
Alloway Dr., Clyde. D 8 5
Alloway Rd. G43 P14 62
Alma St. G40 L19 37
Almond Av., Renf. J 9 32
Almond Cres., Pais. N 3 45
Almond Dr., Lenz. C22 12
Almond Rd. G33 G23 25
Almond Rd., Bear. E11 7
Almond St. G33 J20 37
Almond Vale, Udd. O28 57
  *Hamilton Vw.*
Alness Cres. G52 M12 49
Alpatrick Gdns., John. M 1 44
Alpine Gro., Udd. O27 57
Alsatian Av., Clyde E 8 5
Alston La. G40 L18 36
  *Claythorn St.*
Altnacreag Gdns., Chr. D28 15
Alton Gdns. G12 H14 20
  *Great George St.*
Alton Rd., Pais. M 8 47
Altyre St. G32 M21 54
Alva Gate. G52 N12 49
Alva Gdns. G52 N12 49
Alva Pl., Lenz. D24 13
Alyth Cres., Clark. S16 63
Alyth Gdns. G52 M12 49
Alyth Gdns., Clark. S16 63
Ambassador Way, Renf. J 8 31
  *Cockels Loan*
Amisfield St. G20 G15 21
Amochrie Dr., Pais. O 3 45
Amochrie Rd., Pais. N 3 45
Amulree Pl. G32 M22 54
Amulree St. G32 L22 38
Ancaster Dr. G13 G12 19
Ancaster La. G13 F11 19
  *Great Western Rd.*
Anchor Av., Pais. M 7 47
Anchor Cres., Pais. M 7 47

Anchor Dr., Pais. M 7 47
Anchor Wynd, Pais. M 7 47
Ancroft St. G20 H16 21
Ancrum St. G32 L22 38
Anderson Dr., Renf. H 8 17
Anderson Gdns., Blan. R27 69
  *Station Rd.*
Anderson Quay G3 L15 35
Anderson St. G11 J13 34
Andrew Av., Lenz. D23 13
Andrew Av., Renf. H 9 18
Andrew Dr., Clyde. F 8 17
Andrews St., Pais. L 6 30
Anglegate G14 H11 19
Angus Av. G52 M11 49
Angus Av., Bish. F20 23
Angus Gdns., Udd. O27 57
Angus La. G64 E20 11
Angus Oval G52 M10 48
Angus Pl. G52 M10 48
Angus St. G21 H18 22
Angus St., Clyde. F 9 18
Angus Wk., Udd. O28 57
Annan Dr. G73 O20 53
Annan Dr., Bear. D11 7
Annan Dr., Pais. N 3 45
Annan Pl., John. O08 43
Annan St. G42 O16 51
Annandale St. G42 M16 51
Annbank St. G31 L18 36
Anne Av., Renf. H 8 17
Anne Cres., Lenz. D23 13
Annette St. G42 N16 51
Annfield Gdns., Blan. R26 68
Annfield Pl. G31 K18 36
Annick Dr., Bear. E11 7
Annick St. G32 L22 38
Annick St. G72 P23 67
Anniesdale Av. G33 G23 25
Anniesland Cres. G14 G10 18
Anniesland Mansions G12 19
  G13
Anniesland Rd. G13 G11 19
Anniesland Rd. G14 G10 18
Anson St. G40 M18 52
Anson Way, Renf. J 8 31
  *Britannia Way*
Anstruther St. G32 L21 38
Antonine Gdns., C 7 5
  *Clyde.*
Antonine Rd., Bear. C10 6
Anworth St. G32 M22 54
Appin Rd. G31 K19 37
Appin Way, Udd. Q28 69
  *Bracken Ter.*
Appleby St. G22 H16 21
Applecross Gdns., Chr. D27 15
Applecross St. G22 H16 21
Appledore Cres., Udd. Q28 69
Apsley La. G11 J13 34
Apsley St. G11 J13 34
Aray St. G20 G14 20
Arbroath Av. G52 M10 48
Arcadia St. G40 L18 36
  *Drake St.*
Arcadia St. G40 L18 36
Arcan Cres. G15 E10 6
Arch St. G31 L19 37
Archerfield Av. G32 N22 54
Archerfield Cres. G32 N22 54
Archerfield Dr. G32 N22 54
Archerfield Gro. G32 N22 54
  *Archerfield Av.*
Archerhill Av. G13 F 9 18
Archerhill Cotts. G13 F10 18
  *Archerhill Rd.*
Archerhill Cres. G13 F10 18
Archerhill Gdns. G13 F10 18
  *Archerhill Rd.*
Archerhill Rd. G13 F10 18
Archerhill Sq. G13 F10 18
  *Kelso St.*
Archerhill St. G13 F10 18
  *Archerhill Rd.*
Archerhill Ter. G13 F10 18
  *Archerhill Rd.*
Ard Pl. G42 O18 52
Ard Rd., Renf. H 7 17
Ard St. G32 M22 54
Ardargie Dr. G32 O23 55
  *River Rd.*

Ardargie Pl. G32 O23 55
  *River Rd.*
Ardbeg Av. G73 Q21 66
Ardbeg Av., Bish. E20 11
Ardbeg St. G42 N16 51
Ardconnel St. G46 Q12 61
Arden Av. G46 R12 61
Arden Dr., Giff. R13 62
Arden Pl. G46 R12 61
  *Stewarton Rd.*
Ardencraig Cres. G44 R17 64
Ardencraig Dr. G45 R18 64
Ardencraig La. G45 R17 64
  *Ardencraig Rd.*
Ardencraig Quad. G45 R18 64
Ardencraig Rd. G45 R17 64
Ardencraig St. G45 R19 65
Ardencraig Ter. G45 R18 64
Ardenlea Rd., Udd. O27 57
Ardenlea St. G40 M19 53
Ardery St. G11 J13 34
  *Apsley St.*
Ardessie Pl. G20 G14 20
Ardessie St. G23 E14 8
  *Torrin Rd.*
Ardfern St. G32 M22 54
Ardgay Pl. G32 M22 54
Ardgay St. G32 M22 54
Ardgay Way G73 Q19 65
Ardgour Dr., Linw. L 1 28
Ardgowan Av., Pais. M 6 46
Ardgowan Dr., Udd. O27 57
Ardgowan St., Pais. N 6 46
Ardholm St. G32 L22 38
Ardhu Pl. G15 D 9 6
Ardlamont Sq., Linw. L 2 28
Ardlaw St. G51 L12 33
Ardle Rd. G43 P15 63
Ardlui St. G32 M21 54
Ardmaleish Cres. G45 R18 64
Ardmaleish Rd. G45 R17 64
Ardmaleish St. G45 R18 64
Ardmaleish Ter. G45 R18 64
Ardmay Cres. G44 O17 52
Ardmillan St. G33 K21 38
Ardmore Oval, Pais. L 4 29
Ardmore St. G31 K19 37
Ardmory Av. G42 O17 52
Ardmory La. G42 O18 52
Ardnacross Dr. G33 J23 39
Ardnahoe Av. G42 O17 52
Ardnahoe Pl. G42 O17 52
Ardneil Rd. G51 L12 33
Ardnish St. G51 K12 33
Ardo Gdns. G51 L13 34
Ardoch Gro. G72 P21 66
Ardoch Rd., Bear. C13 8
Ardoch St. G22 H17 22
Ardoch Way, Chr. E27 15
  *Braeside Av.*
Ardshiel Rd. G51 K12 33
Ardsloy La. G14 H10 18
  *Ardsloy Pl.*
Ardsloy Pl. G14 H10 18
Ardtoe Cres. G33 G24 25
Ardtoe Pl. G33 G24 25
Arduthie Rd. G51 K12 33
Ardwell Rd. G52 M12 49
Argosy Way, Renf. J 8 31
  *Britannia Way*
Argyle St. G3 J14 34
Argyle St. G3 K15 35
Argyle St., Pais. M 5 46
Argyll Arc. G2 K16 35
Argyll Av., Renf. H 7 17
Argyll Av., Bear. B12 7
Argyll Rd., Clyde. E 8 5
Arisaig Dr. G52 M12 49
Arisaig Dr., Bear. D13 8
Arisaig Pl. G52 M12 49
Ark La. G31 K18 36
Arkle Ter. G72 Q21 66
Arkleston Cres., Pais. K 7 31
Arkleston Rd., Pais. K 7 31
Arklet Rd. G51 L12 33
Arklie Av., Bear. B12 7
  *Tweedsmuir Cres.*
Arlington St. G3 J15 35
Armadale Ct. G31 K19 37
Armadale Path G31 K19 37
Armadale Pl. G31 K19 37
Armadale St. G31 K19 37

| Street | Ref | Page |
|---|---|---|
| Armour St. G31 | L18 | 36 |
| Armour St., John. | M 1 | 44 |
| Arngask Rd. G51 | K12 | 33 |
| Arnhall Pl. G52 | M12 | 49 |
| Arnholm Pl. G52 | M12 | 49 |
| Arnisdale Pl. G34 | K25 | 40 |
| Arnisdale Rd. G34 | K25 | 40 |
| Arnisdale Way G73 | Q19 | 65 |
| *Shieldaig Dr.* | | |
| Arniston St. G32 | K21 | 38 |
| Arnol Pl. G33 | K24 | 39 |
| Arnold Av., Bish. | E19 | 11 |
| Arnold St. G20 | G16 | 21 |
| Arnott Way G72 | P22 | 66 |
| Arnprior Gdns., Chr. | E27 | 15 |
| *Braeside Av.* | | |
| Arnprior Quad. G45 | Q17 | 64 |
| Arnprior Rd. G45 | Q17 | 64 |
| Arnprior St. G45 | Q17 | 64 |
| Arnside Av., Giff. | Q14 | 62 |
| Arnthern St. G72 | P23 | 67 |
| Arnwood Dr. G12 | G13 | 20 |
| Aron Ter. G72 | Q21 | 66 |
| Aros Dr. G52 | N12 | 49 |
| Arran Dr. G52 | M12 | 49 |
| Arran Dr., Cumb. | D 1 | 70 |
| Arran Dr., Giff. | R13 | 62 |
| Arran Dr., John. | N08 | 43 |
| Arran Dr., Pais. | O 6 | 46 |
| Arran La., Chr. | E28 | 15 |
| *Burnbrae Av.* | | |
| Arran Pl., Clyde. | E 8 | 5 |
| Arran Pl., Linw. | L 1 | 28 |
| Arran Rd., Renf. | J 8 | 31 |
| Arran Ter. G73 | P18 | 64 |
| Arranthrue Cres., Renf. | H 8 | 17 |
| Arranthrue Dr., Renf. | H 8 | 17 |
| Arriochmill Rd. G20 | H14 | 20 |
| *Kelvin Dr.* | | |
| Arrochar Ct. G23 | F15 | 21 |
| *Sunningdale Rd.* | | |
| Arrochar Dr. G23 | E14 | 8 |
| Arrochar St. G23 | F14 | 20 |
| Arrol Pl. G40 | M19 | 53 |
| Arrol St. G52 | K 9 | 32 |
| Arrowchar Ct. G23 | F15 | 21 |
| *Arrowchar St.* | | |
| Arrowchar St. G23 | F14 | 20 |
| Arrowsmith Av. G13 | F11 | 19 |
| Arthur Av., Barr. | R 7 | 59 |
| Arthur Rd., Pais. | O 6 | 46 |
| Arthur St. G3 | J14 | 34 |
| Arthur St., Pais. | L 5 | 30 |
| Arthurlie Av., Barr. | R 8 | 59 |
| Arthurlie Dr., Giff. | R14 | 62 |
| Arthurlie St. G51 | K12 | 33 |
| Arthurlie St., Barr. | R 8 | 59 |
| Arundel Dr. G42 | O16 | 51 |
| Arundel Dr., Bish. | D19 | 11 |
| Asbury Ct., Linw. | L 2 | 28 |
| Ascaig Cres. G52 | N12 | 49 |
| Ascog Rd., Bear. | E12 | 7 |
| Ascog St. G42 | N16 | 51 |
| Ascot Av. G12 | G12 | 19 |
| Ascot Ct. G12 | G13 | 20 |
| Ash Gro., Bish. | E19 | 11 |
| Ash Gro., Lenz. | C22 | 12 |
| Ash Gro., Udd. | O28 | 57 |
| *Douglas Cres.* | | |
| Ash Pl., John. | N 1 | 44 |
| Ash Rd., Bail. | M25 | 56 |
| Ash Rd., Cumb. | A 4 | 71 |
| Ash Rd., Dalm. | C 6 | 4 |
| Ash Wk. G73 | Q20 | 65 |
| Ashburton Rd. G12 | G13 | 20 |
| Ashby Cres. G13 | E12 | 7 |
| Ashcroft Dr. G44 | P18 | 64 |
| Ashdale Dr. G52 | M12 | 49 |
| Ashdene Rd. G22 | F16 | 21 |
| Ashfield St. G22 | H17 | 22 |
| Ashfield, Bish. | D19 | 11 |
| Ashgill Pl. G22 | G17 | 22 |
| Ashgill Rd. G22 | G16 | 21 |
| Ashgrove St. G40 | N19 | 53 |
| Ashgrove, Bail. | L27 | 41 |
| Ashkirk Dr. G52 | M12 | 49 |
| Ashlea Dr., Giff. | Q14 | 62 |
| Ashley La. G3 | J15 | 35 |
| *Woodlands Rd.* | | |
| Ashley St. G3 | J15 | 35 |
| Ashmore Rd. G43 | P15 | 63 |
| Ashton Gdns. G12 | J14 | 34 |
| *Ashton Rd.* | | |
| Ashton La. G12 | J14 | 34 |
| *University Av.* | | |
| Ashton Pl. G12 | H14 | 20 |
| *Byres Rd.* | | |
| Ashton Rd. G12 | J14 | 34 |
| *University Av.* | | |
| Ashton Rd. G73 | N19 | 53 |
| Ashton Ter. G12 | J14 | 34 |
| *Ashton Rd.* | | |
| Ashton Way G78 | O 3 | 45 |
| Ashtree Rd. G43 | O14 | 50 |
| Ashvale Cres. G21 | H18 | 22 |
| Ashvale Row E. G21 | H18 | 22 |
| *Ashvale Row* | | |
| Ashvale Row W. G21 | H18 | 22 |
| *Ashvale Row* | | |
| Aspen Pl., John. | N 1 | 44 |
| Athelstane Dr., Cumb. | D 1 | 70 |
| Athelstane Rd. G13 | F11 | 19 |
| Athena Way, Udd. | O28 | 57 |
| Athol Av. G52 | K 9 | 32 |
| Athol Gdns., Bear. | B12 | 7 |
| Athol Ter., Udd. | N27 | 57 |
| *Lomond Rd.* | | |
| Athole Gdns. G12 | H14 | 20 |
| Athole La. G12 | H14 | 20 |
| *Saltoun St.* | | |
| Atholl Cres., Pais. | L 9 | 32 |
| Atholl Dr., Giff. | S14 | 62 |
| Atholl Gdns. G73 | Q21 | 66 |
| Atholl Gdns., Bish. | D19 | 11 |
| Atholl La., Chr. | E28 | 15 |
| Atholl Pl., Linw. | L 1 | 28 |
| Atlas Pl. G21 | H18 | 22 |
| Atlas Rd. G21 | H18 | 22 |
| Atlas St., Clyde. | F 7 | 17 |
| Attlee Av., Clyde. | E 8 | 5 |
| Attlee Pl., Clyde. | E 8 | 5 |
| *Attlee Av.* | | |
| Attow Rd. G43 | P13 | 62 |
| Auburn Dr., Barr. | R 8 | 59 |
| Auburn Pl. G78 | L20 | 37 |
| Auchans Rd., Linw. | J 1 | 28 |
| Auchencrow St. G34 | K26 | 40 |
| Auchendale, Lenz. | C24 | 13 |
| Auchengeich Rd., Chr. | D26 | 14 |
| Auchengill Path G34 | J26 | 40 |
| *Auchengill Rd.* | | |
| Auchengill Pl. G34 | J26 | 40 |
| Auchengill Rd. G34 | J26 | 40 |
| Auchenglen Dr., Chr. | E27 | 15 |
| Auchenlodment Rd., John. | N 1 | 44 |
| Auchentorlie Quad., Pais. | M 7 | 47 |
| Auchentorlie St. G11 | J12 | 33 |
| Auchentoshan Av., Clyde. | C 6 | 4 |
| Auchentoshan Ter. G21 | J18 | 36 |
| Auchentoshen Cotts., Old K. | C 5 | 4 |
| Auchinairn Rd., Bish. | F18 | 22 |
| Auchinbee Loop Rd., Cumb. | B 1 | 70 |
| Auchinlea Rd. G34 | J24 | 39 |
| Auchinleck Av. G33 | G21 | 24 |
| Auchinleck Cres. G33 | G21 | 24 |
| Auchinleck Dr. G33 | G21 | 24 |
| Auchinleck Gdns. G33 | G21 | 24 |
| Auchinleck Rd. G33 | F21 | 24 |
| Auchinleck Rd., Clyde. | B 7 | 5 |
| Auchinleck Ter., Clyde. | B 7 | 5 |
| *Auchinleck Rd.* | | |
| Auchinloch Rd., Lenz. | D23 | 13 |
| Auchinloch St. G21 | H18 | 22 |
| Auchmannoch Av., Pais. | L 9 | 32 |
| Auckengreoch Av., John. | O08 | 43 |
| Auckengreoch Rd., John. | O08 | 43 |
| Auckland Pl., Dalm. | D 5 | 4 |
| Auckland St. G22 | H16 | 21 |
| Auld Kirk Rd. G72 | Q23 | 67 |
| Auld Rd., The, Cumb. | B 3 | 71 |
| Auld St., Dalm. | D 6 | 4 |
| Auldbar Rd. G52 | M12 | 49 |
| Auldbar Ter., Pais. | N 7 | 47 |
| Auldburn Rd. G43 | P13 | 62 |
| Auldearn Rd. G21 | F20 | 23 |
| Auldgirth Rd. G52 | M12 | 49 |
| Auldhouse Av. G42 | P13 | 62 |
| *Harriet St.* | | |
| Auldhouse Rd. G43 | P13 | 62 |
| Auldhouse Ter. G43 | P14 | 62 |
| *Auldhouse Rd.* | | |
| Aultbea St. G22 | F16 | 21 |
| Aultmore Rd. G33 | K24 | 39 |
| Aurs Cres., Barr. | R 8 | 59 |
| Aurs Dr., Barr. | R 8 | 59 |
| Aurs Pl., Barr. | R 8 | 59 |
| Aurs Rd., Barr. | Q 8 | 59 |
| Aursbridge Dr., Barr. | R 8 | 59 |
| Austen La. G13 | G12 | 19 |
| *Woodend Dr.* | | |
| Austen La. G13 | G12 | 19 |
| *Skaterig La.* | | |
| Austen Rd. G13 | G12 | 19 |
| Avenel Rd. G13 | E12 | 7 |
| Avenue End Rd. G33 | H22 | 24 |
| Avenue St. G40 | L19 | 37 |
| Avenue St. G73 | N19 | 53 |
| Avenue, The, Kilb. | N07 | 42 |
| *Low Barholm* | | |
| Avenuehead Rd., Chr. | D27 | 15 |
| Avenuehead Rd., Gart. | F28 | 27 |
| Avenuepark St. G20 | H15 | 21 |
| Aviemore Gdns., Bear. | C13 | 8 |
| Aviemore Rd. G52 | N12 | 49 |
| Avoch Dr. G46 | Q12 | 61 |
| Avoch St. G34 | J25 | 40 |
| Avon Av., Bear. | D13 | 8 |
| Avon Dr. G64 | F19 | 23 |
| Avon Dr., Linw. | L 1 | 28 |
| Avon Rd., Bish. | F19 | 23 |
| Avon Rd., Giff. | R13 | 62 |
| Avon St. G5 | L15 | 35 |
| Avonbank Rd. G73 | O18 | 52 |
| Avondale Dr., Pais. | L 7 | 31 |
| Avondale St. G33 | J22 | 38 |
| Avonhead Av. G67 | D 1 | 70 |
| *Avonhead Rd.* | | |
| Avonhead Gdns. G67 | D 1 | 70 |
| *Avonhead Rd.* | | |
| Avonhead Pl. G67 | D 1 | 70 |
| *Avonhead Rd.* | | |
| Avonhead Rd. G67 | D 1 | 70 |
| Avonspark St. G21 | H19 | 23 |
| Aylmer Rd. G43 | P15 | 63 |
| Ayr Rd., Giff. | R13 | 62 |
| Ayr St. G21 | H18 | 22 |
| Aytoun Rd. G41 | M14 | 50 |
| Back Causeway G31 | L20 | 37 |
| Back Sneddon St., Pais. | L 6 | 30 |
| Backmuir Rd. G15 | D10 | 6 |
| Bagnell St. G21 | G18 | 22 |
| Bailie Dr., Bear. | C12 | 7 |
| Baillie Dr., Both. | Q28 | 69 |
| Baillieston Rd. G32 | M23 | 55 |
| Baillieston Rd., Udd. | N25 | 56 |
| Bain Sq. G40 | L18 | 36 |
| *Bain St.* | | |
| Bain St. G40 | L18 | 36 |
| Bainsford St. G32 | L21 | 38 |
| Baird Av. G52 | K 9 | 32 |
| Baird Dr., Bear. | C11 | 7 |
| Baird St. G4 | J17 | 36 |
| Bairdsbrae G4 | H16 | 21 |
| *Possil Rd.* | | |
| Baker Pl. G41 | N15 | 51 |
| *Baker St.* | | |
| Baker St. G41 | N15 | 51 |
| Bakewell Rd., Bail. | L25 | 40 |
| Balaclava St. G2 | L16 | 35 |
| *McAlpine St.* | | |
| Balado Rd. G33 | K24 | 39 |
| Balbeg St. G51 | L12 | 33 |
| Balbeggie Pl. G32 | M23 | 55 |
| Balbeggie St. G32 | M23 | 55 |
| Balblair Rd. G52 | N12 | 49 |
| Balcaldine Av., Chr. | E25 | 14 |
| Balcarres Av. G12 | G14 | 20 |
| Balcomie St. G33 | J22 | 38 |
| Baldinnie Rd. G34 | K25 | 40 |
| Baldorran Cres., Cumb. | B 1 | 70 |
| Baldoven Cres. G33 | K24 | 39 |
| Baldovie Rd. G52 | M11 | 49 |
| Baldragon Rd. G34 | J25 | 40 |
| Baldric Rd. G13 | G11 | 19 |
| Baldwin Av. G13 | E11 | 7 |
| Balerno Dr. G52 | M12 | 49 |
| Balfluig St. G34 | J24 | 39 |

| Name | Grid | Pg |
|---|---|---|
| Balfour St. G20 | G14 | 20 |
| Balfron Rd. G51 | K12 | 33 |
| Balfron Rd., Pais. | L 8 | 31 |
| Balgair Dr., Pais. | L 7 | 31 |
| Balgair St. G22 | G16 | 21 |
| Balgair Ter. G32 | L22 | 38 |
| Balglass St. G22 | H16 | 21 |
| Balgonie Av. G78 | N 4 | 45 |
| Balgonie Av., Pais. | N 4 | 46 |
| Balgonie Dr., Pais. | N 5 | 46 |
| Balgonie Rd. G52 | M12 | 49 |
| Balgonie Woods, Pais. | N 5 | 46 |
| Balgownie Cres., Thorn. | R13 | 62 |
| Balgray Cres., Barr. | R 9 | 60 |
| Balgraybank St. G21 | H19 | 23 |
| Balgrayhill Rd. G21 | G18 | 22 |
| Balintore St. G32 | L22 | 38 |
| Baliol La. G3 | J15 | 35 |
| *Woodlands Rd.* | | |
| Baliol St. G3 | J15 | 35 |
| Ballaig Av., Bear. | C11 | 7 |
| Ballaig Cres. G33 | G23 | 25 |
| Ballantay Quad. G45 | Q19 | 65 |
| Ballantay Rd. G45 | Q19 | 65 |
| Ballantay Ter. G45 | Q19 | 65 |
| Ballantyne Rd. G52 | K10 | 32 |
| Ballater Dr., Bear. | E12 | 7 |
| Ballater Dr., Pais. | N 7 | 47 |
| Ballater Dr., Renf. | F 5 | 16 |
| Ballater St. G5 | L17 | 36 |
| Ballayne Dr., Chr. | E28 | 15 |
| Ballindalloch Dr. G31 | K19 | 37 |
| Balloch Gdns. G52 | M12 | 49 |
| Balloch Vw., Cumb. | C 2 | 70 |
| Ballochmill Rd. G73 | O20 | 53 |
| Ballogie Rd. G44 | O16 | 51 |
| Balmarino Pl. G64 | E20 | 11 |
| Balmartin Rd. G23 | E14 | 8 |
| Balmeg Av., Giff. | S14 | 62 |
| Balmerino Pl., Bish. | F20 | 23 |
| *Angus Av.* | | |
| Balmoral Cres. G42 | N16 | 51 |
| *Queens Dr.* | | |
| Balmoral Cres., Renf. | G 6 | 16 |
| Balmoral Dr. G32 | O22 | 54 |
| Balmoral Dr., Bear. | E13 | 8 |
| Balmoral Dr., G72 | P21 | 66 |
| Balmoral Gdns., Blan. | R26 | 68 |
| Balmoral Gdns., Udd. | N27 | 57 |
| *Kilmuir Rd.* | | |
| Balmoral Rd., John. | N 1 | 44 |
| Balmoral St. G14 | H10 | 18 |
| Balmore Pl. | G16 | 21 |
| *Balmore Rd.* | | |
| Balmore Rd. G23 | C15 | 9 |
| Balmore Sq. G22 | G16 | 21 |
| Balmuildy Rd., Bish. | D16 | 9 |
| G23 | | |
| Balornock Rd. G21 | G19 | 23 |
| Balruddery Pl. G64 | F20 | 23 |
| Balshagray Av. G11 | H12 | 19 |
| Balshagray Cres. G11 | J12 | 19 |
| Balshagray Pl. G11 | H12 | 19 |
| *Balshagray Dr.* | | |
| Baltic Ct. G40 | M19 | 53 |
| *Baltic St.* | | |
| Baltic La. G40 | M19 | 53 |
| Baltic Pl. G40 | M18 | 52 |
| Baltic St. G40 | M19 | 53 |
| Balure St. G31 | K20 | 37 |
| Balvaird Cres. G73 | O19 | 53 |
| Balvaird Dr. G73 | O19 | 53 |
| Balveny St. G33 | J23 | 39 |
| Balvicar Dr. G42 | N15 | 51 |
| Balvicar St. G42 | N15 | 51 |
| Balvie Av. G15 | E10 | 6 |
| Balvie Av., Giff. | R14 | 62 |
| Banavie Rd. G11 | H13 | 20 |
| Banchory Av. G43 | P13 | 62 |
| Banchory Av., Renf. | F 5 | 16 |
| Banchory Cres., Bear. | E13 | 8 |
| Banff St. G33 | J22 | 38 |
| Bangorshill St. G46 | Q12 | 61 |
| Bank Rd. G32 | O23 | 55 |
| Bank St. G12 | J15 | 35 |
| Bank St. G72 | P22 | 66 |
| Bank St., Barr. | R 8 | 59 |
| Bank St., Pais. | M 6 | 30 |
| Bankbrae Av. G53 | P10 | 60 |
| Bankend St. G33 | J22 | 38 |
| Bankfoot Dr. G52 | M10 | 48 |
| Bankfoot Rd. G52 | M10 | 48 |
| Bankfoot Rd., Pais. | L 4 | 29 |
| Bankglen Rd. G15 | D10 | 6 |
| Bankhall St. G42 | N16 | 51 |
| Bankhead Av. G13 | G10 | 18 |
| Bankhead Dr. G73 | O19 | 53 |
| Bankhead Rd. G73 | P18 | 64 |
| Bankhead Rd., | B25 | 14 |
| Waterside | | |
| Bankier St. G40 | L18 | 36 |
| Banknock St. G32 | L21 | 38 |
| Bankside Av., John. | M09 | 43 |
| Banling Green Rd. G44 | P16 | 63 |
| *Clarkston Rd.* | | |
| Bannatyne Av. G31 | K19 | 37 |
| Banner Dr. G13 | E11 | 7 |
| Banner Rd. G13 | E11 | 7 |
| Bannercross Av., Bail. | L25 | 40 |
| Bannercross Dr., Bail. | L23 | 40 |
| Bannercross Gdns., Bail. | L25 | 40 |
| *Bannercross Dr.* | | |
| Bannerman Pl., Clyde. | E 8 | 5 |
| Bannerman St., Clyde. | E 7 | 5 |
| Bantaskin St. G20 | F14 | 20 |
| Banton Pl. G33 | K25 | 40 |
| Barassie Ct., Both. | R27 | 69 |
| Barbae Pl., Udd. | Q28 | 69 |
| *Hume Dr.* | | |
| Barbreck Rd. G42 | N15 | 51 |
| *Pollokshaws Rd.* | | |
| Barcaple St. G21 | H18 | 22 |
| Barclay Av., John. | N 1 | 44 |
| Barclay Sq., Renf. | J 7 | 31 |
| Barclay St. G21 | G18 | 22 |
| *Balgrayhill Rd.* | | |
| Barcraigs Dr., Pais. | O 6 | 46 |
| Bard Av. G13 | F10 | 18 |
| Bardowie St. G22 | H16 | 21 |
| Bardrain Av., John. | N 2 | 44 |
| Bardrain Rd., Pais. | O 5 | 46 |
| Bardykes Rd., Blan. | R26 | 68 |
| Barfillan Dr. G52 | L12 | 33 |
| Barfillan Rd. G52 | L12 | 33 |
| Bargaran Rd. G53 | M10 | 48 |
| Bargarron Dr., Pais. | K 7 | 31 |
| Bargeddie St. G33 | J20 | 37 |
| Barhill Cres., Kilb. | N07 | 42 |
| Barholm Sq. G33 | J23 | 39 |
| Barke Rd., Cumb. | B 3 | 71 |
| Barlanark Av. G32 | K23 | 39 |
| Barlanark Pl. G32 | L23 | 39 |
| *Hallhill Rd.* | | |
| Barlanark Pl. G33 | K24 | 39 |
| Barlanark Rd. G33 | K23 | 39 |
| Barlia Dr. G45 | Q18 | 64 |
| Barlia St. G45 | Q18 | 64 |
| Barlia Ter. G45 | Q18 | 64 |
| Barloch St. G22 | H17 | 22 |
| Barlogan Av. G52 | L12 | 33 |
| Barlogan Quad. G52 | L12 | 33 |
| Barmill Rd. G43 | P13 | 62 |
| Barmulloch Rd. G21 | H19 | 23 |
| Barn Grn. G78 | M07 | 42 |
| Barnard Gdns., Bish. | D19 | 11 |
| Barnard Ter. G40 | M19 | 53 |
| Barnbeth Rd. G53 | N10 | 48 |
| Barnes Rd. G20 | G16 | 21 |
| Barnes St., Barr. | R 7 | 59 |
| Barnflat St. G73 | N19 | 53 |
| Barnkirk Av. G15 | D10 | 6 |
| Barns St., Clyde. | E 8 | 5 |
| Barnsford Av., Renf. | H 4 | 16 |
| Barnsford Rd., Pais. | J 4 | 29 |
| Barnton St. G32 | K21 | 38 |
| Barnwell Ter. G51 | K12 | 33 |
| Barochan Rd. G53 | M10 | 48 |
| Baron Rd., Pais. | L 7 | 31 |
| Baron St., Renf. | J 8 | 31 |
| Baronald Dr. G12 | G13 | 20 |
| Baronald Gate G12 | G13 | 20 |
| Baronald St. G73 | N19 | 53 |
| Baronhill, Cumb. | A 3 | 71 |
| Barons Court Rd., John. | M 3 | 45 |
| Barr Cres., Clyde. | C 7 | 5 |
| Barr Pl., Pais. | M 5 | 46 |
| Barr St. G20 | H16 | 21 |
| Barra Av., Renf. | J 8 | 31 |
| Barra St. G20 | F14 | 20 |
| Barrachnie Cres., Bail. | L24 | 39 |
| Barrachnie Rd., Bail. | L24 | 39 |
| Barrack St. G4 | L18 | 36 |
| Barrhead Rd. G43 | O 9 | 48 |
| Barrhead Rd., Pais. | M 7 | 47 |
| Barrie Quad., Clyde. | D 7 | 5 |
| Barrie Rd. G52 | K10 | 32 |
| Barrington Dr. G4 | J15 | 35 |
| Barrisdale Rd. G20 | F14 | 20 |
| Barrisdale Way G73 | Q19 | 65 |
| Barrland Dr., Giff. | Q14 | 62 |
| Barrland St. G41 | M16 | 51 |
| Barrochan Cres., Pais. | M 4 | 45 |
| Barrochan Rd., John. | M09 | 43 |
| Barrowfield St. G40 | L19 | 37 |
| Barrwood St. G33 | J21 | 38 |
| Barshaw Dr., Pais. | L 7 | 31 |
| Barshaw Pl., Pais. | L 8 | 31 |
| Barshaw Rd. G52 | L 9 | 32 |
| Barterholm Rd., Pais. | N 6 | 46 |
| Bartholomew St. G40 | M19 | 53 |
| Bartiebeith Rd. G33 | K24 | 39 |
| Basset Av. G13 | F10 | 18 |
| Basset Cres. G13 | F10 | 18 |
| Bath La. G2 | K16 | 35 |
| *Blythswood St.* | | |
| Bath La. W. G3 | K15 | 35 |
| *North St.* | | |
| Bath St. G2 | K16 | 35 |
| Bathgate St. G31 | L19 | 37 |
| Bathgo Av., Pais. | M 9 | 48 |
| Batson St. G42 | N16 | 51 |
| Battle Pl. G41 | O15 | 51 |
| Battleburn St. G32 | M22 | 54 |
| Battlefield Av. G42 | O16 | 51 |
| Battlefield Cres. G42 | O16 | 51 |
| *Battlefield Gdns.* | | |
| Battlefield Gdns. G42 | O16 | 51 |
| Battlefield Rd. G42 | O16 | 51 |
| Bavelaw St. G33 | J23 | 39 |
| Bayfield Av. G15 | D10 | 6 |
| Bayfield Ter. G15 | D10 | 6 |
| Beaconsfield Rd. G12 | G13 | 20 |
| Beafort Av. G43 | P14 | 62 |
| Beard Cres., Gart. | G27 | 27 |
| Beardmore Cotts., Renf. | G 6 | 16 |
| Beardmore St., Dalm. | D 5 | 4 |
| Beardmore Way, Dalm. | D 5 | 4 |
| Bearford Dr. G52 | L10 | 32 |
| Bearsden Rd., Bear. | E12 | 7 |
| & G13 | | |
| Beaton Rd. G41 | N15 | 51 |
| Beattock St. G31 | L20 | 37 |
| Beatty St., Dalm. | D 4 | 4 |
| Beaufort Gdns., Bish. | E18 | 10 |
| Beauly Dr., Pais. | N 3 | 45 |
| Beauly Pl. G20 | G14 | 20 |
| Beauly Pl., Bish. | E20 | 11 |
| Beauly Pl., Chr. | E26 | 14 |
| Beauly Rd., Bail. | M25 | 56 |
| Beaumont Gate G12 | J14 | 34 |
| Bedale Rd., Bail. | M24 | 55 |
| Bedford Av., Clyde. | E 8 | 5 |
| *Onslow Rd.* | | |
| Bedford La. G5 | L16 | 35 |
| Bedford Row G5 | L16 | 35 |
| *Dunmore St.* | | |
| Bedford St. G5 | L16 | 35 |
| Bedlay Ct., Chr. | D28 | 15 |
| Bedlay St. G21 | H18 | 22 |
| *Petershill Rd.* | | |
| Bedlay St. G21 | H18 | 22 |
| *Linsburn St.* | | |
| Bedlay Wk., Chr. | D28 | 15 |
| Beech Av. G41 | M13 | 50 |
| Beech Av. G72 | P21 | 66 |
| Beech Av. G73 | Q20 | 65 |
| Beech Av., Bail. | L25 | 40 |
| Beech Av., Bear. | C13 | 8 |
| Beech Av., John. | N 2 | 44 |
| Beech Av., Pais. | N 7 | 47 |
| Beech Av. North Av. | P21 | 66 |
| G72 | | |
| Beech Dr., Dalm. | C 7 | 5 |
| Beech Gdns., Bail. | L25 | 40 |
| Beech Gro., Barr. | R 8 | 59 |
| *Arthurlie Av.* | | |
| Beech Pl., Bish. | F19 | 23 |
| Beech Rd., Bish. | F19 | 23 |
| Beech Rd., John. | N08 | 43 |
| Beech Rd., Lenz. | C23 | 13 |
| Beechcroft Pl., Blan. | R27 | 69 |
| Beeches Av., Clyde. | C 6 | 4 |
| Beeches Rd., Clyde. | C 6 | 4 |
| Beeches Ter., Clyde. | C 7 | 4 |
| Beechgrove St. G40 | N19 | 53 |

| | | |
|---|---|---|
| Blythswood Dr., Pais. | L 6 | 30 |
| Blythswood Rd., Renf. | G 8 | 17 |
| Blythswood Sq. G2 | K16 | 35 |
| Blythswood St. G2 | K16 | 35 |
| Boclair Av., Bear. | D12 | 7 |
| Boclair Cres., Bear. | D13 | 8 |
| Boclair Cres., Bish. | E19 | 11 |
| Boclair Rd., Bear. | D13 | 8 |
| Boclair Rd., Bish. | E19 | 11 |
| Boclair St. G13 | F12 | 19 |
| Boden St. G40 | M19 | 53 |
| Bodmin Gdns., Chr. | D27 | 15 |
| *Gartferry Rd.* | | |
| Bogany Ter. G45 | R18 | 64 |
| Bogbain Rd. G34 | K25 | 40 |
| Boghall Pl., Udd. | N25 | 56 |
| Boghall Rd., Udd. | N25 | 56 |
| Boghall St. G33 | J22 | 38 |
| Boghead Rd. G21 | H19 | 23 |
| Boghead Rd., Lenz. | D22 | 12 |
| Bogleshole Rd. G72 | O21 | 54 |
| Bogmoor Rd. G51 | K11 | 33 |
| Bogside Pl., Bail. | K26 | 40 |
| *Whamflet Av.* | | |
| Bogside Rd. G33 | G22 | 24 |
| Bogside St. G40 | M19 | 53 |
| Bogton Av. G44 | Q15 | 63 |
| Bogton Avenue La. G44 | Q15 | 63 |
| *Bogton Av.* | | |
| Boleyn Rd. G41 | N15 | 51 |
| Bolivar Ter. G42 | O17 | 52 |
| Bolton Dr. G42 | O16 | 51 |
| Bon Accord St., Clyde. | F 7 | 17 |
| Bonawe St. G20 | H15 | 21 |
| *Kirkland St.* | | |
| Boness St. G40 | M19 | 53 |
| Bonhill St. G22 | H16 | 21 |
| Bonmore Gdns., Udd. | O27 | 57 |
| Bonnar St. G40 | M19 | 53 |
| Bonnaughton Rd., Bear. | C10 | 6 |
| Bonnyholm Av. G53 | M10 | 48 |
| Bonnyrigg Dr. G43 | P13 | 62 |
| Bonyton Av. G13 | G 9 | 18 |
| Boon Dr. G15 | E10 | 6 |
| Boquhanran Pl., Clyde. | D 7 | 5 |
| *Albert Rd.* | | |
| Boquhanran Rd., Clyde | E 6 | 4 |
| Borden La. G13 | G12 | 19 |
| *Borden Rd.* | | |
| Borden Rd. G13 | G12 | 19 |
| Boreland Dr. G13 | F10 | 18 |
| Boreland Pl. G13 | G10 | 18 |
| Borgie Cres. G72 | P22 | 66 |
| Borland Rd., Bear. | D13 | 8 |
| Borron St. G4 | H17 | 22 |
| Borthwick St. G33 | J22 | 38 |
| Boswell Sq. G52 | K 9 | 32 |
| Botanic Cres. G20 | H14 | 20 |
| Bothlyn Cres., Gart. | F27 | 27 |
| Bothlynn Dr. G33 | G23 | 25 |
| Bothlynn Rd., Chr. | F26 | 26 |
| Bothwell La. G2 | K16 | 35 |
| *West Campbell St.* | | |
| Bothwell Park Rd. G71 | R28 | 69 |
| Bothwell Rd., Udd. & Both. | P27 | 69 |
| Bothwell St. G2 | K16 | 35 |
| Bothwell St. G72 | P21 | 66 |
| Bothwell Ter. G12 | J15 | 35 |
| *Bank St.* | | |
| Bothwick Way, Pais. | O 3 | 45 |
| *Crosbie Dr.* | | |
| Boundary Rd. G73 | N18 | 52 |
| Bourne Cres., Renf. | F 5 | 16 |
| Bourne Ct., Renf. | F 5 | 16 |
| Bourtree Dr. G73 | Q20 | 65 |
| Bouverie St. G14 | G 9 | 18 |
| Bouverie St. G73 | O18 | 52 |
| Bowden Dr. G52 | L10 | 32 |
| Bower St. G12 | H15 | 21 |
| Bowerwalls St., Barr. | Q 9 | 60 |
| Bowes Cres., Bail. | M24 | 55 |
| Bowfield Av. G52 | L 9 | 32 |
| *Bowfield Cres.* | | |
| Bowfield Cres. G52 | L 9 | 32 |
| Bowfield Dr. G52 | L 9 | 32 |
| Bowfield Pl. G52 | L 9 | 32 |
| *Gleddoch Rd.* | | |
| Bowfield Ter. G52 | L 9 | 32 |
| *Bowfield Cres.* | | |
| Bowhouse Way G73 | Q19 | 65 |
| Bowling Green La. G14 | H11 | 19 |
| *Westland Dr.* | | |
| Bowling Green Rd. G14 | H11 | 19 |
| Bowling Green Rd. G32 | M23 | 55 |
| Bowman St. G42 | N16 | 51 |
| Bowmont Gdns. G12 | H14 | 20 |
| Bowmont Hill, Bish. | D19 | 11 |
| Bowmont Ter. G12 | H14 | 20 |
| Bowmore Gdns. G73 | Q21 | 66 |
| Bowmore Rd. G52 | L12 | 33 |
| Boyd St. G42 | N16 | 51 |
| Boydstone Pl. G46 | P12 | 61 |
| Boydstone Rd. G43 | P12 | 61 |
| Boyle St., Clyde. | F 8 | 17 |
| Boyleston Rd., Barr. | Q 7 | 59 |
| Boyndie Path G34 | K25 | 40 |
| Boyndie St. G34 | K25 | 40 |
| Brabloch Cres., Pais. | L 6 | 30 |
| Bracadale Dr., Bail. | M26 | 56 |
| Bracadale Gdns., Bail. | M26 | 56 |
| Bracadale Rd., Bail. | M26 | 56 |
| Bracken Rd., Barr. | P 7 | 59 |
| Bracken St. G22 | G16 | 21 |
| Bracken Ter., Udd. | Q28 | 69 |
| Brackenbrae Av., Bish. | E18 | 10 |
| Brackenbrae Rd., Bish. | E18 | 10 |
| Brackenrig Rd. G46 | R12 | 61 |
| Bracla Av. G13 | F 9 | 18 |
| Bracora Pl. G20 | G14 | 20 |
| *Glenfinnan Dr.* | | |
| Bradan Av. G13 | F 9 | 18 |
| Bradda Av. G73 | Q20 | 65 |
| Bradfield Av. G12 | G14 | 20 |
| Brae Av., Clyde. | B 7 | 5 |
| Brae Cres., Clyde. | B 7 | 5 |
| Braeface Rd., Cumb. | C 2 | 70 |
| Braefield Dr., Thorn. | Q13 | 62 |
| Braefoot Cres., Pais. | O 6 | 46 |
| Braehead Rd., Clyde. | B 7 | 5 |
| Braehead Rd.; Cumb. | B 3 | 71 |
| Braehead Rd., Pais. | P 5 | 58 |
| Braehead St. G5 | M17 | 52 |
| Braemar Av., Dalm. | D 6 | 4 |
| Braemar Cres., Bear. | E12 | 7 |
| Braemar Dr., John. | N 1 | 44 |
| Braemar Rd. G73 | Q21 | 66 |
| Braemar Rd., Renf. | G 5 | 16 |
| Braemar St. G42 | O15 | 51 |
| Braemar Vw., Dalm. | C 6 | 4 |
| Braemount Av., Pais. | P 5 | 58 |
| Braes Av., Clyde. | F 8 | 17 |
| Braeside Av. G73 | O20 | 53 |
| Braeside Av., Chr. | E27 | 15 |
| Braeside Cres., Bail. | L27 | 41 |
| Braeside Cres., Barr. | R 9 | 60 |
| Braeside Dr., Barr. | R 8 | 59 |
| Braeside Pl. G72 | Q22 | 66 |
| Braeside St. G20 | H15 | 21 |
| Braid Gro. G4 | J16 | 35 |
| Braid St. G4 | J16 | 35 |
| Braidbar Farm Rd., Giff. | Q14 | 62 |
| Braidbar Rd., Giff. | Q14 | 62 |
| Braidcraft Rd. G53 | N11 | 49 |
| Braidfauld Gdns. G32 | M21 | 54 |
| Braidfauld Pl. G32 | N21 | 54 |
| Braidfauld St. G32 | N21 | 54 |
| Braidfield Rd., Clyde. | C 7 | 5 |
| Braidholm Cres., Giff. | Q14 | 62 |
| Braidholm Rd., Giff. | Q14 | 62 |
| Braids Rd., Pais. | N 6 | 46 |
| Bramley Pl., Lenz. | D24 | 13 |
| Branchock Av. G72 | Q23 | 67 |
| Brand St. G51 | L14 | 34 |
| Brandon Gdns. G72 | P21 | 66 |
| Brandon St. G31 | L18 | 36 |
| Branscroft G78 | M07 | 42 |
| Brassey St. G20 | G15 | 21 |
| Breadalbane Gdns. G73 | Q20 | 65 |
| Breadalbane St. G3 | K15 | 35 |
| Brech Av., Bail. | L27 | 41 |
| Brechin Rd., Bish. | E20 | 11 |
| Brechin St. G3 | K15 | 35 |
| Breck Av. G78 | O 2 | 44 |
| Brediland Rd., Linw. | L 1 | 28 |
| Brediland Rd., Pais. | N 3 | 45 |
| Bredisholm Dr., Bail. | M26 | 56 |
| Bredisholm Rd., Bail. | M27 | 57 |
| Bredisholm Ter., Bail. | M26 | 56 |
| Brenfield Av. G44 | Q15 | 63 |
| Brenfield Dr. G44 | Q15 | 63 |
| Brentwood Av. G53 | Q10 | 60 |
| Brentwood Dr. G53 | Q10 | 60 |
| Brentwood Sq. G53 | Q10 | 60 |
| *Brentwood Dr.* | | |
| Brentwood Rd. G53 | Q10 | 60 |
| Brereton St. G42 | N17 | 52 |
| Bressey Rd. G33 | L24 | 39 |
| Breval Cres., Clyde. | B 7 | 5 |
| Brewery St., John. | M09 | 43 |
| Brewster Av., Pais. | K 7 | 31 |
| Briar Dr., Clyde. | D 7 | 5 |
| Briar Neuk, Bish. | F19 | 23 |
| Briar Rd. G43 | P14 | 62 |
| Briarlea Dr., Giff. | Q14 | 62 |
| Brick La., Pais. | L 6 | 30 |
| Bridge of Weir Rd. Kilb. & Linw. | L08 | 43 |
| Bridge St., Dalm. | D 6 | 4 |
| Bridge St., G72 | P22 | 66 |
| Bridge St., Linw. | L 2 | 28 |
| Bridge St., Pais. | M 6 | 46 |
| Bridgebar St., Barr. | Q 9 | 60 |
| Bridgeburn Dr., Chr. | E27 | 15 |
| Bridgegate G1 | L17 | 36 |
| Bridgend Rd. G53 | O11 | 49 |
| Bridgeton Cross G40 | L18 | 36 |
| Brigham Pl. G23 | F15 | 21 |
| *Broughton Rd.* | | |
| Brighton Pl. G51 | L13 | 34 |
| Brighton St. G51 | L13 | 34 |
| Brightside Av., Udd. | P28 | 69 |
| Brisbane St. G42 | O16 | 51 |
| Brisbane St., Dalm. | D 5 | 4 |
| Britannia Way, Clyde. | E 7 | 5 |
| Britannia Way, Renf. | J 8 | 31 |
| Briton St. G51 | L13 | 34 |
| Broad Pl. G40 | L18 | 36 |
| *Broad St.* | | |
| Broad St. G40 | L18 | 36 |
| Broadford St. G4 | J17 | 36 |
| *Harvey St.* | | |
| Broadholm St. G22 | G16 | 21 |
| Broadleys Av., Bish. | D18 | 10 |
| Broadlie Dr. G13 | G10 | 18 |
| Broadloan, Renf. | J 8 | 31 |
| Broadwood Dr. G44 | P16 | 63 |
| Brock Oval G53 | P11 | 61 |
| Brock Pl. G53 | O11 | 49 |
| Brock Rd. G53 | O11 | 49 |
| Brock Ter. G53 | P11 | 61 |
| Brock Way G67 | C 3 | 71 |
| *North Carbrain Rd.* | | |
| Brockburn Rd. G53 | N10 | 48 |
| Brockburn Ter. G53 | O11 | 49 |
| Brockville St. G32 | L21 | 38 |
| Brodick Sq. G64 | F19 | 23 |
| Brodick St. G21 | J19 | 37 |
| Brodie Park Av., Pais. | N 6 | 46 |
| Brodie Pl., Renf. | J 7 | 31 |
| Brodie Rd. G21 | F20 | 23 |
| Brogknowe, Udd. | O26 | 56 |
| *Glasgow Rd.* | | |
| Brook St. G40 | L18 | 36 |
| Brooklands Av., Udd. | O27 | 57 |
| Brooklea Dr., Giff. | P14 | 62 |
| Brookside St. G40 | L19 | 37 |
| Broom Cres., Barr. | P 7 | 59 |
| Broom Dr., Clyde. | D 7 | 5 |
| Broom Gdns., Lenz. | C22 | 12 |
| Broom Rd. G43 | P14 | 62 |
| Broom Rd. G67 | A 4 | 71 |
| Broom Ter., John. | N 1 | 44 |
| Broomdyke Way, Pais. | K 5 | 30 |
| Broomfield Av. G21 | H19 | 23 |
| *Broomfield Rd.* | | |
| Broomfield Av. G72 | O20 | 53 |
| Broomfield Pl. G21 | G18 | 22 |
| *Broomfield Rd.* | | |
| Broomfield Rd. G21 | G18 | 22 |
| Broomfield Ter., Udd. | N27 | 57 |
| Broomhill Av. G32 | O22 | 54 |
| Broomhill Cres. G11 | H12 | 19 |
| Broomhill Dr. G11 | H12 | 19 |
| Broomhill Dr. G73 | P19 | 65 |
| Broomhill Gdns. G11 | H12 | 19 |
| Broomhill La. G11 | H12 | 19 |
| Broomhill Path G11 | J12 | 33 |
| Broomhill Pl. G11 | H12 | 19 |
| *Broomhill Dr.* | | |
| Broomhill Rd. G11 | J12 | 33 |
| Broomhill Ter. G11 | J12 | 33 |
| Broomieknowe Dr. G73 | P19 | 65 |
| Broomieknowe Rd. G73 | P19 | 65 |
| Broomielaw G1 | L16 | 35 |

| Name | Grid | Page |
|---|---|---|
| Broomknowe Pl. G66 | D24 | 13 |
| Broomknowe, Cumb. | B 1 | 70 |
| *Logan Dr.* | | |
| Broomknowes Rd. G21 | H19 | 23 |
| Broomlands Rd., Cumb. | D 3 | 71 |
| Broomlands St., Pais. | M 5 | 46 |
| Broomlea Cres., Renf. | F 5 | 16 |
| Broomley Dr. G46 | R14 | 62 |
| Broomley La., Giff. | R14 | 62 |
| Broomloan Ct. G51 | L13 | 34 |
| Broomloan Pl. G51 | L13 | 34 |
| Broomloan Rd. G51 | L13 | 34 |
| Broompark Circus G31 | K18 | 36 |
| Broompark Dr. G31 | K18 | 36 |
| Broompark Dr., Renf. | F 5 | 16 |
| Broompark St. G31 | K18 | 36 |
| Broomton Rd. G21 | F20 | 23 |
| Broomward Dr., John. | M 1 | 44 |
| Brora Dr., Bear. | D13 | 8 |
| Brora Dr., Giff. | R14 | 62 |
| Brora Dr., Renf. | H 9 | 18 |
| Brora Gdns., Bish. | E19 | 11 |
| Brora La. G31 | J20 | 37 |
| *Brora St.* | | |
| Brora Rd., Bish. | E19 | 11 |
| Brora St. G33 | J20 | 37 |
| Broughton Dr. G23 | F15 | 21 |
| Broughton Rd. G23 | F15 | 21 |
| Brown Av., Clyde. | F 8 | 17 |
| Brown Rd., Cumb. | C 2 | 70 |
| Brown St. G2 | K16 | 35 |
| Brown St., Pais. | L 5 | 30 |
| Brown St., Renf. | J 7 | 31 |
| Brownhill Rd. G43 | Q13 | 62 |
| Brownlie St. G42 | O16 | 51 |
| Browns La., Pais. | M 6 | 46 |
| Brownsdale Rd. G73 | O18 | 52 |
| Brownside Av. G72 | P21 | 66 |
| Brownside Av., Barr. | P 7 | 59 |
| Brownside Av., Pais. | O 5 | 46 |
| Brownside Cres., Barr. | P 7 | 59 |
| Brownside Dr. G13 | G 9 | 18 |
| Brownside Dr., Barr. | P 7 | 59 |
| Brownside Gro., Barr. | P 7 | 59 |
| Brownside Rd. G72 & G73 | P20 | 65 |
| Bruce Av., John. | O09 | 43 |
| Bruce Av., Pais. | K 7 | 31 |
| Bruce Rd. G41 | M15 | 51 |
| Bruce Rd., Pais. | L 7 | 31 |
| Bruce Rd., Renf. | J 7 | 31 |
| Bruce St., Clyde. | E 7 | 5 |
| Bruce Ter., Blan. | R27 | 69 |
| Brucefield Pl. G34 | K26 | 40 |
| Brunstance Rd. G34 | J25 | 40 |
| Brunswick Ho., Dalm. | C 5 | 4 |
| *Perth Cres.* | | |
| Brunswick St. G1 | K17 | 36 |
| Brunton St. G44 | P16 | 63 |
| Brunton Ter. G44 | Q15 | 63 |
| Bruntsfield Av. G53 | Q10 | 48 |
| Bruntsfield Gdns. G53 | Q10 | 60 |
| Brydson Pl., Linw. | L 1 | 28 |
| *Fulwood Av.* | | |
| Buccleuch Av. G52 | K 9 | 32 |
| Buccleuch La. G3 | J16 | 35 |
| *Scott St.* | | |
| Buccleuch St. G3 | J16 | 35 |
| Buchan St. G5 | L16 | 35 |
| *Norfolk St.* | | |
| Buchan Ter., G72 | Q21 | 66 |
| Buchanan Cres. G64 | F20 | 23 |
| Buchanan Dr. G64 | F20 | 23 |
| Buchanan Dr. G72 | P21 | 66 |
| Buchanan Dr. G73 | P19 | 65 |
| Buchanan Dr., Bear. | D13 | 8 |
| Buchanan Dr., Bish. | F20 | 23 |
| Buchanan Dr., Lenz. | D23 | 13 |
| Buchanan St. G1 | K16 | 35 |
| Buchanan St., Bail. | M25 | 56 |
| Buchanan St., John. | N09 | 43 |
| Buchlyvie Path G34 | K25 | 40 |
| Buchlyvie Rd., Pais. | L 9 | 32 |
| Buchlyvie St. G34 | K25 | 40 |
| Buckingham Bldgs. G12 | H14 | 20 |
| *Great Western Rd.* | | |
| Buckingham Dr. G32 | O22 | 54 |
| Buckingham Dr. G73 | O20 | 53 |
| Buckingham St. G12 | H14 | 20 |
| Buckingham Ter. G12 | H14 | 20 |
| *Great Western Rd.* | | |
| Bucklaw Gdns. G52 | M11 | 49 |
| Bucklaw Pl. G52 | M11 | 49 |
| Bucklaw Ter. G52 | M11 | 49 |
| Buckley St. G22 | G17 | 22 |
| Bucksburn Rd. G21 | H20 | 23 |
| Buddon St. G40 | M20 | 53 |
| Budhill Av. G32 | L22 | 38 |
| Bulldale St. G14 | G 9 | 18 |
| Bullionslaw Dr. G73 | P20 | 65 |
| Bulloch Av., Giff. | R14 | 62 |
| Bullwood Av. G53 | N 9 | 48 |
| Bullwood Ct. G53 | N 9 | 48 |
| Bullwood Dr. G53 | N 9 | 48 |
| Bullwood Gdns. G53 | N 9 | 48 |
| Bullwood Pl. G53 | N 9 | 48 |
| Bunessan St. G52 | L12 | 33 |
| Bunhouse Rd. G3 | J14 | 34 |
| Burgh Hall La. G11 | J13 | 34 |
| *Fortrose St.* | | |
| Burgh Hall St. G11 | J13 | 34 |
| Burgh La. G12 | H14 | 20 |
| *Vinicombe St.* | | |
| Burghead Dr. G51 | K12 | 33 |
| Burgher St. G31 | L20 | 37 |
| Burleigh Rd., Udd. | Q28 | 69 |
| Burleigh St. G51 | K13 | 34 |
| Burlington Av. G12 | G13 | 20 |
| Burmola St. G22 | H16 | 21 |
| Burn Gdns., Blan. | R26 | 68 |
| Burn Ter. G72 | O21 | 54 |
| Burn Vw., Cumb. | B 4 | 71 |
| Burnacre Gdns., Udd. | O27 | 57 |
| Burnbank Dr., Barr. | R 8 | 59 |
| Burnbank Gdns. G20 | J15 | 35 |
| Burnbank Pl. G4 | K18 | 36 |
| *Drygate* | | |
| Burnbank Ter. G20 | J15 | 35 |
| Burnbrae Av., Bear. | B13 | 8 |
| Burnbrae Av., Chr. | E28 | 15 |
| Burnbrae Av., Linw. | L 2 | 28 |
| *Bridge St.* | | |
| Burnbrae Ct., Lenz. | D23 | 13 |
| *Auchinloch Rd.* | | |
| Burnbrae Dr. G73 | P20 | 65 |
| *East Kilbride Rd.* | | |
| Burnbrae Rd., John. | M 2 | 44 |
| Burnbrae Rd., Lenz. | E24 | 13 |
| Burnbrae St. G21 | H19 | 23 |
| Burnbrae, Clyde. | C 7 | 5 |
| Burncleuch Av., G72 | Q22 | 66 |
| Burncrooks Ct., Clyde. | C 6 | 4 |
| Burndyke G51 | K14 | 34 |
| Burndyke St. G51 | K13 | 34 |
| Burnett Rd. G33 | K24 | 39 |
| Burnfield Av., Giff. | Q13 | 62 |
| Burnfield Cotts., Giff. | Q13 | 62 |
| Burnfield Dr. G43 | Q13 | 62 |
| Burnfield Gdns., Giff. | Q14 | 62 |
| *Burnfield Rd.* | | |
| Burnfield Rd., Giff. | P13 | 62 |
| Burnfoot Cres. G73 | P20 | 65 |
| Burnfoot Cres., Pais. | O 5 | 46 |
| Burnfoot Dr. G52 | L10 | 32 |
| Burngreen Ter., Cumb. | A 3 | 71 |
| Burnham Rd. G14 | H10 | 18 |
| Burnham Ter. G14 | H10 | 18 |
| *Burnham Rd.* | | |
| Burnhead Rd. G43 | P15 | 63 |
| Burnhead Rd., Cumb. | C 1 | 70 |
| Burnhead St., Udd. | O28 | 57 |
| Burnhill Quadrant G73 | O18 | 52 |
| Burnhill St. G73 | O18 | 52 |
| Burnhouse St. G20 | G14 | 20 |
| Burnmouth Ct. G33 | L24 | 39 |
| *Burnmouth Rd.* | | |
| Burnmouth Rd. G33 | L24 | 39 |
| Burnpark Av., Udd. | O26 | 56 |
| Burns Dr., John. | O09 | 43 |
| Burns Gro., Thorn. | R13 | 62 |
| Burns Rd., Cumb. | C 3 | 71 |
| Burns St. G4 | J16 | 35 |
| Burns St., Dalm. | D 6 | 4 |
| Burnside Av., Barr. | Q 7 | 59 |
| Burnside Ct., Dalm. | D 6 | 4 |
| *Scott St.* | | |
| Burnside Gate G73 | P20 | 65 |
| Burnside Gdns., Kilb. | N 7 | 42 |
| Burnside Rd. G73 | P20 | 65 |
| Burnside Rd., John. | N 2 | 44 |
| Burnside Ter. G72 | Q24 | 67 |
| Burntbroom Dr., Bail. | M24 | 55 |
| Burntbroom Gdns., Bail. | M24 | 55 |
| Burntbroom Rd., Udd. & Bail. | M24 | 55 |
| Burntbroom St. G33 | K23 | 39 |
| Burntshields Rd., Kilb. | N06 | 42 |
| Burr Gdns., Bish. | E20 | 11 |
| *Solway Rd.* | | |
| Burrells La. G4 | K18 | 36 |
| *High St.* | | |
| Burrelton Rd. G43 | P15 | 63 |
| Burton La. G43 | N16 | 51 |
| *Langside Rd.* | | |
| Bushes Av., Pais. | N 5 | 46 |
| Busheyhill St. G72 | P22 | 66 |
| Bute Av., Renf. | J 8 | 31 |
| Bute Cres., Bear. | E12 | 7 |
| Bute Cres., Pais. | O 5 | 46 |
| Bute Dr., John. | N08 | 43 |
| Bute Gdns. G12 | J14 | 34 |
| Bute Gdns. G44 | Q16 | 53 |
| Bute Ter. G73 | P19 | 65 |
| Bute Ter., Udd. | O28 | 57 |
| Butterbiggins Rd. G42 | M16 | 51 |
| Butterfield Pl. G41 | N15 | 51 |
| *Pollokshaws Rd.* | | |
| Byrebush Rd. G53 | N11 | 49 |
| Byres Av., Pais. | L 7 | 31 |
| *Byres Cres.* | | |
| Byres Cres., Pais. | L 7 | 31 |
| Byres Rd. G11 | J14 | 34 |
| Byres Rd., John. | N 2 | 44 |
| Byron Ct., Udd. | R28 | 69 |
| *Shelly Dr.* | | |
| Byron La. G11 | J12 | 33 |
| *Sandeman St.* | | |
| Byron St. G11 | J12 | 33 |
| Byron St., Clyde. | D 6 | 4 |
| Byshot St. G22 | H17 | 22 |
| Cable Depot Rd., Dalm. | E 6 | 4 |
| Cadder Ct., Bish. | C19 | 11 |
| Cadder Gro. G20 | F15 | 21 |
| *Cadder Rd.* | | |
| Cadder Pl. G20 | F15 | 21 |
| Cadder Rd. G20 | F15 | 21 |
| Cadder Rd., Bish. | C19 | 11 |
| Cadder Way, Bish. | C19 | 11 |
| Cadoc St., G72 | P22 | 66 |
| Cadogan St. G2 | K16 | 35 |
| Cadzow Av., Giff. | S13 | 62 |
| Cadzow Dr., G72 | P21 | 66 |
| Caird Dr. G11 | J13 | 34 |
| Cairn Av., Renf. | J 9 | 32 |
| Cairn Dr., Linw. | L 1 | 28 |
| Cairn La., Pais. | K 5 | 30 |
| *Mosslands Rd.* | | |
| Cairn St. G21 | G18 | 22 |
| Cairnban St. G51 | L11 | 33 |
| Cairnbrook Rd. G34 | K26 | 40 |
| Cairncraig St. G31 | M20 | 53 |
| Cairndow Av. G44 | Q15 | 63 |
| Cairngorm Cres., Barr. | R 8 | 59 |
| Cairngorm Cres., Bear. | C10 | 6 |
| Cairngorm Cres., Pais. | N 6 | 46 |
| Cairngorm Rd. G43 | P14 | 62 |
| Cairnhill Circus G52 | M 9 | 48 |
| Cairnhill Dr. G52 | M 9 | 48 |
| Cairnhill Pl. G52 | M 9 | 48 |
| *Cairnhill Circus* | | |
| Cairnhill Rd. G61 | E12 | 7 |
| Cairnlea Dr. G51 | L13 | 34 |
| Cairnmuir Rd. G72 | R21 | 66 |
| Cairns Av. G72 | P22 | 66 |
| Cairns Rd. G72 | Q22 | 66 |
| Cairnsmore Pl. G15 | E 9 | 6 |
| Cairnsmore Rd. G15 | E 9 | 6 |
| Cairnswell Av. G72 | Q23 | 67 |
| Cairnswell Pl. G72 | Q23 | 67 |
| Cairntoul Dr. G14 | G10 | 18 |
| Cairntoul Pl. G14 | G10 | 18 |
| Calcots Path G34 | J26 | 40 |
| *Auchengill Rd.* | | |
| Calcots Pl. G34 | J26 | 40 |
| Caldarvan St. G22 | H16 | 21 |
| Calder Av., Barr. | R 8 | 59 |
| Calder Dr. G72 | P22 | 66 |
| Calder Gate, Bish. | D18 | 10 |
| Calder Pl., Bail. | M25 | 56 |
| Calder Rd., Pais. | L 4 | 29 |
| Calder Rd., Udd. | P26 | 68 |
| Calder St. G42 | N16 | 51 |
| Calderbank Vw., Bail. | M26 | 56 |
| Calderbraes Av., Udd. | O27 | 57 |

| Street | Ref | Pg |
|---|---|---|
| Caldercuilt Rd. G20 | F14 | 20 |
| Caldercuilt St. G20 | F14 | 20 |
| Calderpark Av., Udd. | N25 | 56 |
| Caldervale, Udd. | P26 | 68 |
| Calderwood Av., Bail. | M25 | 56 |
| Calderwood Dr., Bail. | M25 | 56 |
| Calderwood Gdns., Bail. | M25 | 56 |
| Calderwood Rd. G73 | O20 | 53 |
| Calderwood Rd., G43 | P14 | 62 |
| Caldwell Av. G13 | G10 | 18 |
| Caldwell Av., Linw. | L 1 | 28 |
| Caledon La. G12 | J14 | 34 |
| *Highburgh Rd.* | | |
| Caledon St. G12 | J14 | 34 |
| Caledonia Av. G5 | M17 | 52 |
| Caledonia Av. G73 | O19 | 53 |
| Caledonia Dr., Bail. | M25 | 56 |
| Caledonia Rd. G5 | M17 | 52 |
| Caledonia Rd., Bail. | M25 | 56 |
| Caledonia St. G5 | M17 | 52 |
| Caledonia St., Dalm. | E 6 | 4 |
| Caledonia St., Pais. | L 5 | 30 |
| Caledonian Circuit G72 | P23 | 67 |
| Caledonian Cotts., Both. | R28 | 69 |
| Caledonian Cres. G12 | H14 | 20 |
| *Great Western Rd.* | | |
| Caledonian Cres. G12 | J15 | 35 |
| Caledonian Mans. G12 | H14 | 20 |
| *Great Western Rd.* | | |
| Caledonian Pl. G72 | P24 | 67 |
| Caley Brae, Udd. | P27 | 69 |
| Calfhill Rd. G53 | M10 | 48 |
| Calfmuir Rd., | C25 | 14 |
| *Chr. & Waterside* | | |
| Calgary St. G4 | J17 | 36 |
| Callander St. G20 | H16 | 21 |
| Callieburn Rd., Bish. | F19 | 23 |
| Cally Av. G15 | D10 | 6 |
| Calside Av., Pais. | M 5 | 46 |
| Calside, Pais. | N 6 | 46 |
| Calton Entry G40 | L18 | 36 |
| *Gallowgate* | | |
| Calvay Cres. G33 | K23 | 39 |
| Calvay Pl. G33 | L24 | 39 |
| Calvay Rd. G33 | K23 | 39 |
| Cambourne Rd., Chr. | D27 | 15 |
| Cambridge Av., Clyde. | D 7 | 5 |
| Cambridge Dr. G20 | G14 | 20 |
| *Glenfinnan Dr.* | | |
| Cambridge La. G3 | J16 | 35 |
| *Cambridge St.* | | |
| Cambridge Rd., Renf. | J 8 | 31 |
| Cambridge St. | K16 | 35 |
| Camburn St. G32 | L21 | 38 |
| Cambus Pl. G32 | J23 | 39 |
| Cambusdoon Rd. G32 | J23 | 39 |
| Cambuskenneth Gdns. G32 | L24 | 39 |
| *Hailes Av.* | | |
| Cambuskenneth Pl. G32 | J23 | 39 |
| Cambuslang Rd. G32 | O21 | 54 |
| Cambuslang Rd. G72 & G73 | N19 | 53 |
| Cambusmore Pl. G32 | J23 | 39 |
| Camden St. G5 | M17 | 52 |
| Camelon St. G32 | L21 | 38 |
| Cameron Dr., Bear. | D13 | 8 |
| Cameron Sq., Clyde. | C 8 | 5 |
| *Glasgow Rd.* | | |
| Cameron St. G20 | H16 | 21 |
| Cameron St. G52 | K 9 | 32 |
| Cameron St., Clyde. | F 8 | 17 |
| Camlachie St. G31 | L19 | 37 |
| Camp Rd. G73 | N18 | 52 |
| Camp Rd., Bail. | L25 | 40 |
| Campbell Dr., Barr. | R 8 | 59 |
| Campbell Dr., Bear. | C11 | 7 |
| Campbell St. G20 | F14 | 21 |
| Campbell St., John. | N09 | 43 |
| Campbell St., Renf. | H 8 | 17 |
| Camperdown St. G20 | H16 | 21 |
| *Garscube Rd.* | | |
| Camphill Av. G41 | O15 | 51 |
| Camphill, Pais. | M 5 | 46 |
| Camps Cres., Renf. | J 9 | 32 |
| Campsie Av., Barr. | R 8 | 59 |
| Campsie Dr., Bear. | B12 | 7 |
| Campsie Dr., Pais. | K 7 | 31 |
| Campsie Dr., Pais. | O 5 | 46 |
| Campsie Pl., Chr. | F26 | 26 |
| Campsie St. G21 | G18 | 22 |
| Campsie Vw., Bail. | L27 | 41 |
| Campsie Vw., Chr. | F26 | 26 |
| Campsie Vw., Cumb. | B 3 | 71 |
| Campston Pl. G33 | J22 | 38 |
| Camstradden Dr. E., Bear. | D11 | 7 |
| Camstradden Dr. W., Bear. | D11 | 7 |
| Camus Pl. G15 | D 9 | 6 |
| Canal Av., John. | M 1 | 44 |
| Canal Rd., John. | N09 | 43 |
| Canal St. G4 | J17 | 36 |
| Canal St., Clyde. | F 7 | 17 |
| Canal St., John. | M 2 | 44 |
| Canal St., Pais. | M 5 | 46 |
| Canal St., Renf. | H 8 | 17 |
| Canal Ter., Pais. | M 6 | 46 |
| Canberra Av., Dalm. | D 5 | 4 |
| Cander Rigg, Bish. | D19 | 11 |
| Candleriggs G1 | L17 | 36 |
| Candren Rd., Linw. | L 2 | 28 |
| Candren Rd., Pais. | M 4 | 45 |
| Canmore Pl. G31 | M20 | 53 |
| Canmore St. G31 | M20 | 53 |
| Cannick Dr., Pais. | N 7 | 47 |
| Canniesburn Rd., Bear. | D11 | 7 |
| Canniesburn Sq., Bear. | E12 | 7 |
| *Macfarlane Rd.* | | |
| Canniesburn Toll, Bear. | D12 | 7 |
| Canonbie St. G34 | J26 | 40 |
| Capelrig St. G46 | Q12 | 61 |
| Caplaw Rd., Pais. | P 5 | 58 |
| Caplethill Rd., | O 6 | 46 |
| *Pais. & Barr.* | | |
| Caprington St. G33 | J22 | 38 |
| Cara Dr. G51 | K12 | 33 |
| Caravelle Way, Renf. | J 8 | 31 |
| *Friendship Way* | | |
| Carberry Rd. G41 | N14 | 50 |
| Carbeth St. G22 | H16 | 21 |
| Carbisdale St. G22 | G18 | 22 |
| Carbost St. G23 | E14 | 8 |
| *Torgyle St.* | | |
| Carbrook St. G21 | J19 | 37 |
| Carbrook St., Pais. | M 5 | 46 |
| Cardarrach St. G21 | H19 | 23 |
| Cardell Dr., Pais. | M 4 | 45 |
| Cardell Rd., Pais. | M 4 | 45 |
| Carding La. G3 | K15 | 35 |
| *Argyle St.* | | |
| Cardonald Dr. G52 | M10 | 48 |
| Cardonald Gdns. G52 | M10 | 48 |
| Cardonald Place Rd. G52 | M10 | 48 |
| Cardow Rd. G21 | H20 | 23 |
| Cardowan Dr. G33 | G23 | 25 |
| Cardowan Rd. G33 | G24 | 25 |
| Cardowan Rd. G33 | L21 | 38 |
| Cardross Ct. G31 | K18 | 36 |
| Cardross St. G31 | K18 | 36 |
| Cardwell St. G41 | M16 | 51 |
| Cardyke St. G21 | H19 | 23 |
| Careston Pl., Bish. | E20 | 11 |
| Carfin St. G42 | N16 | 51 |
| Carfrae St. G3 | K14 | 34 |
| Cargill St. G31 | M21 | 54 |
| Cargill St. G64 | F19 | 23 |
| Carham Cres. G52 | L11 | 33 |
| Carham Dr. G52 | L11 | 33 |
| Carillon Rd. G51 | L14 | 34 |
| Carisbrooke Cres., Bish. | D19 | 11 |
| Carlaverock Rd. G43 | P14 | 62 |
| Carleith Av., Clyde. | C 6 | 4 |
| Carleith Quad. G51 | K11 | 33 |
| Carleith Ter., Clyde. | C 6 | 4 |
| *Carleith Av.* | | |
| Carleston St. G21 | H18 | 22 |
| Carleton Dr., Giff. | Q14 | 62 |
| Carleton Gate, Giff. | Q14 | 62 |
| Carlibar Av. G13 | G 9 | 18 |
| Carlibar Dr., Barr. | Q 8 | 59 |
| Carlibar Gdns., Barr. | Q 8 | 59 |
| *Commercial Rd.* | | |
| Carlibar Rd., Barr. | Q 7 | 59 |
| Carlile La., Pais. | L 6 | 30 |
| *New Sneddon St.* | | |
| Carlile Pl., Pais. | L 6 | 30 |
| Carlisle St. G21 | H17 | 22 |
| Carlowrie Av., Blan. | R26 | 68 |
| Carlton Ct. G5 | L16 | 35 |
| Carlton Pl. G5 | L16 | 35 |
| Carlton Ter. G20 | H15 | 21 |
| *Wilton St.* | | |
| Carlyle Av. G52 | K 9 | 32 |
| Carlyle Rd., Pais. | L 6 | 30 |
| Carlyle Ter. G73 | N19 | 53 |
| Carmaben Rd. G33 | K24 | 39 |
| Carment Dr. G41 | O14 | 50 |
| Carment La. G41 | O14 | 50 |
| Carmichael Pl. G42 | O15 | 51 |
| Carmichael St. G51 | L13 | 34 |
| Carmunnock By-pass G44 | R17 | 64 |
| Carmunnock La. G44 | P16 | 63 |
| *Madison Av.* | | |
| Carmunnock Rd. G44 | O16 | 51 |
| Carmyle Av. G32 | N22 | 54 |
| Carna Dr. G44 | P17 | 64 |
| Carnarvon St. G3 | J15 | 35 |
| Carnbooth Ct. G42 | R18 | 64 |
| Carnbroe St. G20 | J16 | 35 |
| Carnegie Rd. G52 | L10 | 32 |
| Carnock Cres., Barr. | R 7 | 59 |
| Carnock Rd. G53 | O11 | 49 |
| Carnoustie Cres., Bish. | E20 | 11 |
| Carnoustie St., Both. | R27 | 69 |
| Carnoustie St. G5 | L15 | 35 |
| Carntyne Pl. G32 | K20 | 37 |
| Carntyne Rd. G31 | L20 | 37 |
| Carntynehall Rd. G32 | K21 | 38 |
| Carnwadric Rd. G46 | Q12 | 61 |
| Carnwath Av. G43 | P15 | 63 |
| Caroline St. G31 | L21 | 38 |
| Carolside Dr. G15 | D10 | 6 |
| Carradale Gdns., Bish. | E20 | 11 |
| *Thrums Av.* | | |
| Carradale Pl., Linw. | L 1 | 28 |
| Carrbridge Dr. G20 | G14 | 20 |
| *Glenfinnan Dr.* | | |
| Carriagehill Dr., Pais. | N 6 | 46 |
| Carrick Cres., Giff. | R14 | 62 |
| Carrick Dr. G32 | M24 | 55 |
| Carrick Dr. G73 | P19 | 65 |
| Carrick Gro. G32 | M24 | 55 |
| Carrick Rd. G73 | P18 | 64 |
| Carrick Rd., Bish. | E20 | 11 |
| Carrick Rd., Cumb. | B 3 | 71 |
| Carrick St. G2 | K16 | 35 |
| Carrickarden Rd., Bear. | D12 | 7 |
| Carrickstone Vw., Cumb. | A 2 | 70 |
| *Eastfield Rd.* | | |
| Carriden Pl. G33 | K24 | 39 |
| Carrington St. G4 | J15 | 35 |
| Carroglen Gdns. G32 | L23 | 39 |
| Carroglen Gro. G32 | L23 | 39 |
| Carron Cres. G22 | G17 | 22 |
| Carron Cres. G66 | D24 | 13 |
| Carron Cres., Bear. | D11 | 7 |
| Carron Cres., Bish. | E19 | 11 |
| Carron Ct. G72 | P23 | 67 |
| Carron La., Pais. | K 7 | 31 |
| *Kilearn Rd.* | | |
| Carron Pl. G22 | G18 | 22 |
| Carron St., G22 | G18 | 22 |
| Carrour Gdns., Bish. | E18 | 10 |
| Carsaig Dr. G52 | L12 | 33 |
| Carse View Dr., Bear. | C13 | 8 |
| Carsebrook Av., Chr. & Waterside | C25 | 14 |
| *Chryston Rd.* | | |
| Carsegreen Av., Pais. | O 4 | 45 |
| Carstairs St. G40 | N19 | 53 |
| Carswell Gdns. G41 | N15 | 51 |
| Cart St., Clyde. | F 7 | 17 |
| Cartartan Rd., Pais. | L 9 | 32 |
| Cartcraigs Rd. G43 | P13 | 62 |
| Cartha Cres., Pais. | M 7 | 47 |
| Cartha St. G41 | O15 | 51 |
| Cartside Av., John. | N08 | 43 |
| Cartside Quad. G42 | O16 | 51 |
| Cartside St. G42 | O15 | 51 |
| Cartside St., Kilb. | N08 | 43 |
| *Kilbarchan Rd.* | | |
| Cartvale La., Pais. | L 6 | 30 |
| Cartvale Rd. G42 | O15 | 51 |
| Caskie Dr., Blan. | R27 | 69 |
| Cassley Av., Renf. | J 9 | 32 |
| Castle Av., Both. | R27 | 69 |
| Castle Av., John. | N 1 | 44 |
| Castle Av., Udd. | P27 | 69 |
| Castle Chimmins Av. G72 | Q23 | 67 |

Castle Chimmins Rd. Q23 67
G72
Castle Cres. North Court K17 36
*Royal Exchange Sq.*
Castle Gdns., Chr. E27 15
Castle Pl., Udd. P27 69
*Ferry Rd.*
Castle Rd. G78 M 2 44
*Main Rd.*
Castle Rd., John. M 2 44
Castle Sq., Dalm. D 6 4
Castle St. G4 K18 36
Castle St. G73 O19 53
Castle St., Bail. M25 56
Castle St., Dalm. D 6 4
Castle St., Pais. M 5 46
Castle Vw., Clyde. D 7 5
*Granville St.*
Castle Way, Cumb. B 4 71
Castlebank Cres., G11 J13 34
*Meadowside St.*
Castlebank Ct. G13 G12 19
*Munro Pl.*
Castlebank Gdns. G13 G12 19
*Munro Pl.*
Castlebank St. G11 J12 33
Castlebank Vill. G13 G12 19
*Munro Pl.*
Castlebay Dr. G22 E17 10
Castlebay Pl. G22 F17 22
Castlebay St. G22 F17 22
Castlecroft Gdns., Udd. P27 69
Castlefern Rd. G73 Q19 65
Castlehill Cres., Renf. H 8 17
*Ferry Rd.*
Castlehill Rd., Bear. C10 6
Castlelaw Gdns. G32 L22 38
Castlelaw Pl. G32 L22 38
Castlelaw St. G32 L22 38
Castlemilk Cres. G44 P18 64
Castlemilk Dr. G45 Q18 64
Castlemilk Mews G44 P18 64
*Castlemilk Rd.*
Castlemilk Rd. G44 O18 52
Castleton Av. G21 F18 22
*Colston Rd.*
Castleton Ct. G42 R18 64
Cathay St. G22 F17 22
Cathcart Cres., Pais. M 7 47
Cathcart Pl. O18 52
Cathcart Rd. G42 O16 51
Cathcart Rd. G73 O18 52
Cathedral Ct. G4 K17 36
*Rottenrow East*
Cathedral La. G4 K17 36
*Cathedral St.*
Cathedral Sq. G4 K18 36
Cathedral St. G1 K17 36
Cathedral St. G4 K18 36
Catherine Pl. G3 K15 35
*Hydepark St.*
Cathkin Av. G72 P21 66
Cathkin Av. G73 O20 53
Cathkin By-pass G73 Q20 65
Cathkin Ct. G42 R18 64
Cathkin Gdns., Udd. N27 57
Cathkin Pl., G72 P21 66
Cathkin Rd. G42 O15 51
Cathkin Rd., E.K. R19 65
Cathkin Rd., Udd. N27 57
Cathkin Vw. G32 O22 54
Cathkinview Rd. G42 O16 51
Catrine Av., Clyde. D 8 5
Causewayside St. N22 54
G32
Causeyside St., Pais. M 6 46
Cavendish Pl. G5 M16 51
Cavendish St. G5 M16 51
Cavin Dr. G45 Q18 64
Cavin Rd. G45 Q18 64
Caxton St. G13 G12 19
Cayton Gdns., Bail. M24 55
Cecil Pl. G11 L15 35
*Paisley Rd. W.*
Cecil St. G12 H14 20
Cedar Av. G78 O 1 44
Cedar Av., Dalm. D 5 4
Cedar Ct. G20 J16 35
Cedar Ct. G78 M07 42
Cedar Dr., Lenz. C23 13
Cedar Gdns. G73 Q20 65
Cedar Pl., Barr. R 8 59

Cedar Pl., Blan. R26 68
Cedar Rd., Bish. F19 23
Cedar Rd., Cumb. B 4 71
Cedar St. G20 J16 35
Cedar Wk., Bish. F19 23
Cedric Pl. G13 F11 19
*Cedric Rd.*
Cedric Rd. G13 F11 19
Celtic Pl. G20 F14 20
*Maryhill Rd.*
Cemetery Rd. G32 L23 39
Cemetery Rd. G52 M11 49
*Paisley Rd. W.*
Cemetery Rd., John. N 1 44
Central Av. G11 J12 33
*Broomhill Ter.*
Central Av. G32 M23 55
Central Av. G72 P21 66
Central Av., Udd. P29 69
Central Chambers G2 K16 35
*Hope St.*
Central Way, Cumb. D 2 70
Central Way, Pais. L 6 30
Centre St. G5 L16 35
Centre, The, Barr. R 7 59
Ceres Gdns. G64 E20 11
Cessnock Rd. G33 G22 24
Cessnock St. G51 L14 34
Cessnock St., Clyde. D 8 5
Chachan Dr. G51 K12 33
*Skipness Dr.*
Chalmers Ct. G40 L18 36
Chalmers Gate G40 L18 36
Chalmers Pl. G40 L18 36
*Claythorn St.*
Chalmers St. G40 L18 36
Chalmers St., Clyde. E 7 5
Chamberlain La. G13 G12 19
Chamberlain Rd. G13 G12 19
Chancellor St. G11 J13 34
Chapel Rd., Clyde. C 7 5
Chapel St. G20 G15 21
Chapel St. G73 O18 52
Chapelhill Rd., Pais. N 7 47
Chapelton Av., Bear. D12 7
Chapelton Gdns., Bear. D12 7
Chapelton St., G22 G16 21
Chaplet Av., G13 F11 19
Chapman St. G42 N16 51
*Allison St.*
Chappel St., Barr. Q 7 59
Charing Cross G2 J15 35
Charing Cross La. G3 K15 35
*Granville St.*
Charles Av., Renf. H 8 17
Charles Cres., Lenz. D23 13
Charles St. G21 J18 36
Charlotte La. G1 L17 36
*London Rd.*
Charlotte La. S. G1 L17 36
*Charlotte St.*
Charlotte Pl., Pais. N 6 46
Charlotte St., G1 L17 36
Chatelherault Av. G72 P21 66
Chatton St. G23 E14 8
Cheapside St. G3 K15 35
Chelmsford Dr. G12 G13 20
Cherry Bank, Lenz. C22 12
Cherry Cres., Clyde. D 7 5
Cherry Pl., Bish. F19 23
Cherry Pl., John. N 1 44
Cherrybank Rd. G43 P15 63
Chester St. G32 L22 38
Chesterfield Av. G12 G13 20
Chesters Pl. G73 O19 53
Chesters Rd., Bear. D11 7
Chestnut Dr., Dalm. C 7 5
Chestnut Dr., Lenz. C22 12
Chestnut Pl., John. O 1 44
Chestnut St. G22 G17 22
Cheviot Av., Barr. R 8 59
Cheviot Rd., G43 P14 62
Cheviot Rd., Pais. O 6 46
Chirnside Pl. G52 L10 32
Chirnside Rd. G52 L10 32
Chisholm St. G1 L17 36
Christian St. G43 O14 50
Christie La., Pais. L 6 30
*New Sneddon St.*
Christie Pl. G72 P22 66
Christie St., Pais. L 6 30
Christopher St. G21 J19 37

Chryston Rd., C25 14
Waterside & Chr.
Chryston Rd., Chr. F26 26
Church Av. G33 G23 25
Church Av. G73 P20 65
Church Dr., Lenz. C23 13
Church Hill, Pais. L 6 30
Church La. G42 N16 51
*Victoria Rd.*
Church Rd., Chr. F26 26
Church Rd., Giff. R14 62
Church St. G11 J14 34
Church St., Bail. M26 56
Church St., Clyde. D 7 5
Church St., John. M09 43
Church St., Kilb. M07 42
Church St., Udd. P27 69
Churchill Av., John. O08 43
Churchill Cres., Udd. Q28 69
Churchill Dr. G11 H12 19
Churchill Pl., Kilb. M07 42
Churchill Way, Bish. E18 10
*Kirkintilloch Rd.*
Churchill Way, Bish. E18 10
*Kirkintilloch Rd.*
Circus Dr. G31 K18 36
Circus Pl. G31 K18 36
Circus Place La. G31 K18 36
*Circus Pl.*
Civic Way, Lenz. B23 13
*Kirkintilloch Rd.*
Clachan Dr. G51 K12 33
*Skipness Dr.*
Claddens Pl., Lenz. D24 13
Claddens Quad. G22 G17 22
Claddens St. G22 G16 21
Claddens Wynd G66 D24 13
Claddon Vw., Clyde. D 8 5
*Kirkoswald Dr.*
Clair Rd., Bish. E20 11
Clairmont Gdns. G3 J15 35
Clare St. G21 J19 37
Claremont Av., Giff. R14 62
Claremont Pl. G3 J15 35
*Claremont Ter.*
Claremont St. G3 K15 35
Claremont Ter. G3 J15 35
Claremont Terrace La. J15 35
G3
*Clifton St.*
Clarence Dr. G11 H13 20
Clarence Gdns. G11 H13 20
Clarence St., Clyde. D 8 5
Clarence St., Pais. L 7 31
Clarendon La., G20 J16 35
*Clarendon St.*
Clarendon Pl. G20 J16 35
Clarendon St. G20 J16 35
Clarion Cres. G13 F10 18
Clarion Rd. G13 F10 18
Clark St. G41 L15 35
*Tower St.*
Clark St., Dalm. D 6 4
Clark St., John. M09 43
Clark St., Pais. L 5 30
Clark St., Renf. H 7 17
Clarkston Av. G44 Q15 63
Clarkston Rd. G44 R15 63
Clathic Av., Bear. D13 8
Claude Av. G72 Q24 67
Claude Rd., Pais. L 7 31
Claudhall Av., Gart. F27 27
Clavens Rd. G52 L 9 32
Claverhouse Pl., Pais. M 7 47
Claverhouse Rd. G52 K 9 32
Clavering St. E., Pais. L 5 30
*Well St.*
Clavering St. W., Pais. L 5 30
*King St.*
Clayhouse Rd. G33 G24 25
Claypotts Pl. G33 J22 38
Claypotts Rd. G33 J22 38
Clayslaps Rd. G3 J14 34
*Argyle St.*
Claythorn Av. G40 L18 36
Claythorn Circus G40 L18 36
*Claythorn Av.*
Claythorn Ct. G40 L18 36
*Claythorn Pk.*
Claythorn Pk. G40 L18 36
Claythorn Ter. G40 L18 36
*Claythorn Pk.*

| Street | Grid | Page |
|---|---|---|
| Clayton Ter. G31 | K18 | 36 |
| Cleddans Cres., Clyde. | C 8 | 5 |
| Cleddans Ct., Bish. | E10 | 11 |
| Cleddans Rd., Clyde. | C 8 | 5 |
| Cleeves Pl. G53 | P10 | 60 |
| Cleeves Quadrant G53 | P10 | 60 |
| Cleeves Rd. G53 | P10 | 60 |
| Cleghorn St. G22 | H16 | 21 |
| Cleland La. G5 | L17 | 36 |
| *Cleland St.* | | |
| Cleland St. G5 | L17 | 36 |
| Clelland Av., Bish. | F19 | 23 |
| Clerwood St. G32 | L20 | 37 |
| Cleveden Cres. G12 | G13 | 20 |
| Cleveden Cres. La. G12 | G13 | 20 |
| *Cleveden Dr.* | | |
| Cleveden Dr. G12 | G13 | 20 |
| Cleveden Dr. G73 | P20 | 65 |
| Cleveden Gdns. G12 | G14 | 20 |
| Cleveden Pl. G12 | G13 | 20 |
| Cleveden Rd. G12 | G13 | 20 |
| Cleveland St. G3 | K15 | 35 |
| Cliff Rd. G3 | J15 | 35 |
| Clifford Gdns. G51 | L13 | 34 |
| Clifford La. G51 | L14 | 34 |
| *Gower St.* | | |
| Clifford Pl. G51 | L14 | 34 |
| *Clifford St.* | | |
| Clifford St. G51 | L13 | 34 |
| Clifton Pl. G3 | J15 | 35 |
| *Clifton St.* | | |
| Clifton Rd., Giff. | Q13 | 62 |
| Clifton St. G3 | J15 | 35 |
| Clifton Ter. G72 | Q21 | 66 |
| Clifton Ter., John. | N 1 | 44 |
| Clincart Rd. G42 | O16 | 51 |
| Clincarthill Rd. G73 | O19 | 53 |
| Clinton Av., Udd. | P27 | 69 |
| Clippens Rd., Linw. | L 1 | 28 |
| Cloan Av. G15 | E10 | 6 |
| Cloan Cres., Bish. | D19 | 11 |
| Cloberhill Rd. G13 | E11 | 7 |
| Cloch St. G33 | K22 | 38 |
| Clochoderick Av., Kilb. | N07 | 43 |
| *Mackenzie Dr.* | | |
| Clonbeith St. G33 | J24 | 39 |
| Closeburn St. G22 | G17 | 22 |
| Cloth St., Barr. | R 8 | 59 |
| Clouden Rd., Cumb. | C 3 | 71 |
| Cloudhowe Ter., Blan. | R26 | 68 |
| Clouston Ct. G20 | H15 | 21 |
| Clouston La. G20 | H14 | 20 |
| *Clouston St.* | | |
| Clouston St. G20 | H14 | 20 |
| Clova Pl., Udd. | P27 | 69 |
| Clova St. G46 | Q12 | 61 |
| Clover Av., Bish. | E18 | 10 |
| Cloverbank St. G21 | J19 | 37 |
| Clunie Rd. G52 | M12 | 49 |
| Cluny Av., Bear. | E13 | 8 |
| Cluny Dr., Bear. | E13 | 8 |
| Cluny Dr., Pais. | L 7 | 31 |
| Cluny Gdns. G14 | H12 | 19 |
| Cluny Gdns., Bail. | M25 | 56 |
| Cluny Vill. G14 | H11 | 19 |
| *Westland Dr.* | | |
| Clutha St. G51 | L15 | 35 |
| *Paisley Rd. W.* | | |
| Clyde Av., Barr. | R 8 | 59 |
| Clyde Av., Both. | R27 | 69 |
| Clyde Cres., Blan. | S26 | 68 |
| Clyde Ct., Dalm. | D 6 | 4 |
| *Little Holm* | | |
| Clyde Pl. G5 | L16 | 35 |
| Clyde Pl. G72 | Q23 | 67 |
| Clyde Pl., John. | O08 | 43 |
| Clyde Rd., Pais. | K 7 | 31 |
| Clyde St. G1 | L16 | 35 |
| Clyde St., Clyde. | F 8 | 17 |
| Clyde St., Renf. | G 8 | 17 |
| Clyde Ter., Both. | R28 | 69 |
| Clyde Vale G71 | R28 | 69 |
| Clyde Vw. G71 | R28 | 69 |
| Clyde Vw., Pais. | N 7 | 47 |
| Clydebrae Dr. G71 | R28 | 69 |
| Clydebrae St. G51 | K13 | 34 |
| Clydeford Dr. G32 | M21 | 54 |
| Clydeford Dr., Udd. | O26 | 56 |
| Clydeford Rd. G72 | O22 | 54 |
| Clydeham Ter., Clyde. | F 8 | 17 |
| Clydeholm Rd. G14 | J12 | 33 |
| Clydeneuk Dr., Udd. | O26 | 56 |
| Clydesdale Av., Pais. & Renf. | J 7 | 31 |
| Clydeside Expressway G14 | H11 | 19 |
| Clydeside Rd. G73 | N18 | 52 |
| Clydesmill Dr. G32 | O22 | 54 |
| Clydesmill Gro. G32 | O22 | 54 |
| Clydesmill Pl. G32 | O22 | 54 |
| Clydesmill Rd. G32 | O22 | 54 |
| Clydeview G11 | J13 | 34 |
| *Dumbarton Rd.* | | |
| Clydeview La. G11 | J12 | 33 |
| *Broomhill Ter.* | | |
| Clydeview Ter. G32 | O23 | 55 |
| Clydeview Ter. G40 | M18 | 52 |
| *Newhall St.* | | |
| Clynder St. G51 | L13 | 34 |
| Clyth Dr., Giff. | R14 | 62 |
| Coalhill St. G31 | L19 | 37 |
| Coatbridge Rd., Bail. | L27 | 40 |
| Coatbridge Rd., Gart. | H27 | 27 |
| Coates Cres. G53 | O11 | 49 |
| Coats Cres., Bail. | L25 | 40 |
| Coatshill Av., Blan. | R26 | 68 |
| Cobbleriggs Way, Udd. | P27 | 69 |
| Cobinshaw St. G32 | L22 | 38 |
| Cobinton Pl. G38 | J22 | 38 |
| Coburg St. G5 | L16 | 35 |
| *Bedford St.* | | |
| Coburg St. G5 | L16 | 35 |
| Cochno Rd., Clyde. | B 7 | 5 |
| Cochno St., Clyde. | F 8 | 17 |
| Cochran St., Pais. | M 6 | 46 |
| Cochrane St. G1 | K17 | 36 |
| Cochrane St., Barr. | R 7 | 59 |
| Cochranemill Rd., John. | N08 | 43 |
| Cockels Loan, Renf. | J 7 | 31 |
| Cockenzie St. G32 | L22 | 38 |
| Cockmuir St. G21 | H19 | 23 |
| Cogan Rd. G43 | P14 | 62 |
| Cogan St. G43 | O14 | 50 |
| Cogan St., Barr. | R 7 | 59 |
| Colbert St. G40 | M18 | 52 |
| Colbreggan Ct., Clyde. | C 8 | 5 |
| *St. Helena Cres.* | | |
| Colbreggan Gdns., Clyde. | C 8 | 5 |
| Colchester Dr. G12 | G13 | 20 |
| Coldingham Av. G14 | G 9 | 18 |
| Coldstream Dr. G73 | P20 | 65 |
| Coldstream Dr., Pais. | N 4 | 45 |
| Coldstream Pl. G21 | H17 | 22 |
| *Keppochhill Rd.* | | |
| Coldstream Rd., Clyde. | E 7 | 5 |
| Colebrook St. G72 | P22 | 66 |
| Colebrook Ter. G12 | H15 | 21 |
| *Colebrooke St.* | | |
| Colebrooke La. G12 | H15 | 21 |
| *Colebrooke St.* | | |
| Colebrooke Pl. G12 | H15 | 21 |
| *Belmont St.* | | |
| Colebrooke St. G12 | H15 | 21 |
| Coleridge, Udd. | Q28 | 69 |
| Colfin St. G34 | J26 | 40 |
| Colgrain St. G20 | G16 | 21 |
| Colinbar Circle, Barr. | R 7 | 59 |
| Colinslee Av., Pais. | N 6 | 46 |
| Colinslee Cres., Pais. | N 6 | 46 |
| Colinslee Dr., Pais. | N 6 | 46 |
| Colinslie Rd. G53 | O11 | 49 |
| Colinton Pl. G32 | K22 | 38 |
| Colintraive Av. G33 | H21 | 24 |
| *Mossbank Dr.* | | |
| Coll Av., Renf. | J 8 | 31 |
| Coll Pl. G21 | J19 | 37 |
| Coll St. G21 | J19 | 37 |
| Colla Gdns., Bish. | E20 | 11 |
| College La. G1 | L17 | 36 |
| *High St.* | | |
| College St. G1 | K17 | 36 |
| Collessie Dr. G33 | J23 | 39 |
| Collier St., John. | M09 | 43 |
| Collina St. G20 | G14 | 20 |
| Collins St. G4 | K18 | 36 |
| Collins St., Clyde. | C 8 | 5 |
| Collylin Rd., Bear. | D12 | 7 |
| Colmonell Av. G13 | F 9 | 18 |
| Colonsay Av., Renf. | J 8 | 31 |
| Colonsay Rd. G52 | L12 | 33 |
| Colonsay Rd., Pais. | O 5 | 46 |
| Colquhoun Av. G52 | K10 | 32 |
| Colquhoun Dr., Bear. | C11 | 7 |
| Colston Av., Bish. | F18 | 22 |
| Colston Dr., Bish. | F18 | 22 |
| Colston Gdns., Bish. | F18 | 22 |
| Colston Path, Bish. | F18 | 22 |
| *Colston Gdns.* | | |
| Colston Pl., Bish. | F18 | 22 |
| Colston Rd., Bish. | F18 | 22 |
| Coltmuir St. G22 | G16 | 21 |
| Coltness La. G33 | K23 | 39 |
| Coltness St. G33 | K23 | 39 |
| Coltpark Av., Bish. | F18 | 22 |
| Coltpark La., Bish. | F18 | 22 |
| Columba Path, Clyde. | E 8 | 5 |
| *Onslow Rd.* | | |
| Columba St. G51 | K13 | 34 |
| Colvend Dr. G73 | Q19 | 65 |
| Colvend St. G40 | M18 | 52 |
| Colville Dr. G73 | P20 | 65 |
| Colwood Av. G53 | Q10 | 60 |
| Colwood Gdns. G53 | Q10 | 60 |
| *Colwood Av.* | | |
| Colwood Path G53 | Q10 | 60 |
| *Parkhouse Rd.* | | |
| Colwood Pl. G53 | Q10 | 60 |
| Colwood Sq. G53 | Q10 | 60 |
| *Colwood Av.* | | |
| Comedie Rd. G33 | H24 | 25 |
| Comely Park St. G31 | L19 | 37 |
| Comley Pl. G31 | L19 | 37 |
| *Gallowgate* | | |
| Commerce St. G5 | L16 | 35 |
| Commercial Ct. G5 | L17 | 36 |
| Commercial Rd. G5 | M17 | 52 |
| Commercial Rd., Barr. | Q 8 | 59 |
| Commonhead Rd. G34 | K26 | 40 |
| Commonhead Rd., Bail. | K27 | 41 |
| Commore Av., Barr. | R 8 | 59 |
| Commore Dr. G13 | F10 | 18 |
| Comrie Rd. G33 | G23 | 25 |
| Comrie St. G32 | M22 | 54 |
| Cona St. G46 | Q12 | 61 |
| Conan Ct. G72 | P23 | 67 |
| Condorrat Ring Rd., Cumb. | D 1 | 70 |
| Congleton St. G53 | P 9 | 60 |
| *Nitshill Rd.* | | |
| Conifer Pl., Lenz. | C22 | 12 |
| Conisborough Path G34 | J24 | 39 |
| *Balfluig St.* | | |
| Conisborough Rd. G34 | J24 | 39 |
| Connal St. G40 | M19 | 53 |
| Conniston St. G32 | K21 | 38 |
| Conon Av., Bear. | D11 | 7 |
| Consett La. G33 | K23 | 39 |
| Consett St. G33 | K23 | 39 |
| *Consett La.* | | |
| Contin Pl. G12 | G14 | 20 |
| Convair Way, Renf. | J 8 | 31 |
| *Lismore Av.* | | |
| Conval Way, Pais. | K 5 | 30 |
| *Abbotsburn Way* | | |
| Cook St. G5 | L16 | 35 |
| Coopers Well La. G11 | J14 | 34 |
| *Dumbarton Rd.* | | |
| Coopers Well St. G11 | J14 | 34 |
| *Dumbarton Rd.* | | |
| Copland Pl. G51 | L13 | 34 |
| Copland Quad. G51 | L13 | 34 |
| Copland Rd. G51 | L13 | 34 |
| Coplaw St. G42 | M16 | 51 |
| Copperfield La., Udd. | O28 | 57 |
| *Hamilton Vw.* | | |
| Corbett St. G32 | M22 | 54 |
| Corbiston Way, Cumb. | C 3 | 71 |
| Cordiner St. G44 | O16 | 51 |
| Corkerhill Gdns. G52 | M12 | 49 |
| Corkerhill Pl. G52 | N11 | 49 |
| Corkerhill Rd. G52 | N11 | 49 |
| Corlaich Av. G42 | O18 | 52 |
| Corlaich Dr. G42 | O18 | 52 |
| Corn St. G4 | J16 | 35 |
| Cornaig Rd. G53 | O10 | 48 |
| Cornalee Gdns. G53 | O10 | 48 |
| Cornalee Pl. G53 | O10 | 48 |
| Cornalee Rd. G53 | O10 | 48 |
| Cornhill St. G21 | G19 | 23 |
| Cornoch St. G23 | E14 | 8 |
| *Torrin Rd.* | | |
| Cornock Cres., Clyde. | D 7 | 5 |
| Cornock St., Clyde. | D 7 | 5 |
| Cornwall Av. G73 | P20 | 65 |
| Cornwall St. G41 | L14 | 34 |

| | | |
|---|---|---|
| Coronation Pl., Gart. | F27 | 27 |
| Coronation Way, Bear. | E13 | 8 |
| Corpach Pl. G34 | J26 | 40 |
| Corran St. G32 | K21 | 38 |
| Corrie Dr., Pais. | M 9 | 48 |
| Corrie Gro. G44 | Q15 | 63 |
| Corrie Pl., Lenz. | D24 | 13 |
| Corrour Rd. G43 | O14 | 50 |
| Corse Ford Av., John. | O08 | 43 |
| Corse Rd. G52 | L 9 | 32 |
| Corsebar Av., Pais. | N 5 | 46 |
| Corsebar Cres, Pais. | N 5 | 46 |
| Corsebar Dr., Pais. | N 5 | 46 |
| Corsebar La. G78 | N 4 | 45 |
| *Balgonie Av.* | | |
| Corsebar Rd., Pais. | N 5 | 46 |
| Corsehill Pl. G34 | K26 | 40 |
| Corsehill St. G34 | K26 | 40 |
| Corselet Rd. G53 | Q10 | 60 |
| Corsewall Av. G32 | M24 | 55 |
| Corsford Dr. G53 | P11 | 61 |
| Corsock St. G31 | K20 | 37 |
| Corston St. G33 | K20 | 37 |
| Cortachy Pl., Bish. | E20 | 11 |
| Coruisk Way | O 3 | 45 |
| *Spencer Dr.* | | |
| Coruisk Way, Pais. | O 3 | 45 |
| *Spencer Dr.* | | |
| Corunna St. G3 | K15 | 35 |
| Coshneuk Rd. G33 | G22 | 24 |
| Cottar St. G20 | F15 | 21 |
| Cotton Av., Linw. | L 1 | 28 |
| Cotton St. G40 | N19 | 53 |
| Cotton St., Pais. | M 6 | 46 |
| Coulters La. G40 | L18 | 36 |
| Countess Wk., Bail. | L28 | 41 |
| County Av. G72 | O20 | 53 |
| County Pl., Pais. | L 6 | 30 |
| *Moss St.* | | |
| County Sq., Pais. | L 6 | 30 |
| Couper St. G4 | J17 | 36 |
| Courthill Av. G44 | P16 | 63 |
| Coustonhill St. G43 | O14 | 50 |
| *Pleasance St.* | | |
| Coustonholm Rd. G43 | O14 | 50 |
| Coventry Dr. G31 | K19 | 37 |
| Cowal Dr., Linw. | L 1 | 28 |
| Cowal St. G20 | F14 | 20 |
| Cowan Clo., Barr. | Q 8 | 59 |
| Cowan Cres. | R 8 | 59 |
| Cowan La. G12 | J15 | 35 |
| *Cowan St.* | | |
| Cowan Rd., Cumb. | A 1 | 70 |
| Cowan St. G12 | J15 | 35 |
| Cowan Wilson Av., | S26 | 68 |
| Blan. | | |
| Cowcaddens Rd. G2 | J16 | 35 |
| Cowden Dr., Bish. | D19 | 11 |
| Cowden St. G51 | K11 | 33 |
| Cowdenhill Circus G13 | F11 | 19 |
| Cowdenhill Pl. G13 | F11 | 19 |
| Cowdenhill Rd. G13 | F11 | 19 |
| Cowdie St., Pais. | K 5 | 30 |
| Cowdray Cres., Renf. | H 8 | 17 |
| Cowell Vw., Clyde. | D 7 | 5 |
| *Granville St.* | | |
| Cowglen Pl. G53 | O11 | 49 |
| *Cowglen Rd.* | | |
| Cowglen Rd. G53 | O11 | 49 |
| Cowglen Ter. G53 | O11 | 49 |
| Cowie St. G41 | L15 | 35 |
| Cowlairs Rd. G21 | H18 | 22 |
| Coxhill St. G21 | H17 | 22 |
| Coxton Pl. G33 | J23 | 39 |
| Coylton Rd. G43 | P15 | 63 |
| Craggan Dr. G14 | G 9 | 18 |
| Cragielea St. G31 | K19 | 37 |
| Crags Av., Pais. | N 6 | 46 |
| Crags Cres., Pais. | N 6 | 46 |
| Crags Rd., Pais. | N 6 | 46 |
| Craig Rd. G44 | P16 | 63 |
| Craig Rd., Linw. | K 1 | 28 |
| Craigallian Av. G72 | Q23 | 67 |
| Craiganour La. G43 | P14 | 62 |
| Craiganour Pl. G43 | P14 | 62 |
| Craigard Pl. G73 | Q21 | 66 |
| *Inverclyde Gdns.* | | |
| Craigbank Dr. G53 | P10 | 60 |
| Craigbank St. G22 | H17 | 22 |
| Craigbarnet Cres. G33 | H22 | 24 |
| Craigbo Av. G23 | E14 | 8 |
| Craigbo Ct. G23 | F14 | 20 |

| | | |
|---|---|---|
| Craigbo Dr. G23 | F14 | 20 |
| Craigbo Pl. G23 | F14 | 20 |
| Craigbo Rd. G23 | F14 | 20 |
| Craigbo St. G23 | E14 | 8 |
| Craigbog Av., John. | N08 | 43 |
| Craigellan Rd. G43 | P14 | 62 |
| Craigenbay Cres., Lenz. | C23 | 13 |
| Craigenbay Rd., Lenz. | D23 | 13 |
| Craigenbay St. G21 | H19 | 23 |
| Craigencart Ct., Clyde. | C 6 | 4 |
| *Gentle Row* | | |
| Craigend Dr., Coat. | M29 | 57 |
| Craigend Pl. G13 | G12 | 19 |
| Craigend St. G13 | G12 | 19 |
| Craigendmuir Rd. G33 | H24 | 25 |
| Craigendmuir St. G33 | J20 | 37 |
| Craigendon Oval, Pais. | P 5 | 58 |
| Craigendon Rd., Pais. | P 5 | 58 |
| Craigends Dr., Kilb. | M07 | 42 |
| *High Barholm* | | |
| Craigenfeoch Av., John. | N08 | 43 |
| Craigfaulds Av., Pais. | N04 | 45 |
| Craigflower Gdns. G53 | Q10 | 60 |
| Craigflower Rd. G53 | Q10 | 60 |
| Craighalbert Rd. G68 | B 1 | 70 |
| Craighall Rd. G4 | J16 | 35 |
| Craighead Av. G33 | H20 | 23 |
| Craigheads St., Barr. | R 7 | 59 |
| Craighouse St. G33 | J22 | 38 |
| Craigie Pk. G66 | C24 | 13 |
| Craigie St. G42 | N16 | 51 |
| Craigiebar Dr., Pais. | O 5 | 46 |
| Craigieburn Gdns. G20 | F13 | 20 |
| Craigieburn Rd., Cumb. | C 2 | 70 |
| Craigiehall Pl. G51 | L14 | 34 |
| Craigielea Dr., Pais. | L 5 | 30 |
| Craigielea Rd. G81 | B 6 | 4 |
| Craigielea Rd., Renf. | H 8 | 17 |
| Craigielinn Av., Pais. | P 5 | 58 |
| Craigievar St. G33 | J24 | 39 |
| Craigleith St. G32 | L21 | 38 |
| Craiglockhart St. G33 | J23 | 39 |
| Craigmaddie Ter. La. G3 | K15 | 35 |
| *Derby St.* | | |
| Craigmillar Rd. G42 | O16 | 51 |
| Craigmont Dr. G20 | G15 | 21 |
| Craigmont St. G20 | G15 | 21 |
| Craigmore Rd., Bear. | B10 | 6 |
| Craigmore St. G31 | L20 | 37 |
| Craigmount Av., Pais. | P 5 | 58 |
| Craigmuir Cres. G52 | L 9 | 32 |
| Craigmuir Pl. G52 | L 9 | 32 |
| *Craigmuir Rd.* | | |
| Craigmuir Rd. G52 | L 9 | 32 |
| Craigneil St. G33 | J24 | 39 |
| Craignestock St. G40 | L18 | 36 |
| Craignethan Gdns. G11 | J13 | 34 |
| *Lawrie St.* | | |
| Craignure Rd. G73 | Q19 | 65 |
| Craigpark Dr. G31 | K19 | 37 |
| Craigpark St. G31 | K19 | 37 |
| Craigpark Ter. G31 | K19 | 37 |
| *Craigpark* | | |
| Craigpark Way, Udd. | O28 | 57 |
| *Newton Dr.* | | |
| Craigs Av., Clyde. | C 8 | 5 |
| Craigston Pl., John. | N09 | 43 |
| Craigston Rd., John. | N09 | 43 |
| Craigton Av., Barr. | R 9 | 60 |
| Craigton Dr. G51 | L12 | 33 |
| Craigton Dr., Barr. | R 9 | 60 |
| Craigton Pl. G51 | L12 | 33 |
| *Craigton Dr.* | | |
| Craigton Pl., Blan. | R26 | 68 |
| Craigton Rd. G51 | L12 | 33 |
| Craigvicar Gdns. G32 | L23 | 39 |
| *Hailes Av.* | | |
| Craigview Av., John. | O08 | 43 |
| Craigwell Av. G73 | P20 | 65 |
| Crail St. G31 | L20 | 37 |
| Cramond Av., Renf. | J 9 | 32 |
| Cramond St. G5 | N17 | 52 |
| Cramond Ter. G32 | L22 | 38 |
| Cranborne Rd. G12 | G13 | 20 |
| Cranbrooke Dr. G20 | F14 | 20 |
| Cranhill St. G33 | J20 | 37 |
| Cranston St. G3 | K15 | 35 |
| *Great George St.* | | |
| Cranworth La. G12 | H14 | 20 |
| *Great George St.* | | |
| Cranworth St. G12 | H14 | 20 |
| Crarae Av., Bear. | E12 | 7 |
| Crathie Dr. G11 | J13 | 34 |

| | | |
|---|---|---|
| Crathie La. G11 | J13 | 34 |
| *Exeter Dr.* | | |
| Craw Rd., Pais. | M 5 | 46 |
| Crawford Av., Lenz. | D23 | 13 |
| Crawford Cres., Blan. | R26 | 68 |
| Crawford Cres., Udd. | O27 | 57 |
| Crawford Ct., Giff. | R13 | 62 |
| *Milverton Rd.* | | |
| Crawford Dr. G15 | E 9 | 6 |
| Crawford St. G11 | J13 | 34 |
| Crawford Dr., Pais. | L 4 | 29 |
| Crawfurd Gdns. G73 | Q19 | 65 |
| Crawfurd Rd. G73 | Q19 | 65 |
| Crawriggs Av., Lenz. | C23 | 13 |
| Crebar Dr., Barr. | R 8 | 59 |
| Crebar St. G46 | Q12 | 61 |
| Credon Gdns. G73 | Q20 | 65 |
| Cree Av., Bish. | E20 | 11 |
| Cree Gdns. G32 | L21 | 38 |
| *Kilmany Dr.* | | |
| Creran St. G40 | L18 | 36 |
| *Tobago St.* | | |
| Crescent Ct., Dalm. | D 6 | 4 |
| *Swindon St.* | | |
| Crescent Rd. G13 | G10 | 18 |
| Cresswell La. G12 | H14 | 20 |
| *Great George St.* | | |
| Cresswell St. G12 | H14 | 20 |
| Cressy St. G11 | K12 | 33 |
| Crest Av. G13 | F10 | 18 |
| Crestlea Av., Pais. | O 6 | 46 |
| Creswell Ter., Udd. | O27 | 57 |
| *Kylepark Dr.* | | |
| Crichton Ct. G42 | R18 | 64 |
| Crichton St. G21 | H18 | 22 |
| Crieff Ct. G3 | K15 | 35 |
| *North St.* | | |
| Criffell Gdns. G32 | M23 | 55 |
| Criffell Rd. G32 | M23 | 55 |
| Crimea St. G2 | K16 | 35 |
| Crinan Gdns., Bish. | E19 | 11 |
| Crinan Rd., Bish. | E19 | 11 |
| Crinan St. G31 | K19 | 37 |
| Cripps Av., Clyde. | E 8 | 5 |
| Croft Rd. G73 | P22 | 66 |
| Croft St. G31 | L19 | 37 |
| Croft Wynd, Udd. | P28 | 69 |
| Croftbank Av. G71 | R28 | 69 |
| Croftbank Cres., Both. | R28 | 69 |
| Croftbank Cres., Udd. | P27 | 69 |
| Croftbank St. G21 | H18 | 22 |
| Croftbank St., Udd. | P27 | 69 |
| Croftburn Dr. G44 | Q17 | 64 |
| Croftcroighn Rd. G33 | J22 | 38 |
| Croftend Av. G44 | P18 | 64 |
| Croftfoor Av. G44 | Q17 | 64 |
| Croftfoot Cotts., Gart. | G28 | 27 |
| Croftfoot Cres. G45 | Q19 | 65 |
| Croftfoot Dr. G45 | Q18 | 64 |
| Croftfoot Quad. G45 | Q18 | 64 |
| Croftfoot Rd. G45 | Q17 | 64 |
| Croftfoot St. G45 | Q19 | 65 |
| Croftfoot Ter. G45 | Q18 | 64 |
| Crofthead St., Udd. | P27 | 69 |
| Crofthill Av., Udd. | P27 | 69 |
| Crofthill Rd. G44 | P17 | 64 |
| Crofthouse Dr. G44 | Q18 | 64 |
| Croftmont Av. G44 | Q18 | 64 |
| Croftmoraig Av., Chr. | D28 | 15 |
| Crofton Av. G44 | Q17 | 64 |
| Croftpark Av. G44 | Q17 | 64 |
| Croftpark Rd., Clyde. | B 7 | 5 |
| Croftside Av. G44 | Q18 | 64 |
| Croftspar Av. G32 | L23 | 39 |
| Croftspar Dr. G32 | L23 | 39 |
| Croftspar Pl. G32 | L23 | 39 |
| Croftwood Av. G44 | Q17 | 64 |
| Croftwood, Bish. | D19 | 11 |
| Cromart Pl., Chr. | E26 | 14 |
| Cromarty Av. G43 | P15 | 63 |
| Cromarty Av., Bish. | E20 | 11 |
| Cromarty Gdns., Clark. | R16 | 63 |
| Crombie Gdns., Bail. | M25 | 56 |
| Cromdale St. G51 | L12 | 33 |
| Cromer La., Pais. | K 5 | 30 |
| *Abbotsburn Way* | | |
| Cromer St. G20 | G15 | 21 |
| Cromer Way, Pais. | K 5 | 30 |
| *Mosslands Rd.* | | |
| Crompton Av. G44 | P16 | 63 |
| Cromwell La. G20 | J16 | 35 |
| *Cromwell St.* | | |

| | | |
|---|---|---|
| Cromwell St. G20 | J16 | 35 |
| Cronberry Quad. G52 | M 9 | 48 |
| Cronberry Ter. G52 | M 9 | 48 |
| Crookedshields Rd. G72 | R22 | 66 |
| Crookston Av. G52 | M10 | 48 |
| Crookston Ct. G52 | M10 | 48 |
| Crookston Dr. G52 | M 9 | 48 |
| Crookston Gdns. G52 | M 9 | 48 |
| Crookston Gro. G52 | M10 | 48 |
| Crookston Pl. G52 | M 9 | 48 |
| Crookston Quad. G52 | M 9 | 48 |
| Crookston Rd. G52 | N10 | 48 |
| Crookston Ter. G52 | M10 | 48 |
| *Crookston Rd.* | | |
| Crosbie Dr. G78 | O 3 | 45 |
| Crosbie St. G20 | F14 | 20 |
| Crosbie Woods, Pais. | N 4 | 45 |
| Cross Arthurlie St., | R 7 | 59 |
| Barr. | | |
| Cross Rd., Pais. | N 4 | 45 |
| Cross St. G32 | N23 | 55 |
| Cross St. G43 | O13 | 50 |
| Cross St., Pais. | M 5 | 46 |
| Cross, The, G1 | L17 | 36 |
| Cross, The, Pais. | L 6 | 30 |
| Crossbank Av. G42 | N18 | 52 |
| Crossbank Dr. G42 | N18 | 52 |
| Crossbank Rd. G42 | N17 | 52 |
| Crossbank Ter. G42 | N17 | 52 |
| Crossflat Cres., Pais. | L 7 | 31 |
| Crossford Dr. G23 | E15 | 9 |
| Crosshill Av. G42 | N16 | 51 |
| Crosshill Av., Lenz. | C23 | 13 |
| Crosshill Dr. G73 | P19 | 65 |
| Crosshill Rd., | C20 | 11 |
| Bish. & Lenz. | | |
| Crosshill Sq., Bail. | M26 | 56 |
| Crosslee St. G52 | L12 | 33 |
| Crosslees Ct., Thorn. | Q12 | 61 |
| *Main St.* | | |
| Crosslees Dr., Thorn. | Q12 | 61 |
| Crosslees Pk., Thorn. | Q12 | 61 |
| Crosslees Rd., Thorn. | R12 | 61 |
| Crossloan Pl. G51 | K12 | 33 |
| Crossloan Rd. G51 | K12 | 33 |
| Crossloan Ter. G51 | K12 | 33 |
| Crossmill Av., Barr. | Q 8 | 59 |
| Crosspoint Dr. G23 | E15 | 9 |
| *Invershiel Rd.* | | |
| Crosstobs Rd. G53 | N10 | 48 |
| Crovie Rd. G53 | O10 | 48 |
| Crow Ct., The, Bish. | E18 | 10 |
| *Kenmure Av.* | | |
| Crow La. G13 | G12 | 19 |
| Crow Rd. G11 | H12 | 19 |
| Crow Wood Rd., Chr. | F25 | 26 |
| Crowflats Rd., Udd. | P27 | 69 |
| *Lady Isle Cres.* | | |
| Crowhill Rd. G64 | F18 | 22 |
| Crowhill St. G22 | G17 | 22 |
| Crowlin Cres. G33 | K22 | 38 |
| Crown Av., Clyde. | D 7 | 5 |
| Crown Circuit G12 | H13 | 20 |
| *Crown Rd.* | | |
| Crown Circus G12 | H13 | 20 |
| *Crown Rd. S.* | | |
| Crown Ct. G1 | K17 | 36 |
| *Virginia St.* | | |
| Crown Gdns. G12 | H13 | 20 |
| *Crown Rd. N.* | | |
| Crown Mansions G11 | H13 | 20 |
| *North Gardner St.* | | |
| Crown Rd. N. G12 | H13 | 20 |
| Crown Rd. S. G12 | H13 | 20 |
| Crown St. G5 | M17 | 52 |
| Crown St., Bail. | M24 | 55 |
| Crown Ter. G12 | H13 | 20 |
| *Crown Rd. S.* | | |
| Crownpoint Rd. G40 | L18 | 36 |
| Crowpoint Rd. G40 | L19 | 37 |
| *Alma St.* | | |
| Crowwood Ter., Chr. | F25 | 26 |
| Croy Pl. G21 | G20 | 23 |
| *Croy Rd.* | | |
| Croy Pl. G21 | G20 | 23 |
| *Rye Rd.* | | |
| Croy Rd. G21 | G20 | 23 |
| Croydon St. G31 | L20 | 37 |
| Cruachan Av., Renf. | J 8 | 31 |
| Cruachan Cres., Pais. | O 6 | 46 |
| Cruachan Dr., Barr. | R 8 | 59 |
| Cruachan Rd. G73 | Q20 | 65 |
| Cruachan Rd., Bear. | B10 | 6 |
| *Ledi Dr.* | | |
| Cruachan St. G46 | Q12 | 61 |
| Cruachan Way, Barr. | R 8 | 59 |
| Cruden St. G51 | L12 | 33 |
| Crum Av., Thorn. | Q13 | 62 |
| Crusader Av. G13 | E11 | 7 |
| Cubie St. G40 | L18 | 36 |
| *Crownpoint Rd.* | | |
| Cuilhill Rd., Bail. | K27 | 41 |
| Cuillin Way, Barr. | R 8 | 59 |
| Cuillins Rd. G73 | Q20 | 65 |
| Cuillins, The, Udd. | N26 | 56 |
| Culbin Dr. G13 | F 9 | 18 |
| Cullen St. G32 | M22 | 54 |
| Cullins, The, Chr. | D28 | 15 |
| Culloden St. G31 | K19 | 37 |
| Culrain St. G32 | L22 | 38 |
| Culross La. G32 | M23 | 55 |
| Culross St. G32 | M23 | 55 |
| Cult Rd., Lenz. | D24 | 13 |
| Cults St. G51 | L12 | 33 |
| Culzean Cres., Bail. | M25 | 56 |
| *Huntingtower Rd.* | | |
| Culzean Dr. G32 | M23 | 39 |
| *Hailes Av.* | | |
| Cumberland Ct. G1 | L17 | 36 |
| *Gallowgate* | | |
| Cumberland La. G5 | M16 | 51 |
| *Cumberland St.* | | |
| Cumberland Pl. G5 | M17 | 52 |
| Cumberland Pl., Pais. | M 6 | 46 |
| *Laigh Kirk La.* | | |
| Cumberland St. G5 | L16 | 35 |
| Cumberland St. G5 | M17 | 52 |
| Cumbernauld Rd. G31 | K20 | 37 |
| Cumbrae Ct., Clyde. | E 7 | 5 |
| *Montrose St.* | | |
| Cumbrae Rd., Pais. | O 6 | 46 |
| Cumbrae Rd., Renf. | J 8 | 31 |
| Cumbrae St. G33 | K22 | 38 |
| Cumlodden Dr. G20 | F14 | 20 |
| Cumming Dr. G42 | O16 | 51 |
| Cumnock Dr., Renf. | R 8 | 59 |
| Cunard St., Clyde. | F 8 | 17 |
| Cunningham Dr., Clyde. | C 6 | 4 |
| Cunningham Dr., Giff. | Q15 | 63 |
| Cunningham Rd. G73 | O20 | 53 |
| *Cambuslang Rd.* | | |
| Cunningham Rd., G52 | K 9 | 32 |
| Cunningham St. G1 | K17 | 36 |
| *Parliamentary Rd.* | | |
| Cunninghame Rd., Kilb. | M07 | 42 |
| Curfew Rd. G13 | E11 | 7 |
| Curle St. G14 | J11 | 33 |
| Curlew Pl., John. | O08 | 43 |
| Curling Cres. G44 | O17 | 52 |
| Currie St. G20 | G15 | 21 |
| Curtis Av. G44 | O17 | 52 |
| Curzon St. G20 | G15 | 21 |
| Cut, The, Udd. | P27 | 69 |
| Cuthbert St., Udd. | O28 | 57 |
| *Oakdene Av.* | | |
| Cuthbertson St. G42 | N16 | 51 |
| Cuthelton Dr. G31 | M21 | 54 |
| *Cuthelton St.* | | |
| Cuthelton St. G31 | M20 | 53 |
| Cuthelton Ter. G31 | M20 | 53 |
| Cypress Av., Blan. | S26 | 68 |
| Cypress Av., Udd. | O28 | 57 |
| *Myrtle Rd.* | | |
| Cypress Ct., Lenz. | C22 | 12 |
| Cypress St. G22 | G17 | 22 |
| Cyprus Av., John. | N 1 | 44 |
| Cyprus St., Clyde. | F 8 | 17 |
| Cyril St., Pais. | M 7 | 47 |
| | | |
| Daer Av., Renf. | J 9 | 32 |
| Dairsie Gdns., Bish. | F20 | 23 |
| Dairsie St. G44 | Q15 | 63 |
| Daisy St. G42 | N16 | 51 |
| Dakota Way, Renf. | J 8 | 31 |
| *Friendship Way* | | |
| Dalbeth Rd. G32 | N21 | 54 |
| Dalchurn Path G34 | K25 | 40 |
| *Dalchurn Pl.* | | |
| Dalchurn Pl. G34 | K25 | 40 |
| Dalcraig Cres., Blan. | R26 | 68 |
| Dalcross La. G11 | J14 | 34 |
| *Byres Rd.* | | |
| Dalcross St. G11 | J14 | 34 |
| Dalcruin Gdns. G69 | D28 | 15 |
| Daldowie Av. G32 | M23 | 55 |
| Dale Path G40 | M18 | 52 |
| Dale St. G40 | M18 | 52 |
| Dale Way G73 | Q19 | 65 |
| Daleview Av. G12 | G13 | 20 |
| Dalfoil Ct. G52 | M 9 | 48 |
| Dalgarroch Av. G13 | F 9 | 18 |
| Dalgleish Av., Clyde. | C 6 | 4 |
| Dalhousie Gdns., Bish. | E18 | 10 |
| Dalhousie La. G3 | J16 | 35 |
| *Scott St.* | | |
| Dalhousie La. W. G3 | J16 | 35 |
| *Buccleuch St.* | | |
| Dalhousie Rd., Kilb. | N07 | 42 |
| Dalhousie St. G3 | J16 | 35 |
| Dalilea Dr. G34 | J26 | 40 |
| Dalilea Path G34 | J26 | 40 |
| *Dalilea Dr.* | | |
| Dalilea Pl. G34 | J26 | 40 |
| Dalintober St. G5 | L16 | 35 |
| Dalkeith Av. G41 | M13 | 50 |
| Dalkeith Av., Bish. | D19 | 11 |
| Dalkeith Rd., Bish. | D19 | 11 |
| Dalmahoy St. G32 | K21 | 38 |
| Dalmally St. G20 | H15 | 21 |
| Dalmarnock Ct. G40 | M19 | 53 |
| *Baltic St.* | | |
| Dalmary Dr., Pais. | L 7 | 31 |
| Dalmeny Av., Giff. | Q14 | 62 |
| Dalmeny Dr., Barr. | R 7 | 59 |
| Dalmeny St. G5 | N18 | 52 |
| Dalmuir Ct., Dalm. | D 6 | 4 |
| *Stewart St.* | | |
| Dalnair St. G3 | J14 | 34 |
| Dalness Pass. G32 | M22 | 54 |
| *Ochil St.* | | |
| Dalness St. G32 | M22 | 54 |
| Dalnottar Hill Rd., | C 4 | 4 |
| Old.K. | | |
| Dalreoch Av., Bail. | L26 | 40 |
| Dalriada St. G40 | M20 | 53 |
| Dalry Rd., Udd. | O28 | 57 |
| *Myrtle Rd.* | | |
| Dalry St. G32 | M22 | 54 |
| Dalserf Cres., Giff. | R13 | 62 |
| Dalserf St. G31 | L19 | 37 |
| Dalsetter Av. G15 | E 9 | 6 |
| Dalsetter Pl. G15 | E10 | 6 |
| Dalsholm Rd. G20 | F13 | 20 |
| Dalskeith Av., Pais. | L 4 | 29 |
| Dalskeith Cres., Pais. | L 4 | 29 |
| Dalskeith Rd., Pais. | M 4 | 45 |
| Dalswinton Pl. G34 | K26 | 40 |
| *Dalswinton St.* | | |
| Dalswinton St. G34 | K26 | 40 |
| Dalton Av., Clyde. | E 9 | 6 |
| Dalton St. G31 | L21 | 38 |
| Dalveen Av., Udd. | O27 | 57 |
| Dalveen Ct., Barr. | R 8 | 59 |
| Dalveen St. G32 | L21 | 38 |
| Dalveen Way G73 | Q20 | 65 |
| Dalwhinnie Av., Blan. | R26 | 68 |
| Daly Gdns., Blan. | R27 | 69 |
| Dalziel Dr. G41 | M14 | 50 |
| Dalziel Quadrant G41 | M14 | 50 |
| *Dalziel Dr.* | | |
| Dalziel Rd. G52 | K 9 | 32 |
| Damshot Cres. G53 | N11 | 49 |
| Damshot Rd. G53 | O11 | 49 |
| Danes Cres. G14 | G10 | 18 |
| Danes Dr. G14 | G10 | 18 |
| Danes La. S. G14 | H11 | 19 |
| *Dunglass Av.* | | |
| Dargarvel Av. G41 | M13 | 50 |
| Darkwood Cres., Pais. | L 4 | 29 |
| Darleith St. G32 | L21 | 38 |
| Darluith Rd., Linw. | L 1 | 28 |
| Darnaway Av. G33 | J23 | 39 |
| Darnaway St. G33 | J23 | 39 |
| Darnick St. G21 | H19 | 23 |
| *Hobden St.* | | |
| Darnley Cres., Bish. | D18 | 10 |
| Darnley Gdns. G41 | N15 | 51 |
| Darnley Pl. G41 | N15 | 51 |
| *Darnley Rd.* | | |
| Darnley Rd. G41 | N15 | 51 |
| Darnley Rd., Barr. | Q 9 | 60 |
| Darnley St. G41 | N15 | 51 |
| Darroch Way, Cumb. | B 3 | 71 |
| Dartford St. G22 | H16 | 21 |
| Darvaar Rd., Renf. | J 8 | 31 |

| Street | Map | Page |
|---|---|---|
| Darvel Cres., Pais. | M 8 | 47 |
| Darvel St. G53 | P 9 | 60 |
| Darwin Pl., Dalm. | D 5 | 4 |
| Dava St. G51 | K13 | 34 |
| Davaar Rd., Pais. | O 6 | 46 |
| Davaar St. G40 | M19 | 53 |
| Daventry Dr. G12 | G13 | 20 |
| David Pl., Bail. | M24 | 55 |
| David Pl., Pais. | K 7 | 31 |
| *Killarn Way* | | |
| David St. G40 | L19 | 37 |
| David Way, Pais. | K 7 | 31 |
| *Killarn Way* | | |
| Davidson Gdns. G14 | H11 | 19 |
| *Westland Dr.* | | |
| Davidson Quad., Clyde. | B 6 | 4 |
| Davidson St. G40 | N19 | 53 |
| Davidson St., Clyde. | F 9 | 18 |
| Davidston Pl., Lenz. | D24 | 13 |
| Davieland Rd., Giff. | R13 | 62 |
| Daviot St. G51 | L11 | 33 |
| Dawes La. N. G14 | H11 | 19 |
| *Upland Dr.* | | |
| Dawson Pl. G4 | H16 | 21 |
| *Dawson Rd.* | | |
| Dawson Rd. G4 | H16 | 21 |
| Dealston Rd., Barr. | Q 7 | 59 |
| Dean Park Av. G72 | Q23 | 67 |
| Dean Park Rd., Renf. | J 9 | 32 |
| Dean St., Clyde. | E 8 | 5 |
| Deanbrae St., Udd. | P27 | 69 |
| Deanfield Quad. G52 | L 9 | 32 |
| Deanpark Av., Udd. | Q28 | 69 |
| Deans Av. G72 | Q23 | 67 |
| Deanside La. G4 | K17 | 36 |
| *Rotton Row* | | |
| Deanside Rd., Renf. | K10 | 32 |
| Deanston Dr. G41 | O15 | 51 |
| Deanwood Av. G44 | Q15 | 63 |
| Deanwood Rd. G44 | Q15 | 63 |
| Debdale Cotts. G13 | G12 | 19 |
| *Whittingehame Dr.* | | |
| Dechmont Av. G72 | Q23 | 67 |
| Dechmont Gdns., Blan. | R26 | 68 |
| Dechmont Gdns., Udd. | N27 | 57 |
| Dechmont Pl. G72 | Q23 | 67 |
| Dechmont Rd., Udd. | N27 | 57 |
| Dechmont St. G31 | M20 | 53 |
| Dechmont Vw., Udd. | O28 | 57 |
| *Hamilton Vw.* | | |
| Dee Av. G78 | N 3 | 45 |
| Dee Av., Renf. | H 9 | 18 |
| Dee Dr., Pais. | N 3 | 45 |
| Dee Pl., John. | O08 | 43 |
| Dee St. G33 | J20 | 37 |
| Deepdene Rd., Bear. | E11 | 7 |
| Deepdene Rd., Chr. | E28 | 15 |
| Delburn St. G31 | M20 | 53 |
| Delhi Av., Dalm. | D 5 | 4 |
| Delhmont Vw., Udd. | O28 | 57 |
| *Hamilton Vw.* | | |
| Delny Pl. G33 | K24 | 39 |
| Delvin Rd., G44 | P16 | 63 |
| Denbeck St. G32 | L21 | 38 |
| Denbrae St. G32 | L21 | 38 |
| Dene Wk., Bish. | F20 | 23 |
| Denewood Av., Pais. | O 5 | 46 |
| Denham St. G22 | H16 | 21 |
| Denholme Dr., Giff. | R14 | 62 |
| Denkenny Sq. G15 | D 9 | 6 |
| Denmark St. G22 | H17 | 22 |
| Denmilne Path G34 | K26 | 40 |
| Denmilne Pl. G34 | K26 | 40 |
| Denmilne St. G34 | K26 | 40 |
| Derby St. G3 | K15 | 35 |
| Derby Terrace La. G3 | K15 | 35 |
| *Derby St.* | | |
| Dervaig St. G31 | L20 | 37 |
| Derwent St. G22 | H16 | 21 |
| Despard Av. G32 | M24 | 55 |
| Despard Gdns. G32 | M24 | 55 |
| Deveron Av., Giff. | R14 | 62 |
| Deveron Rd., Bear. | E11 | 7 |
| Deveron St. G33 | J20 | 37 |
| Devol Cres. G53 | O10 | 48 |
| Devon Gdns. G12 | H13 | 20 |
| *Hyndland Rd.* | | |
| Devon Gdns., Bish. | D18 | 10 |
| Devon Pl. G42 | M16 | 51 |
| Devon St. G5 | M16 | 51 |
| Devondale Av., Blan. | R26 | 68 |
| Devonshire Gdns. G12 | H13 | 20 |
| Devonshire Gdns. La. G12 | H13 | 20 |
| *Hyndland Rd.* | | |
| Devonshire Ter. G12 | H13 | 20 |
| Devonshire Ter. La. G12 | H13 | 20 |
| *Hughenden Rd.* | | |
| Diana Av. G13 | F10 | 18 |
| Dick St. G20 | H15 | 21 |
| *Henderson St.* | | |
| Dickens Av., Clyde. | D 6 | 4 |
| Dilwara Av. G14 | J12 | 33 |
| Dimity St., John. | N09 | 43 |
| Dinard Dr., Giff. | Q14 | 62 |
| Dinart St. G33 | J20 | 37 |
| Dinduff St. G34 | J26 | 40 |
| Dingwall St. G3 | K14 | 34 |
| *Kelvinhaugh St.* | | |
| Dinmont Pl. G41 | N15 | 51 |
| *Norham St.* | | |
| Dinmont Rd. G41 | N14 | 50 |
| Dinwiddie St. G21 | J20 | 37 |
| Dipple Pl. G15 | E10 | 6 |
| Dirleton Av. G41 | O15 | 51 |
| Dirleton Dr., Pais. | N 4 | 45 |
| Dirleton Gate, Bear. | E11 | 7 |
| Divernia Way, Barr. | S 8 | 59 |
| Dixon Av. G42 | N16 | 51 |
| Dixon Rd. G42 | N17 | 52 |
| Dixon St. G1 | L16 | 35 |
| Dixon St., Pais. | M 6 | 46 |
| Dobbies Loan G4 | J16 | 35 |
| Dobbies Loan Pl. G4 | K17 | 36 |
| Dochart Av., Renf. | J 9 | 32 |
| Dochart St. G33 | J21 | 38 |
| Dock St., Clyde. | F 8 | 17 |
| Dodhill Pl. G13 | G10 | 18 |
| Dodside Gdns. G32 | M23 | 55 |
| Dodside Pl. G32 | M23 | 55 |
| Dodside St. G32 | M23 | 55 |
| Dolan St., Bail. | L25 | 40 |
| Dollar Ter. G20 | F14 | 20 |
| *Crosbie St.* | | |
| Dolphin Rd. G41 | N14 | 50 |
| Don Av., Renf. | J 9 | 32 |
| Don Dr., Pais. | N 3 | 45 |
| Don Pl., John. | O08 | 43 |
| Don St. G33 | K20 | 37 |
| Donald Way, Udd. | O28 | 57 |
| Donaldson Dr., Renf. | H 8 | 17 |
| *Ferguson St.* | | |
| Donaldswood Rd., Pais. | O 5 | 46 |
| Doncaster St. G20 | H16 | 21 |
| Doon Cres., Bear. | D11 | 7 |
| Doon Side, Cumb. | C 3 | 71 |
| Doon St., Clyde. | D 8 | 5 |
| Doonfoot Rd. G43 | P14 | 62 |
| Dora St. G40 | M19 | 53 |
| Dorchester Av., G12 | G13 | 20 |
| Dorchester Ct. G12 | G13 | 20 |
| *Dorchester Av.* | | |
| Dorchester Pl. G12 | G13 | 20 |
| Dorian Dr., Clark. | S14 | 62 |
| Dorlin Rd. G33 | G24 | 25 |
| Dormanside Rd. G53 | M10 | 48 |
| Dornal Av. G13 | F 9 | 18 |
| Dornford Av. G32 | N23 | 55 |
| Dornford Rd. G32 | N23 | 55 |
| Dornie Dr. G46 | Q12 | 61 |
| Dornoch Av., Giff. | R14 | 62 |
| Dornoch Pl., Bish. | E20 | 11 |
| Dornoch Pl., Chr. | E26 | 14 |
| Dornoch Rd., Bear. | E11 | 7 |
| Dornoch St. G40 | L18 | 36 |
| Dorset Sq. G3 | K15 | 35 |
| *Dorset St.* | | |
| Dorset St. G3 | K15 | 35 |
| Dosk Av. G13 | F 9 | 18 |
| Dosk Pl. G13 | F 9 | 18 |
| Douglas Av. G32 | N22 | 54 |
| Douglas Av. G73 | P20 | 65 |
| Douglas Av., Giff. | R14 | 62 |
| Douglas Av., John. | N 1 | 44 |
| Douglas Av., Lenz. | C23 | 13 |
| Douglas Ct., Lenz. | C23 | 13 |
| Douglas Dr. G15 | E 9 | 6 |
| Douglas Dr. G72 | P21 | 66 |
| Douglas Dr., Bail. | L24 | 39 |
| Douglas Dr., Both. | R28 | 69 |
| Douglas Gdns., Bear. | D12 | 7 |
| Douglas Gdns., Giff. | R14 | 62 |
| Douglas Gdns., Lenz. | C23 | 13 |
| Douglas Gdns., Udd. | P27 | 69 |
| Douglas La. G2 | K16 | 35 |
| *West George St.* | | |
| Douglas Park Cres., Bear. | C13 | 8 |
| Douglas Pl., Bear. | C12 | 7 |
| Douglas Pl., Lenz. | C23 | 13 |
| Douglas Rd., Pais. & Renf. | K 7 | 31 |
| Douglas St. G2 | K16 | 35 |
| Douglas St., Pais. | L 5 | 30 |
| Douglas St., Udd. | O28 | 57 |
| Douglas Ter. G41 | M15 | 51 |
| *Shields Rd.* | | |
| Douglas Ter., Pais. | J 6 | 30 |
| Douglaston Rd. G23 | E15 | 9 |
| Dougrie Dr. G45 | Q17 | 64 |
| Dougrie Pl. G45 | Q18 | 64 |
| Dougrie Rd. G45 | R17 | 64 |
| Dougrie St. G45 | Q18 | 64 |
| Dougrie Ter. G45 | Q17 | 64 |
| Doune Cres., Bish. | D19 | 11 |
| Doune Gdns. G20 | H15 | 21 |
| Doune Quad. G20 | H15 | 21 |
| Dove St. G53 | P10 | 60 |
| Dovecot G43 | O14 | 50 |
| *Shawhill Rd.* | | |
| Dovecothall St., Barr. | Q 8 | 59 |
| Dowanhill Rd., Cumb. | C 2 | 70 |
| Dowanhill Pl. G11 | J14 | 34 |
| *Old Dumbarton Rd.* | | |
| Dowanhill St. G11 | J14 | 34 |
| Dowanside La. G12 | H14 | 20 |
| *Byres Rd.* | | |
| Dowanside Rd. G12 | H14 | 20 |
| Dowanvale Ter. G11 | J13 | 34 |
| *White St.* | | |
| Down St. G21 | H18 | 22 |
| Downcraig Dr. G45 | R17 | 64 |
| Downcraig Rd. G45 | R17 | 64 |
| Downcraig Ter. G45 | R17 | 64 |
| Downfield Gdns., Both. | R27 | 69 |
| Downfield St. G32 | M21 | 54 |
| Downiebrae Rd. G73 | N19 | 53 |
| Dowrie Cres. G53 | N10 | 48 |
| Dows Pl. G4 | H16 | 21 |
| *Possil Rd.* | | |
| Drainie St. G34 | K25 | 40 |
| *Westerhouse Rd.* | | |
| Drake St. G40 | L18 | 36 |
| Drakemire Av. G45 | Q17 | 64 |
| Drakemire Dr. G45 | Q17 | 64 |
| Dreghorn St. G31 | K20 | 37 |
| Drem Pl. G11 | J13 | 34 |
| *Merkland St.* | | |
| Drimnin Rd. G33 | G24 | 25 |
| Drive Gdns., John. | M 3 | 45 |
| Drive Rd. G51 | K12 | 33 |
| Drochil St. G34 | J25 | 40 |
| Drumbeg Dr. G53 | P10 | 60 |
| Drumbeg Pl. G53 | P10 | 60 |
| Drumbottie Rd. G21 | G19 | 23 |
| Drumby Cres., Clark. | S14 | 62 |
| Drumby Dr., Clark. | S14 | 62 |
| Drumcavel Rd., Chr. & Gart. | F26 | 26 |
| Drumchapel Gdns. G15 | E10 | 6 |
| Drumchapel Pl. G15 | E10 | 6 |
| Drumchapel Rd. G15 | E10 | 6 |
| Drumclog Gdns. G33 | G21 | 24 |
| *Auchinleck Av.* | | |
| Drumclutha Dr., Both. | R28 | 69 |
| Drumcross Rd. G53 | N11 | 49 |
| Drumilaw Rd. G73 | P19 | 65 |
| Drumilaw Way G73 | P19 | 65 |
| Drumlaken Av. G23 | E14 | 8 |
| Drumlaken Ct. G23 | E14 | 8 |
| Drumlaken St. G23 | E14 | 8 |
| Drumlanrig Av. G34 | J26 | 40 |
| Drumlanrig Pl. G34 | J26 | 40 |
| Drumlanrig Quad. G34 | J26 | 40 |
| Drumlochy Rd. G33 | J22 | 38 |
| Drummond Av. G73 | O18 | 52 |
| Drummond Dr., Pais. | M 8 | 47 |
| Drummond Gdns. G13 | G12 | 19 |
| *Crow Rd.* | | |
| Drummore Rd. G15 | D10 | 6 |
| Drummyne Pl. G51 | L12 | 33 |
| *Drumoyne Circus* | | |
| Drumover Dr. G31 | M21 | 54 |
| Drumoyne Av. G51 | K12 | 33 |
| Drumoyne Circus G51 | L12 | 33 |
| Drumoyne Dr. G51 | K12 | 33 |

| | | |
|---|---|---|
| Drumoyne Quad. G51 | L12 | 33 |
| Drumoyne Rd. G51 | L12 | 33 |
| Drumoyne Sq. G51 | K12 | 33 |
| Drumpark St. G46 | Q12 | 61 |
| Drumpark St., Coat. | M28 | 57 |
| *Dunnachie Dr.* | | |
| Drumpeller Rd., Bail. | M25 | 56 |
| Drumpellier Av., Bail. | M25 | 56 |
| Drumpellier Pl., Bail. | M25 | 56 |
| Drumpellier St. G33 | J20 | 37 |
| Drumreoch Dr. G42 | O18 | 52 |
| Drumreoch Pl. G42 | O18 | 52 |
| Drumry Pl. G15 | E 9 | 6 |
| Drumry Rd. E. G15 | E 9 | 6 |
| Drumry Rd., Clyde. | D 7 | 5 |
| Drums Av., Pais. | L 5 | 30 |
| Drums Cres., Pais. | L 5 | 30 |
| Drums Rd. G53 | M10 | 48 |
| Drumsabgard Rd. G73 | P20 | 65 |
| Drumsack Av., Chr. | F26 | 26 |
| Drumshaw Dr. G32 | O23 | 55 |
| Drumvale Dr., Chr. | E27 | 15 |
| Drury St. G2 | K16 | 35 |
| Dryad St. G42 | P12 | 61 |
| Dryborough Av., John. | N 4 | 45 |
| Dryburgh Av. G73 | O19 | 53 |
| Dryburgh Gdns. G20 | H15 | 21 |
| Dryburgh Rd., Bear. | C11 | 7 |
| Dryburn Av. G52 | L10 | 32 |
| Drygate G4 | K18 | 36 |
| Drygrange Rd. G33 | J23 | 39 |
| Drymen Pl., Lenz. | D23 | 13 |
| Drymen Rd., Bear. | C11 | 7 |
| Drymen St. G52 | L12 | 33 |
| *Morven St.* | | |
| Drymen Wynd, Bear. | D12 | 7 |
| Drynoch Pl. G22 | F16 | 21 |
| Duart Dr., John. | N 1 | 44 |
| Duart St. G20 | F14 | 20 |
| Dubs Rd., Barr. | Q 9 | 60 |
| Dubton St. G34 | J25 | 40 |
| Duchall Pl. G14 | H10 | 18 |
| Duchess Pl. G73 | O20 | 53 |
| Duchess Rd. G73 | N20 | 53 |
| Duchray Dr., Pais. | M 9 | 48 |
| Duchray La. G31 | J20 | 37 |
| *Duchray St.* | | |
| Duchray St. G33 | J20 | 37 |
| Ducraig St. G32 | L22 | 38 |
| Dudhope St. G33 | J23 | 39 |
| Dudley Dr. G12 | H13 | 20 |
| Duffus Pl. G32 | O23 | 55 |
| Duffus St. G34 | J25 | 40 |
| Duffus Ter. G32 | O23 | 55 |
| Duke St., G4 | K18 | 36 |
| Duke St., Pais. | N 6 | 46 |
| Duke St., Linw. | L 2 | 28 |
| Dukes Rd. G72 & G73 | P20 | 65 |
| Dukes Rd., Bail. | L28 | 41 |
| Dulsie Rd. G21 | G20 | 23 |
| Dumbarton Rd. G11 | G 9 | 18 |
| Dumbarton Rd., Clyde. | C 6 | 4 |
| Dumbarton Rd., Old.K. | D 5 | 4 |
| Dalm. & Clyde. | | |
| Dumbreck Av. G41 | M13 | 50 |
| Dumbreck Ct. G41 | M13 | 50 |
| Dumbreck Pl., Lenz. | D24 | 13 |
| Dumbreck Rd. G41 | M13 | 50 |
| Dumbreck Sq. G41 | M13 | 50 |
| *Dumbreck Av.* | | |
| Dunagoil Rd. G45 | R17 | 64 |
| Dunagoil St. G45 | R18 | 64 |
| Dunagoil Ter. G45 | R18 | 64 |
| Dunalastair Dr. G33 | G22 | 24 |
| Dunalistair Av. G33 | G22 | 24 |
| Dunan Pl. G33 | K24 | 39 |
| Dunard Rd. G73 | O19 | 53 |
| Dunard St. G20 | H15 | 21 |
| Dunard Way, Pais. | K 5 | 30 |
| *Mosslands Rd.* | | |
| Dunaskin St. G11 | J14 | 34 |
| Dunbar Av. G73 | O20 | 53 |
| Dunbar Av., John. | O09 | 43 |
| Dunbar Rd., Pais. | N 4 | 45 |
| Dunbar St. G31 | L20 | 37 |
| Dunbeith Pl. G20 | G14 | 20 |
| Dunblane St. G4 | J16 | 35 |
| Dunbrach Rd., Cumb. | B 1 | 70 |
| Duncan Av. G14 | H11 | 19 |
| Duncan La. G14 | H11 | 19 |
| *Duncan Av.* | | |

| | | |
|---|---|---|
| Duncan La. N. G14 | H11 | 19 |
| *Ormiston Av.* | | |
| Duncan St., Clyde. | D 7 | 5 |
| Duncansby Rd. G33 | L23 | 39 |
| Dunchatt St. G31 | K18 | 36 |
| Dunchattan Pl. G31 | K18 | 36 |
| *Duke St.* | | |
| Dunchurch Rd., Pais. | L 8 | 31 |
| Dunclutha Dr., Both. | R28 | 69 |
| Dunclutha St. G40 | N19 | 53 |
| Duncombe St. G20 | F14 | 20 |
| Duncombe Vw., Clyde. | D 8 | 5 |
| *Kirkoswald Dr.* | | |
| Duncraig Cres., John. | O08 | 43 |
| Duncrub Dr., Bish. | E18 | 10 |
| Duncruin St. G20 | F14 | 20 |
| Duncryne Av. G32 | M23 | 55 |
| Duncryne Gdns. G32 | M24 | 55 |
| Duncryne Pl., Bish. | F18 | 22 |
| Dundas La. G1 | K17 | 36 |
| Dundas St. G1 | K17 | 36 |
| Dundasvale Ct. G4 | J16 | 35 |
| *Maitland St.* | | |
| Dundasvale Rd. G4 | J16 | 35 |
| *Maitland St.* | | |
| Dundee Dr. G52 | M10 | 48 |
| Dundonald Av., John. | N08 | 43 |
| Dundonald Rd. G12 | H14 | 20 |
| Dundonald Rd., Pais. | K 7 | 31 |
| Dundrennan Rd. G42 | O15 | 51 |
| Dunearn Pl., Pais. | M 7 | 47 |
| Dunearn St. G4 | J15 | 35 |
| Dunegoin St. G51 | K13 | 34 |
| *Sharp St.* | | |
| Dunellan Dr., Clyde. | B 7 | 5 |
| Dunellan St. G52 | L12 | 33 |
| Dunera Av. G14 | J11 | 33 |
| Dungeonhill Rd. G34 | K26 | 40 |
| Dunglass Av. G14 | H11 | 19 |
| Dunglass Av. N. G14 | H11 | 19 |
| *Verona Av.* | | |
| Dungoil Av., Cumb. | B 1 | 70 |
| Dungoil Rd., Lenz. | D24 | 13 |
| Dungoyne St. G20 | F14 | 20 |
| Dunira St. G32 | M21 | 54 |
| Dunivaig St. G33 | K24 | 39 |
| Dunkeld Av. G73 | O19 | 53 |
| Dunkeld Dr., Bear. | D13 | 8 |
| Dunkeld Gdns., Bish. | E19 | 11 |
| Dunkeld La., Chr. | E28 | 15 |
| *Burnbrae Av.* | | |
| Dunkeld St. G31 | M20 | 53 |
| Dunkenny Pl. G15 | D 9 | 6 |
| Dunkenny Rd. G15 | D 9 | 6 |
| Dunlop Cres., Both. | R28 | 69 |
| Dunlop Cres., Renf. | H 8 | 17 |
| *Hairst St.* | | |
| Dunlop St. G1 | L17 | 36 |
| Dunlop St. G72 | P24 | 67 |
| Dunlop St., Linw. | L 2 | 28 |
| Dunlop St., Renf. | H 8 | 17 |
| *Hairst St.* | | |
| Dunmore La. G5 | L16 | 35 |
| *Norfolk St.* | | |
| Dunmore St. G5 | L16 | 35 |
| Dunmore St., Clyde. | F 8 | 17 |
| Dunn St. G40 | M19 | 53 |
| Dunn St., Clyde. | C 6 | 4 |
| Dunn St., Dalm. | D 6 | 4 |
| Dunn St., Pais. | M 7 | 47 |
| Dunnachie Dr., Coat. | M28 | 57 |
| Dunnichen Pl., Bish. | E20 | 11 |
| Dunning St. G31 | M20 | 53 |
| Dunolly St. G21 | J19 | 37 |
| Dunottar St. G33 | J22 | 38 |
| Dunottar St., Bish. | E20 | 11 |
| Dunphail Dr. G34 | K26 | 40 |
| Dunphail Rd. G34 | K26 | 40 |
| Dunragit St. G31 | K20 | 37 |
| Dunroamin Av., | N 1 | 44 |
| John. | | |
| Dunrobin St. G31 | L19 | 37 |
| Dunrod St. G32 | M22 | 54 |
| Dunside Dr. G53 | P10 | 60 |
| Dunskaith Pl. G34 | K26 | 40 |
| Dunskaith St. G34 | K26 | 40 |
| Dunsmuir St. G51 | K13 | 34 |
| Dunster Gdns., Bish. | D19 | 11 |
| Dunswin Av., Dalm. | D 6 | 4 |
| Dunswin Ct., Dalm. | D 6 | 4 |
| *Dunswin Av.* | | |
| Dunsyre Pl. G23 | E15 | 9 |

| | | |
|---|---|---|
| Dunsyre Pl. G23 | F15 | 21 |
| *Broughton Rd.* | | |
| Dunsyre St. G33 | K21 | 38 |
| Duntarvie Cres. G34 | K26 | 40 |
| Duntarvie Pl. G34 | K25 | 40 |
| Duntarvie Quad. G34 | K26 | 40 |
| Duntarvie Rd. G34 | K25 | 40 |
| Dunterle Ct., Barr. | Q 8 | 59 |
| Dunterlie Av. G13 | G10 | 18 |
| Duntiglennan Rd., Clyde. | C 7 | 5 |
| Duntocher Rd., | D 6 | 4 |
| Dalm. & Clyde. | | |
| Duntocher Rd., Bear. | C10 | 6 |
| Duntocher Rd., Clyde. | C 7 | 5 |
| Duntocher St. G21 | H18 | 22 |
| *Northcroft Rd.* | | |
| Duntreath Av. G13 | F 9 | 18 |
| Duntroon St. G31 | K19 | 37 |
| Dunure Dr. G73 | P18 | 64 |
| Dunure St. G20 | F14 | 20 |
| Dunvegan Av., John. | N 2 | 44 |
| Dunvegan Ct. G13 | G10 | 18 |
| *Kintillo Dr.* | | |
| Dunvegan Dr., Bish. | D19 | 11 |
| Dunvegan Quad., Renf. | H 7 | 17 |
| *Kirklandneuk Rd.* | | |
| Dunvegan St. G51 | K13 | 34 |
| *Sharp St.* | | |
| Dunwan Av. G13 | F 9 | 18 |
| Dunwan Pl. G13 | F 9 | 18 |
| Durban Av., Dalm. | D 5 | 4 |
| Durness Av., Bear. | C13 | 8 |
| Durno Path G33 | K24 | 39 |
| Duror St. G32 | L22 | 38 |
| Durris Gdns. G32 | M23 | 55 |
| Durrockstock Rd., Pais. | O 3 | 45 |
| Durward Av. G41 | N14 | 50 |
| Durward Cres., Pais. | N 3 | 45 |
| Duthil St. G51 | L11 | 33 |
| Dyce La. G11 | J13 | 34 |
| Dyers La. G1 | L17 | 36 |
| *Turnbull St.* | | |
| Dyers Wynd, Pais. | L 6 | 30 |
| *Gilmour St.* | | |
| Dyke Pl. G13 | F10 | 18 |
| Dyke Rd. G13 | G 9 | 18 |
| Dyke St., Bail. | L26 | 40 |
| Dykebar Av. G13 | G10 | 18 |
| Dykebar Cres., Pais. | N 7 | 47 |
| Dykefoot Dr. G53 | O11 | 49 |
| Dykehead La. G33 | K23 | 39 |
| Dykehead Rd., Bail. | L27 | 41 |
| Dykehead St. G33 | K23 | 39 |
| Dykemuir Pl. G21 | H19 | 23 |
| Dykemuir Quadrant G21 | H19 | 23 |
| *Dykemuir St.* | | |
| Dykemuir St. G21 | H19 | 23 |
| | | |
| Eagle Cres., Bear. | C10 | 6 |
| Eagle St. G4 | J17 | 36 |
| Eaglesham Ct. G51 | L15 | 35 |
| *Blackburn St.* | | |
| Eaglesham Pl. G51 | L15 | 35 |
| Earl Haig Rd. G52 | K 9 | 32 |
| Earl Pl. G14 | H11 | 19 |
| Earl St. G14 | H10 | 18 |
| Earlbank Av. G14 | H11 | 19 |
| Earlbank La. N. G14 | H11 | 19 |
| *Vancouver Rd.* | | |
| Earlbank La. N. G14 | H11 | 19 |
| *Dunglass Av.* | | |
| Earlbank La. S. G14 | H11 | 19 |
| *Verona Av.* | | |
| Earls Ct., Chr. | E27 | 15 |
| *Longdale Rd.* | | |
| Earls Gate, Both. | R27 | 69 |
| Earls Hill G68 | B 1 | 70 |
| Earlsburn Rd., Lenz. | D24 | 13 |
| Earlspark Av. G43 | O15 | 51 |
| Earn Av., Bear. | D13 | 8 |
| Earn Av., Renf. | J 9 | 32 |
| *Almond Av.* | | |
| Earn St. G33 | J21 | 38 |
| Earnock St. G33 | H20 | 23 |
| Earnside St. G32 | L22 | 38 |
| Easdale Dr. G32 | M22 | 54 |
| East Av., Renf. | H 8 | 17 |
| East Av., Udd. | P29 | 69 |
| East Barns St., Clyde. | F 8 | 17 |
| East Bath La. G2 | K16 | 35 |
| *Sauchiehall St.* | | |
| East Buchanan St., Pais. | L 6 | 30 |

| Street | Grid | Page |
|---|---|---|
| East Campbell St. G1 | L18 | 36 |
| East Fulton Holdings, Linw. | K 1 | 28 |
| East Greenlees Av. G72 | Q23 | 67 |
| East Greenlees Cres. G72 | Q22 | 66 |
| East Greenlees Dr. G72 | Q22 | 66 |
| East Greenlees Rd. G72 | Q22 | 66 |
| East Hallhill Rd., Bail. | L25 | 40 |
| East Kilbride Expressway G72 | R22 | 66 |
| East Kilbride Rd. G73 | P20 | 65 |
| East La., Pais. | M 7 | 47 |
| East Reid St. G73 | O20 | 53 |
| East Springfield Ter., Bish. | F19 | 23 |
| East St., Kilb. | M07 | 42 |
| East Thomson St., Clyde. | D 7 | 5 |
| Eastburn Rd. G21 | G19 | 23 |
| Eastcote Av. G14 | H12 | 19 |
| Eastcroft G73 | O19 | 53 |
| Eastcroft Ter. G21 | H19 | 23 |
| Easter Av., Udd. | P27 | 69 |
| Easter Garngaber Rd. G66 | C24 | 13 |
| Easter Ms., Udd. | P27 | 69 |
| *Church St.* | | |
| Easter Queenslie Rd. G33 | K24 | 39 |
| Eastercraigs G31 | K19 | 37 |
| Easterhill Pl. G32 | M21 | 54 |
| Easterhill St. G32 | M21 | 54 |
| Easterhouse Path G34 | K26 | 40 |
| Easterhouse Pl. G34 | K26 | 40 |
| Easterhouse Quad. G34 | K26 | 40 |
| Easterhouse Rd. G34 | K26 | 40 |
| Eastfield Av. G72 | P21 | 66 |
| Eastfield Rd. G21 | H18 | 22 |
| Eastgate, Gart. | G28 | 27 |
| Eastmuir St. G32 | L22 | 38 |
| Eastvale Pl. G3 | K14 | 34 |
| Eastwood Av. G41 | O14 | 50 |
| Eastwood Av., Giff. | R14 | 62 |
| Eastwood Cres., Thorn. | Q12 | 61 |
| Eastwood Ct., Thorn. | Q12 | 61 |
| *Main St.* | | |
| Eastwood Rd., Chr. | E27 | 15 |
| Eastwood Vw. G72 | P24 | 67 |
| Eastwoodmains Rd., Giff. & Clark. | R14 | 62 |
| Easwald Bank, Kilb. | N07 | 42 |
| Eccles St. G22 | G18 | 22 |
| Eckford St. G32 | M22 | 54 |
| Eday St. G22 | G17 | 22 |
| Edderton Pl. G33 | K25 | 40 |
| Eddleston Pl. G72 | P24 | 67 |
| Eddlewood Path G33 | K24 | 39 |
| Eddlewood Rd. G33 | K24 | 39 |
| Edelweiss Ter. G11 | J13 | 34 |
| *Gardner St.* | | |
| Eden La. G33 | J20 | 37 |
| Eden Pl., Both. | R27 | 69 |
| Eden Pl. G72 | P23 | 67 |
| Eden Pl., Renf. | J 9 | 32 |
| Eden St. G33 | J20 | 37 |
| Edenwood St. G33 | L21 | 38 |
| Edgam Dr. G52 | L11 | 33 |
| Edgefauld Av. G21 | H18 | 22 |
| Edgefauld Dr. G21 | H18 | 22 |
| Edgefauld Pl. G21 | G18 | 22 |
| *Balgrayhill Rd.* | | |
| Edgefauld Rd. G21 | H18 | 22 |
| Edgehill La. G11 | H13 | 20 |
| *Marlborough Av.* | | |
| Edgehill Rd. G11 | H13 | 20 |
| Edgehill Rd., Bear. | C12 | 7 |
| Edgemont St. G41 | O15 | 51 |
| Edina St. G31 | K19 | 37 |
| Edinbeg Av. G42 | O18 | 52 |
| Edinbeg Pl. G42 | O18 | 52 |
| Edington Gdns., Chr. | D27 | 15 |
| Edington St. G4 | J16 | 35 |
| Edison St. G52 | K 9 | 32 |
| Edmiston Dr. G51 | L12 | 33 |
| Edmiston Dr., Linw. | L 1 | 28 |
| Edmiston St. G31 | M20 | 53 |
| Edmondstone Ct., Clyde. | F 8 | 17 |
| *Yokerburn Ter.* | | |
| Edrom Path G32 | L21 | 38 |
| *Edrom St.* | | |
| Edrom St. G32 | L21 | 38 |
| Edward Av., Renf. | H 9 | 18 |
| Edward St. G3 | K14 | 34 |
| *Lumsden St.* | | |
| Edward St., Bail. | L27 | 41 |
| Edward St., Clyde. | F 8 | 17 |
| Edwin St. G51 | L14 | 34 |
| Edzell Dr., John. | N 2 | 44 |
| Edzell Gdns., Bish. | F20 | 23 |
| Edzell St. G14 | J11 | 33 |
| Egidia Av., Giff. | R13 | 62 |
| Egilsay Cres. G22 | F17 | 22 |
| Egilsay Pl. G22 | F17 | 22 |
| Egilsay St. G22 | F17 | 22 |
| Egilsay Ter. G22 | F17 | 22 |
| Eglinton Ct. G5 | L16 | 35 |
| Eglinton Dr., Giff. | R14 | 62 |
| Eglinton La. G5 | M16 | 51 |
| *Eglinton St.* | | |
| Eglinton St. G5 | M16 | 51 |
| Egunton Ct. G5 | M16 | 51 |
| *Cumberland St.* | | |
| Eighth St., Udd. | N27 | 57 |
| Eildon Dr., Barr. | R 8 | 59 |
| Eileen Gdns., Bish. | E19 | 11 |
| Elba La. G31 | L20 | 37 |
| Elcho St. G40 | L18 | 36 |
| Elder Gro., Udd. | O28 | 57 |
| *Burnhead St.* | | |
| Elder Park Gdns. G51 | K12 | 33 |
| *Greenfield St.* | | |
| Elder Park Gro. G51 | K12 | 33 |
| *Greenfield St.* | | |
| Elder St. G51 | K12 | 33 |
| Elderpark St. G51 | K12 | 33 |
| Elderslie St. G3 | J15 | 35 |
| Eldon Gdns., Bish. | E18 | 10 |
| Eldon Pl., John. | N 1 | 44 |
| Eldon St. G3 | J15 | 35 |
| Eldon Ter. G11 | J13 | 34 |
| *Caird Dr.* | | |
| Elgin Dr., Linw. | L 1 | 28 |
| Elgin St. G40 | L19 | 37 |
| Elibank St. G33 | J22 | 38 |
| Elie St. G11 | J14 | 34 |
| Elizabeth Cres., Thorn. | Q13 | 62 |
| Elizabeth St. G51 | L14 | 34 |
| Elizabethan Way, Renf. | J 8 | 31 |
| *Cockels Loan* | | |
| Ellangowan Rd. G41 | O14 | 50 |
| Ellergreen Rd., Bear. | D12 | 7 |
| Ellerslie St., John. | M 1 | 44 |
| Ellesmere St. G22 | H16 | 21 |
| Ellinger Ct., Dalm. | D 6 | 4 |
| *Scott St.* | | |
| Elliot Av. G78 | O 3 | 45 |
| Elliot Av., Giff. | R14 | 62 |
| Elliot Dr., Giff. | Q14 | 62 |
| Elliot La. G3 | K15 | 35 |
| *Elliot St.* | | |
| Elliot Pl. G3 | J15 | 35 |
| Elliot St. G3 | K15 | 35 |
| Ellisland Av., Clyde. | D 8 | 5 |
| Ellisland Cres. G73 | P18 | 64 |
| Ellisland Rd. G43 | P14 | 62 |
| Ellisland Rd., Cumb. | C 3 | 71 |
| Ellismuir Farm Rd., Bail. | M26 | 56 |
| Ellismuir Pl., Bail. | M26 | 56 |
| Ellismuir Rd., Bail. | M26 | 56 |
| Elliston Av. G53 | P11 | 61 |
| Elliston Dr. G53 | P11 | 61 |
| Elliston Pl. G53 | P11 | 61 |
| *Ravenscraig Dr.* | | |
| Elm Av., Lenz. | C23 | 13 |
| Elm Av., Renf. | H 8 | 17 |
| Elm Bank, Bish. | E19 | 11 |
| Elm Dr., John. | O09 | 43 |
| Elm Gdns., Bear. | C12 | 7 |
| Elm Rd. G73 | Q19 | 65 |
| Elm Rd., Dalm. | C 7 | 5 |
| Elm Rd., Pais. | N 7 | 47 |
| Elm St. G14 | H11 | 19 |
| Elm Wk., Bear. | C12 | 7 |
| Elmbank Av., Udd. | O28 | 57 |
| Elmbank Cres. G2 | K16 | 35 |
| Elmbank La. G3 | K15 | 35 |
| *North St.* | | |
| Elmbank St. G2 | K16 | 35 |
| Elmbank Street La. G3 | K15 | 35 |
| *North St.* | | |
| Elmfoot St. G5 | N17 | 52 |
| Elmore Av. G44 | P16 | 63 |
| Elmore La. G44 | P16 | 63 |
| Elmslie Ct., Bail. | M25 | 56 |
| Elmvale Row E. G21 | H18 | 22 |
| *Elmvale Row* | | |
| Elmvale Row G21 | H18 | 22 |
| Elmvale Row W. G21 | H18 | 22 |
| *Elmvale Row* | | |
| Elmvale St. G21 | G18 | 22 |
| Elmwood Av. G11 | H12 | 19 |
| Elmwood Ct., Both. | R28 | 69 |
| *Blantyre Mill Rd.* | | |
| Elmwood Gdns. G11 | H12 | 19 |
| *Randolph Rd.* | | |
| Elmwood Gdns., Kirk. | C22 | 12 |
| Elmwood La. G11 | H11 | 19 |
| *Elmwood Av.* | | |
| Elmwood Ter. G11 | H12 | 19 |
| *Crow Rd.* | | |
| Elphin St. G23 | E14 | 8 |
| *Invershiel Rd.* | | |
| Elphinstone Pl. G51 | K14 | 34 |
| Elrig Rd. G44 | P16 | 63 |
| Elspeth Gdns., Bish. | E19 | 11 |
| Eltham St. G22 | H16 | 21 |
| Elvan Ct. G32 | L21 | 38 |
| *Edrom St.* | | |
| Elvan St. G32 | L21 | 38 |
| Embo Dr. G13 | G10 | 18 |
| Emerson Rd., Bish. | E19 | 11 |
| Emerson St. G20 | G16 | 21 |
| Emily Pl. G31 | L18 | 36 |
| Endfield Av. G12 | G13 | 20 |
| Endrick Bank, Bish. | D19 | 11 |
| Endrick Dr., Bear. | D12 | 7 |
| Endrick Dr., Pais. | L 7 | 31 |
| Endrick St. G21 | H17 | 22 |
| Endsleigh Gdns. G11 | H13 | 20 |
| *Partickhill Rd.* | | |
| Ennerdale St. G32 | L21 | 38 |
| Ensay St. G22 | F17 | 22 |
| Enterkin St. G32 | M21 | 54 |
| Ericht Rd. G43 | P14 | 62 |
| Eriska Av. G14 | G10 | 18 |
| Erradale St. G22 | F16 | 21 |
| Erriboll Pl. G22 | F16 | 21 |
| Erriboll St. G22 | F16 | 21 |
| Errogie St. G34 | K25 | 40 |
| Erskine Av. G41 | M13 | 50 |
| Erskine Sq. G52 | K 9 | 32 |
| Erskine Vw., Clyde. | D 7 | 5 |
| *Singer St.* | | |
| Erskinefauld Rd., Linw. | L 1 | 28 |
| Ervie St. G34 | K26 | 40 |
| Esk Av., Renf. | J 9 | 32 |
| Esk Dr., Pais. | N 3 | 45 |
| Esk St. G14 | G 9 | 18 |
| Esk Way, Pais. | N 3 | 45 |
| Eskbank St. G32 | L22 | 38 |
| Eskdale Dr. G73 | O20 | 53 |
| Eskdale Rd., Bear. | E11 | 7 |
| Eskdale St. G42 | N16 | 51 |
| Esmond St. G3 | J14 | 34 |
| Espedair St., Pais. | M 6 | 46 |
| Essenside Av. G15 | E11 | 7 |
| Essex Dr. G14 | H12 | 19 |
| Essex La. G14 | H11 | 19 |
| *Orleans Av.* | | |
| Essex La. G14 | H12 | 19 |
| Esslemont Av. G14 | G10 | 18 |
| Estate Quad. G32 | O23 | 55 |
| Estate Rd. G32 | O23 | 55 |
| Etive Av., Bear. | D13 | 8 |
| Etive Cres., Bish. | E19 | 11 |
| Etive Ct., Clyde. | C 8 | 5 |
| Etive Dr., Giff. | R14 | 62 |
| Etive St. G32 | L22 | 38 |
| Eton Gdns. G12 | J15 | 35 |
| *Oakfield Av.* | | |
| Eton La. G12 | J15 | 35 |
| *Great George St.* | | |
| Eton Pl. G12 | J15 | 35 |
| *Oakfield Av.* | | |
| Eton Ter. G12 | J15 | 35 |
| *Oakfield Av.* | | |
| Ettrick Av., Renf. | J 9 | 32 |
| Ettrick Cres. G73 | O20 | 53 |
| Ettrick Ct. G72 | Q24 | 67 |
| *Gateside Av.* | | |
| Ettrick Oval, Pais. | O 3 | 45 |
| Ettrick Pl. G43 | O14 | 50 |
| Ettrick Ter., John. | OO8 | 43 |
| Ettrick Way, Renf. | J 9 | 32 |
| Evan Cres., Giff. | R14 | 62 |
| Evan Dr., Giff. | R14 | 62 |

| | | |
|---|---|---|
| Evanton Dr. G46 | R12 | 61 |
| Evanton Pl. G46 | Q12 | 61 |
| *Evanton Dr.* | | |
| Everard Dr. G21 | F18 | 22 |
| Everard Pl. G21 | F18 | 22 |
| Everard Quad. G21 | F18 | 22 |
| Everglades, The, Chr. | F25 | 26 |
| Eversley St. G32 | M22 | 54 |
| Everton Rd. G53 | N11 | 49 |
| Ewart Pl. G3 | K14 | 34 |
| *Kelvinhaugh St.* | | |
| Ewing Pl. G31 | L20 | 37 |
| Ewing St. G73 | O19 | 53 |
| Ewing St., Kilb. | M07 | 42 |
| Exchange Pl. G1 | K17 | 36 |
| *Buchanan St.* | | |
| Exeter Dr. G11 | J13 | 34 |
| Exeter La. G11 | J13 | 34 |
| *Exeter Dr.* | | |
| Eynort St. G22 | F16 | 21 |
| | | |
| Fagan Ct., Blan. | R27 | 69 |
| Faifley Rd., Clyde. | C 7 | 5 |
| Fairbairn Cres., Thorn. | R13 | 62 |
| Fairbairn Path G40 | M19 | 53 |
| *Ruby St.* | | |
| Fairbairn St. G40 | M19 | 53 |
| *Dalmarnock Rd.* | | |
| Fairburn St. G32 | M21 | 54 |
| Fairfax Av. G44 | P17 | 64 |
| Fairfield Gdns. G51 | K12 | 33 |
| Fairfield Pl. G51 | K12 | 33 |
| Fairfield Pl. G71 | R28 | 69 |
| Fairfield St. G51 | K12 | 33 |
| Fairhaven Dr. G23 | F14 | 20 |
| Fairhill Av. G53 | O11 | 49 |
| Fairholm St. G32 | M21 | 54 |
| Fairley St. G51 | L13 | 34 |
| Fairlie Park Dr. G11 | J13 | 34 |
| Fairway Av., Pais. | O 5 | 46 |
| Fairways, Bear. | C10 | 6 |
| Fairyknowe Gdns. G71 | R28 | 69 |
| Falcon Cres., Pais. | L 4 | 29 |
| Falcon Rd., John. | O08 | 43 |
| Falcon Ter. G20 | F14 | 20 |
| Falfield St. G5 | M16 | 51 |
| Falkland Cres., Bish. | F20 | 23 |
| Falkland Mansions G12 | H13 | 20 |
| *Clarence Dr.* | | |
| Falkland St. G12 | H13 | 20 |
| Falloch Rd., Bear. | E11 | 7 |
| Fallside Rd., Both. | R28 | 69 |
| Falside Av., Pais. | N 6 | 46 |
| Falside Rd. G32 | M22 | 54 |
| Falside Rd., Pais. | N 5 | 46 |
| Fara St. G23 | F15 | 21 |
| Farie St. G73 | O19 | 53 |
| Farm Ct., Both. | Q28 | 69 |
| *Fallside Rd.* | | |
| Farm La., Udd. | P28 | 69 |
| *Myers Cres.* | | |
| Farm Pk., Lenz. | D23 | 13 |
| Farm Rd. G41 | M13 | 50 |
| Farm Rd., Blan. | R26 | 68 |
| Farm Rd., Clyde. | C 7 | 5 |
| Farm Rd., Dalm. | D 5 | 4 |
| Farme Cross G73 | N19 | 53 |
| Farmeloan Rd. G73 | O19 | 53 |
| Farmington Av. G32 | L23 | 39 |
| Farmington Gate G32 | L23 | 39 |
| Farmington Gdns. G32 | L23 | 39 |
| Farmington Gro. G32 | L23 | 39 |
| Farne Dr. G44 | Q16 | 63 |
| Farnell St. G4 | J16 | 35 |
| Farrier Ct., John. | M09 | 43 |
| Faskally Av., Bish. | D18 | 10 |
| Faskin Cres. G53 | O 9 | 48 |
| Faskin Pl. G53 | O 9 | 48 |
| Faskin Rd. G53 | O 9 | 48 |
| Fasque Pl. G15 | D 9 | 6 |
| Fastnet St. G33 | K22 | 38 |
| Faulbswood Cres., Pais. | N 4 | 45 |
| Fauldhouse St. G5 | M17 | 52 |
| Faulds Gdns., Bail. | L26 | 40 |
| Faulds, Bail. | L26 | 40 |
| Fauldshead Rd., Renf. | H 8 | 17 |
| Fauldspark Cres., Bail. | L26 | 40 |
| Fauldswood Cres., Pais. | N 4 | 45 |
| Fauldswood Dr,. Pais. | N 4 | 45 |
| Fearnmore Rd. G20 | F14 | 20 |
| Fendoch St. G32 | M22 | 54 |
| Fenella St. G32 | L22 | 38 |
| Fennsbank Av. G73 | Q20 | 65 |
| Fenwick Dr., Barr. | R 8 | 59 |
| Fenwick Pl., Giff. | R13 | 62 |
| Fenwick Rd., Giff. | R14 | 62 |
| Fereneze Av., Barr. | Q 7 | 59 |
| Fereneze Av., Pais. | K 7 | 31 |
| Ferenze Cres. G13 | F10 | 18 |
| Ferenze Dr., Pais. | O 5 | 46 |
| Fergus Ct. G20 | H15 | 21 |
| Fergus Dr. G20 | H15 | 21 |
| Ferguslie Park Av., Pais. | L 4 | 29 |
| Ferguslie Park Cres., Pais. | M 4 | 45 |
| Ferguslie Pk. | L 3 | 29 |
| Ferguslie Wk., Pais. | M 4 | 45 |
| Ferguslie, Pais. | M 4 | 45 |
| Ferguson Av., Renf. | H 8 | 17 |
| Ferguson St., John. | M09 | 43 |
| Ferguson St., Renf. | H 8 | 17 |
| Fergusson Rd., Cumb. | C 2 | 70 |
| Fern Av., Bish. | F19 | 23 |
| Fern Av., Lenz. | C23 | 13 |
| Fern Dr., Barr. | Q 7 | 59 |
| Fern Hill Grange G71 | R28 | 69 |
| Fernan St. G32 | L21 | 38 |
| Fernbank Av. G72 | Q23 | 67 |
| Fernbank St. G22 | G18 | 22 |
| Fernbrae Rd. G46 | Q20 | 65 |
| Fernbrae Way G73 | Q19 | 65 |
| Ferncroft Dr. G44 | P17 | 64 |
| Ferndale Ct. G23 | F14 | 20 |
| *Rothes Dr.* | | |
| Ferndale Dr. G23 | F14 | 20 |
| Ferndale Gdns. G23 | F14 | 20 |
| Ferndale Pl. G23 | F14 | 20 |
| *Rothes Drive* | | |
| Ferness Oval G21 | F20 | 23 |
| Ferness Pl. G21 | F20 | 23 |
| Ferness Rd. G21 | G20 | 23 |
| Ferngrove Av. G12 | G13 | 20 |
| Fernhill Rd. G73 | Q19 | 65 |
| Fernleigh Pl., Chr. | E27 | 15 |
| Fernleigh Rd. G43 | P14 | 62 |
| Fernslea Av. G72 | S26 | 68 |
| Ferry Rd. G3 | K13 | 34 |
| Ferry Rd., Both. | R28 | 69 |
| Ferry Rd., Renf. | H 8 | 17 |
| Ferry Rd., Udd. | P26 | 68 |
| Ferryden St. G14 | J12 | 33 |
| Fersit St. G43 | P14 | 62 |
| Fetlar Dr. G44 | P17 | 64 |
| Fettercairn Av. G15 | D 9 | 6 |
| Fettercairn Gdns., Bish. | E20 | 11 |
| Fettes St. G33 | K21 | 38 |
| Fidra St. G33 | K21 | 38 |
| Fielden Pl. G40 | L19 | 37 |
| Fielden St. G40 | L19 | 37 |
| Fieldhead Dr. G43 | P13 | 62 |
| Fieldhead Sq. G43 | P13 | 62 |
| Fife Av. G52 | M10 | 48 |
| Fife Cres., Both. | R28 | 69 |
| Fifeway, Bish. | F20 | 23 |
| Fifth Av. G12 | G12 | 19 |
| Fifth Av. G33 | G22 | 24 |
| Fifth Av., Lenz. | E23 | 13 |
| Fifth Av., Renf. | J 8 | 31 |
| Finart Dr., Pais. | N 7 | 47 |
| Finch Pl., John. | O08 | 43 |
| Findhorn Av., Renf. | H 9 | 18 |
| Findhorn Cres., Pais. | N 3 | 45 |
| Findhorn St. G33 | K20 | 37 |
| Findochty St. G33 | J23 | 39 |
| Fingal La. G20 | F14 | 20 |
| *Fingal St.* | | |
| Fingal St. G20 | F14 | 20 |
| Fingask St. G32 | M23 | 55 |
| Finglas Av., Pais. | N 7 | 47 |
| Fingleton Av., Barr. | R 8 | 59 |
| Finhaven St. G32 | M21 | 54 |
| Finlarig St. G34 | K26 | 40 |
| Finlas St. G22 | H17 | 22 |
| Finlay Dr. G31 | K19 | 37 |
| Finlay Dr., Linw. | L 1 | 28 |
| Finnart Sq. G40 | M18 | 52 |
| Finnart St. G40 | M18 | 52 |
| Finnieston Pl. G3 | K15 | 35 |
| *Finnieston St.* | | |
| Finnieston St. G3 | K15 | 35 |
| Finsbay St. G51 | L12 | 33 |
| Fintry Av., Pais. | O 6 | 46 |
| Fintry Cres., Barr. | R 8 | 59 |
| Fintry Cres., Bish. | E20 | 11 |
| Fintry Dr. G44 | O17 | 52 |
| Fir Pl. G72 | P23 | 67 |
| *Caledonian Circuit* | | |
| Fir Pl., Bail. | M25 | 56 |
| Fir Pl., John. | N 1 | 44 |
| Firbank Ter., Barr. | R 9 | 60 |
| Firdon Cres. G15 | E10 | 6 |
| Firhill Rd. G20 | H16 | 21 |
| Firhill St. G20 | H16 | 21 |
| Firpark Pl. G31 | K18 | 36 |
| *Firpark St.* | | |
| Firpark Rd., Bish. | F19 | 23 |
| Firpark St. G31 | K18 | 36 |
| Firpark Ter. G31 | K18 | 36 |
| *Ark La.* | | |
| First Av. G33 | H22 | 24 |
| First Av. G44 | R15 | 63 |
| First Av., Bear. | D13 | 8 |
| First Av., Lenz. | E23 | 13 |
| First Av., Renf. | J 8 | 31 |
| First Av., Udd. | O27 | 57 |
| First Gdns. G41 | M13 | 50 |
| First St., Udd. | O27 | 57 |
| First Ter., Clyde. | D 7 | 5 |
| Firwood Dr. G44 | P17 | 64 |
| Fishcoates Gdns. G73 | P20 | 65 |
| *Fishcoates Av.* | | |
| Fisher Cres., Clyde. | C 7 | 5 |
| Fisher Ct. G31 | K18 | 36 |
| Fishers Rd., Renf. | G 8 | 17 |
| Fishescoates Av. G73 | Q20 | 65 |
| Fitzalan Dr., Pais. | L 7 | 31 |
| Fitzalan Rd., Renf. | J 7 | 31 |
| Fitzroy La. G3 | K15 | 35 |
| *Claremont St.* | | |
| Fitzroy Pl. G3 | K15 | 35 |
| *Claremont St.* | | |
| Fitzroy Pl. G3 | K15 | 35 |
| *Sauchiehall St.* | | |
| Flax Rd., Udd. | P28 | 69 |
| Fleet Av., Renf. | J 9 | 32 |
| Fleet St. G32 | M22 | 54 |
| Fleming Av., Chr. | F26 | 26 |
| Fleming Av., Clyde. | F 8 | 17 |
| Fleming Rd., Cumb. | C 2 | 70 |
| Fleming St. G31 | L19 | 37 |
| Fleming St., Pais. | K 6 | 30 |
| Flemington Rd. G72 | R24 | 67 |
| Flemington St. G21 | H18 | 22 |
| Fleurs Av. G41 | M13 | 50 |
| Fleurs Rd. G41 | M13 | 50 |
| Floors St., John. | N09 | 43 |
| Floorsburn Cres., John. | N09 | 43 |
| Flora Gdns., Bish. | E20 | 11 |
| Florence Dr., Giff. | R14 | 62 |
| Florence Gdns. G73 | Q20 | 65 |
| Florence St. G5 | L17 | 36 |
| Florence St. G73 | M17 | 52 |
| Florentine Pl. G12 | J15 | 35 |
| *Gibson St.* | | |
| Florentine Ter. G12 | J15 | 35 |
| *Southpark Av.* | | |
| Florida Av. G42 | O16 | 51 |
| Florida Cres. G42 | O16 | 51 |
| Florida Dr. G42 | O16 | 51 |
| Florida Gdns., Bail. | L25 | 40 |
| Florida Sq. G42 | O16 | 51 |
| Florida St. G42 | O16 | 51 |
| Fochabers Dr. G52 | L11 | 33 |
| Fogo Pl. G20 | G14 | 20 |
| Forbes Dr. G40 | L18 | 36 |
| Forbes Pl., Pais. | M 6 | 46 |
| Forbes St. G40 | L18 | 36 |
| Ford Rd. G12 | H14 | 20 |
| Fordneuk St. G40 | L19 | 37 |
| Fordoun St. G34 | K26 | 40 |
| Fordyce St. G11 | J13 | 34 |
| Fore St. G14 | H11 | 19 |
| Forehouse Rd., Kilb. | MO6 | 42 |
| Forest Dr., Udd. | Q28 | 69 |
| Forest Gdns., Lenz. | D22 | 12 |
| Forest Pl., Lenz. | D22 | 12 |
| Forest Pl., Pais. | N 6 | 46 |
| *Brodie Park Av.* | | |
| Forest Rd., Cumb. | C 4 | 71 |
| Forest Vw., Cumb. | B 4 | 71 |
| Forfar Av. G52 | M10 | 48 |
| Forfar Cres., Bish. | F20 | 23 |
| Forgan Gdns., Bish. | F20 | 23 |
| Forge St. G21 | J19 | 37 |

Forglen St. G34 — J25 40  
Formby Dr. G23 — E14 8  
Forres Av. G46 — Q14 62  
Forres Gate, Giff. — R14 62  
*Forres Av.*  
Forres St. G23 — E15 9  
*Tolsta St.*  
Forrest St. G40 — L19 37  
Forrestfield St. G21 — J19 37  
Fortevoit Av., Bail. — L26 40  
Fortevoit Pl., Bail. — L26 40  
Forth Av., Renf. — J 8 31  
*Third Av.*  
Forth Ave., Pais. — N 3 45  
Forth Pl., John. — O08 43  
Forth Rd. G61 — C11 7  
Forth Rd., Bear. — E11 7  
Forth St. G41 — M15 51  
Fortingall Av. G12 — G14 20  
*Grandtully Dr.*  
Fortingall Pl. G12 — G14 20  
Fortrose St. G11 — J13 34  
Foswell Pl. G15 — C 9 6  
Fotheringay La. G41 — N15 51  
*Beaton Rd.*  
Fotheringay Rd. G41 — N14 50  
Foulis La. G13 — G12 19  
Foulis St. G13 — G12 19  
Foundry La., Barr. — R 7 59  
*Main St.*  
Foundry Open G31 — L19 37  
Fountain St. G31 — L18 36  
Fountainwell Av. G.21 — J17 36  
Fountainwell Dr. G21 — J17 36  
Fountainwell Pl. G21 — J17 36  
Fountainwell Rd. G21 — J17 36  
Fountainwell Sq. G21 — J18 36  
Fountainwell Ter. G21 — J18 36  
Fourth Av., G33 — G22 24  
Fourth Av., Lenz. — E23 13  
Fourth Av., Renf. — J 8 31  
*Third Av.*  
Fourth Gdns. G41 — M13 50  
Fourth St., Udd. — N27 57  
Fox La. G1 — L17 36  
Fox St. G1 — L16 35  
Foxbar Cres., Pais. — O 3 45  
Foxbar Dr. G13. — G10 18  
Foxbar Dr. G78 — O 3 45  
Foxbar Rd., Pais. — O 3 45  
Foxes Gro. G66 — C24 13  
Foxhills Pl. G23 — E15 9  
Foxley St. G.32 — N23 55  
Foyers Ct. G13 — G10 18  
*Kirkton Av.*  
Foyers Ter. G21 — H19 23  
Francis St. G5 — M16 51  
Frankfield Rd. G33 — G24 25  
Frankfield St. G33 — J20 37  
Frankfort St. G41 — N15 51  
Franklin St. G40 — M18 52  
Fraser Av. G73 — O20 53  
Fraser Av., John. — N 1 44  
Fraser St. G40 — L19 37  
Fraser St. G72 — P21 66  
Fraserbank St. G21 — H17 22  
*Keppochill Rd.*  
Frazer St. G31 — L20 37  
Frederick Path G1 — K17 36  
Freeland Dr., Renf. — G 5 16  
Freelands Cres., Old K — C 5 4  
Freelands Ct., Old K. — C 5 4  
Freelands Pl., Old K. — D 5 4  
Freelands Rd., Old K. — C 5 4  
French St. G40 — M18 52  
French St., Dalm. — D 6 4  
French St., Renf. — J 7 31  
Freuchie St. G34 — K25 40  
Friar Av., Bish. — D19 11  
Friars Court Rd., Chr. — E25 14  
Friars Pl. G13 — F11 19  
Friarscourt Av. G13 — E11 7  
Friarscourt La. G13 — F11 19  
*Arrowsmith Av.*  
Friarton Rd. G43 — P15 63  
Friendship Way, — J 8 31  
Renf.  
Fruin Pl. G22 — H17 22  
Fruin Rd. G15 — E 9 6  
Fruin St. G22 — H17 22  
Fulbar Av., Renf. — H 8 17  

Fulbar Ct., Renf. — H 8 17  
*Fulbar Av.*  
Fulbar La., Renf. — H 8 17  
Fulbar Rd. G51 — K11 33  
Fulbar Rd., Pais. — M 3 45  
Fulbar St., Renf. — H 8 17  
Fullarton Av. G32 — N22 54  
Fullarton Rd. G32 — O21 54  
Fullerton St., Pais — K 5 30  
Fullerton Ter., Pais. — K 6 30  
Fulmar Ct., Bish. — F18 22  
Fulmar Pl., John. — O08 43  
Fulton Cres., Kilb. — M07 42  
Fulton St. G13 — F11 19  
Fulwood Av. G13 — F 9 18  
Fulwood Av., Linw. — L 1 28  
Fulwood Pl. G13 — F 9 18  
Fynloch Pl., Clyde — B 6 4  
Fyvie Av. G43 — P13 62  
Gadie Av., Renf. — J 9 32  
Gadie St. G33 — K20 37  
Gadloch Av., Lenz. — E23 13  
Gadloch Gdns., Lenz. — D23 13  
Gadloch St. G22 — G17 22  
Gadloch Vw. G66 — E23 13  
Gadsburn Ct. G21 — G20 23  
*Wallacewell Quadrant*  
Gadshill St. G21 — J18 36  
Gailes Pk., Both. — R27 69  
*Eden Pk.*  
Gailes St. G40 — M19 53  
Gairbraid Av. G20 — G14 20  
Gairbraid Ct. G20 — G14 20  
Gairbraid Pl. G20 — G14 20  
Gairbraid Ter., Bail. — L28 41  
Gairn St. G11 — J13 34  
*Castlebank St.*  
Gala Av., Renf. — J 9 32  
Gala St. G33 — J21 38  
Galbraith Av. G51 — K12 33  
*Burghead Dr.*  
Galbraith Dr. G51 — K11 33  
Galbraith St. G51 — K11 33  
*Moss Rd.*  
Galdenoch St. G33 — J22 38  
Gallacher Av., John. — N 3 45  
Gallacher Av., Pais. — N 4 45  
Gallan Av. G23 — E15 9  
Galloway Dr. G73 — Q19 65  
Galloway St. G21 — G18 22  
Gallowflat St. G73 — O19 53  
Gallowgate G1 — L17 36  
Gallowhill Av., Lenz. — C23 13  
Gallowhill Gro., Lenz. — C23 13  
Gallowhill Rd., Lenz. — C23 13  
Gallowhill Rd., Pais. — L 6 30  
Galston St. G53 — P 9 60  
Gamrie Dr. G53 — O10 48  
Gamrie Gdns. G53 — O10 48  
Gamrie Rd. G53 — O10 48  
Gannochy Dr., Bish. — E20 11  
Gantock Cres. G33 — K22 38  
Gardenside Av. G32 — O22 54  
Gardenside Av., Udd. — P27 69  
Gardenside Cres. G32 — O22 54  
Gardenside Pl. G32 — O22 54  
Gardenside St., Udd. — P27 69  
Gardner La., Bail. — M26 56  
*Church St.*  
Gardner St. G11 — J13 34  
Gardyne St. G34 — J25 40  
Garfield St. G31 — L19 37  
Garforth Rd., Bail. — M24 55  
Gargrave Av., Bail. — M24 55  
Garion Dr. G13 — G10 18  
*Talbot Dr.*  
Garion Dr. G13 — G10 18  
Garlieston Rd. G33 — L24 39  
Garmouth Ct. G51 — K12 33  
*Elder St.*  
Garmouth Gdns. G51 — K12 33  
Garmouth St. G51 — K12 33  
Garnet La. G3 — J16 35  
*Garnet St.*  
Garnet St. G3 — J16 35  
Garnethill St. G3 — J16 35  
Garngaber Av., Lenz. — C23 13  
Garngaber Ct. G66 — C24 13  
*Woodleigh Rd.*  
Garnkirk La. G33 — G24 25  
Garnkirk St. G21 — J18 36  

Garnock St. G21 — J18 36  
Garrell Way, Cumb. — C 2 70  
Garrioch Cres. G20 — G14 20  
Garrioch Dr. G20 — G14 20  
Garrioch Gate G20 — G14 20  
Garrioch Quad. G20 — G14 20  
Garrioch Rd. G20 — H14 20  
Garriochmill Rd. G20 — H15 21  
*Raeberry St.*  
Garriochmill Way G20 — H15 21  
*Woodside Rd.*  
Garrowhill Dr., Bail. — M24 55  
Garry Av., Bear. — E13 8  
Garry Dr., Pais. — N 4 45  
Garry St. G44 — O16 51  
Garscadden G13 — F10 18  
Garscadden Rd. G15 — E10 6  
Garscadden Vw., Clyde. — D 8 5  
*Kirkoswald Dr.*  
Garscube Rd. G20 — H16 21  
Garscube Ter., Pais. — M 7 47  
Gartcarron Hill, Cumb. — B 1 70  
*Dunbrach Rd.*  
Gartconnel Dr., Bear. — C12 7  
Gartconnel Gdns., Bear. — C12 7  
Gartconnel Rd., Bear. — C12 7  
Gartcosh Rd., — K28 41  
Bail. & Gart.  
Gartcraig Rd. G33 — K21 38  
Gartferry Av., Chr. — E27 15  
Gartferry St. G21 — H19 23  
Garth St. G1 — K17 36  
Garthamlock Rd. G33 — J24 39  
Garthland Dr. G31 — K19 37  
Garthland La., Pais. — L 6 30  
Gartliston Ter., Bail. — L28 41  
Gartloch Cotts., Chr. — G25 26  
Gartloch Cotts., Gart. — H27 27  
Gartloch Rd. G33 — J21 38  
Gartly St. G44 — Q15 63  
*Clarkston Rd.*  
Gartmore Gdns., Udd. — O27 57  
Gartmore La., Chr. — E28 15  
Gartmore Rd., Pais. — M 8 47  
Gartmore Ter. G72 — Q21 66  
Gartness St. G31 — K19 37  
Gartocher Rd. G32 — L23 39  
Gartochmill Rd. G20 — H15 21  
Gartons Rd. G21 — H20 23  
Gartshore Rd., — C27 15  
Drumbreck  
Garturk St. G42 — N16 51  
Garvald Ct. G40 — M19 53  
*Baltic St.*  
Garvald St. G40 — M19 53  
Garve Av. G44 — Q16 63  
Garvel Cres. G33 — L24 39  
Garvel Rd. G33 — L24 39  
Garvock Dr. G43 — P13 62  
Gas St., John. — M 1 44  
Gask Pl. G13 — F 9 18  
Gatehouse St. G32 — L22 38  
Gateside Av. G72 — P23 67  
Gateside Cres., Barr. — R 7 59  
Gateside Pl., Kilb. — M07 42  
Gateside Rd., Barr. — R 7 59  
Gateside St. G31 — L19 37  
Gauldry Av. G52 — M11 49  
Gauze St., Pais. — L 6 30  
Gavins Rd., Clyde. — C 7 5  
Gavinton St. G44 — Q15 63  
Gear Ter. G40 — N19 53  
Geary St. G23 — E14 8  
*Torrin Rd,.*  
Geddes Rd. G21 — F20 23  
Gelston St. G32 — M22 54  
General Terminus Quay — L15 35  
G51  
Generals Gate, Udd. — P27 69  
*Cobbleriggs Way*  
Gentle Row, Clyde. — C 6 4  
George Av., Clyde. — D 8 5  
*Robert Burns Av.*  
George Cres., Clyde. — D 8 5  
George Gray St. G73 — O20 53  
George Mann Ter. G73 — P19 65  
George Pl., Pais. — M 6 46  
George Reith Av. G12 — G12 19  
George Sq. G2 — K17 36  
George St. G1 — K17 36  
George St., Bail. — M25 56

George St., Barr. Q 7 59
George St., John. M09 43
George St., Pais. M 5 46
Gertrude Pl., Barr. R 7 59
Gibb St. G21 J18 36
*Royston Rd.*
Gibson Cres., John. N09 43
Gibson Rd., Renf. J 7 31
Gibson St. G12 J15 35
Gibson St. G40 L18 36
Giffnock Park Av., Giff. Q14 62
Gifford Dr. G52 L10 32
Gilbert St. G3 K14 34
Gilbertfield Pl. G33 J22 38
Gilbertfield Rd. G72 Q23 67
Gilbertfield St. G33 J22 38
Gilfillan Way, Pais. O 3 45
*Ashton Way*
Gilhill St. G20 F14 20
Gilia St. G72 P21 66
Gillies La., Bail. M26 56
*Bredisholm Rd.*
Gills Ct. G31 L19 37
Gilmerton Rd., Linw. L 1 28
Gilmerton St. G32 M22 54
Gilmour Av., Clyde. C 7 5
Gilmour Cres. G73 O18 52
Gilmour Pl. G5 M17 52
Gilmour St., Clyde. D 8 5
Gilmour St., Pais. L 6 30
Girthon St. G32 M23 55
Girvan St. G33 J20 37
Gladney Av. G13 F 9 18
Gladsmuir Rd. G52 L10 32
Gladstone Av., Barr. R 7 59
Gladstone St. G4 J16 35
Gladstone St., Dalm. E 6 4
Glaive Rd. G13 E11 7
Glamis Av., John. N 1 44
Glamis Gdns., Bish. D19 11
Glamis Pl. G31 M20 53
*Glamis Rd.*
Glamis Rd. G31 M20 53
Glanderston Av., Barr. R 9 60
Glanderston Dr. G13 F10 18
Glaselune St. G34 K26 40
*Lochdochart Rd.*
Glasgow Bridge B21 12
Glasgow Av. G72 P21 66
Glasgow Rd. G72 & E.K. R21 66
Glasgow Rd. G73 N18 52
Glasgow Rd., Bail. M24 55
Glasgow Rd., Barr. Q 8 59
Glasgow Rd., Blan. R26 68
Glasgow Rd., Clyde. C 7 5
Glasgow Rd., Clyde. F 7 17
Glasgow Rd., Cumb. B 3 71
Glasgow Rd., Cumb. D 1 70
Glasgow Rd., Pais. L 7 31
Glasgow Rd., Renf. H 9 18
Glasgow Rd., Udd. O26 56
Glasgow St. G12 H15 21
Glassel Rd. G34 J26 40
Glasserton Pl. G43 P15 63
Glasserton Rd. G43 P15 63
Glassford St. G1 K17 36
Glebe Av. G71 R28 69
*Green St.*
Glebe Ct. G4 K17 36
Glebe Hollow G71 R28 69
*Glebe Wynd*
Glebe Pl. G72 P22 66
Glebe Pl. G73 O18 52
Glebe St. G4 J17 36
*Kennedy St.*
Glebe St. G4 J17 36
Glebe St., Renf. H 8 17
Glebe Wynd G71 R28 69
Glebe, The, Both. R28 69
Gleddoch Rd. G52 L 9 32
Glen Affric Av. G53 Q11 61
Glen Affric Dr. G53 Q11 61
Glen Affric Pl. G53 Q11 61
Glen Alby Pl. G53 Q11 61
Glen Av. G32 L22 38
Glen Av., Chr. E27 15
Glen Clunie Av. G53 Q11 61
Glen Clunie Dr. G53 Q11 61
Glen Clunie Pl. G53 Q11 61
Glen Cona Dr. G53 P11 61
Glen Cres. G13 F 9 18
Glen Esk Dr. G53 Q11 61

Glen Gdns., John. M 2 44
Glen La., Pais. L 6 30
Glen Livet Pl. G53 Q11 61
Glen Loy Pl. G53 Q11 61
Glen Mallie Dr. G53 Q11 61
Glen Markie Dr. G53 Q11 61
Glen Moriston Rd., Thorn. G53 Q11 61
Glen Nevis Pl. G73 R20 65
Glen Ogle St. G32 M23 55
Glen Orchy Dr. G53 Q11 61
Glen Orchy Pl. G53 Q11 61
Glen Park Av., Thorn. R12 61
Glen Rd. G32 K22 38
Glen Sax Dr., Renf. J 9 32
Glen Sq. G33 H22 24
Glen St. G72 Q23 67
Glen St., Barr. O 8 59
Glen St., Pais. L 6 30
Glen Vw., Cumb. B 4 71
Glenacre Cres., Udd. O27 57
Glenacre Dr. G45 Q17 64
Glenacre Quad. G45 Q17 64
Glenacre Rd., Cumb. D 2 70
Glenacre St. G45 Q17 64
Glenacre Ter. G45 Q17 64
Glenallan Way, Pais. O 3 45
Glenalmond Rd. G73 Q20 65
Glenalmond St. G32 M22 54
Glenapp Av., Pais. N 7 47
Glenapp Rd., Pais. N 7 47
Glenapp St. G41 M15 51
Glenarkley Dr., Pais. N 7 47
Glenartney Row, Chr. E26 14
Glenasdale Way, Pais. N 7 47
*Glenbrittle Dr.*
Glenavon Av. G73 Q20 65
Glenavon Rd. G20 F14 20
*Thornton St.*
Glenavon Ter. G11 J13 34
*Crow Rd.*
Glenbank Av., Lenz. D23 13
Glenbank Dr., Thorn. R12 61
Glenbank Rd., Lenz. D23 13
Glenbarr St. G21 J18 36
Glenbervie Pl. G23 E14 8
Glenbrittle Dr., Pais. N 7 47
Glenbrittle Way, Pais. N 6 46
Glenbuck Av. G33 G21 24
Glenbuck Dr. G33 G21 24
Glenburn Av. G73 P20 65
Glenburn Av., Bail. L26 40
Glenburn Av., Chr. E27 15
Glenburn Cres., Pais. O 5 46
Glenburn Gdns., Bish. E18 10
Glenburn Rd., Bear. C11 7
Glenburn Rd., Giff. R13 62
Glenburn Rd., Pais. O 4 45
Glenburn St. G20 F15 21
Glenburnie Pl. G34 K25 40
Glencairn Dr. G41 N14 50
Glencairn Dr. G73 O18 52
Glencairn Dr., Chr. E27 15
Glencairn Gdns. G41 N15 51
*Glencairn Dr.*
Glencairn Rd., Cumb. C 4 71
Glencairn Rd., Pais. K 7 31
Glencally Av., Pais. N 7 47
Glencart Gro., John. N08 43
*Milliken Park Rd.*
Glenclora Dr., Pais. N 7 47
Glencloy St. G20 F14 20
Glencoe Pl. G13 F12 19
Glencoe Rd. G73 Q20 65
Glencoe St. G13 F12 19
Glencorse Av., Pais. N 5 46
Glencorse Rd., Pais. N 5 46
Glencorse St. G32 K21 38
Glencroft Av., Udd. O27 57
Glencroft Rd. G44 P17 64
Glencryan Rd., Cumb. D 3 71
Glendale Cres., Bish. F20 23
Glendale Dr., Bish. F20 23
Glendale Pl. G31 L19 37
*Glendale St.*
Glendale Pl. G64 F20 23
Glendale St. G31 L19 37
Glendaruel Av., Bear. D13 8
Glendaruel Rd. G73 R21 66
Glendee Gdns., Renf. J 8 31
Glendee Rd., Renf. J 8 31
Glendenning Rd. G13 E12 7

Glendevon Pl., Dalm. D 6 4
Glendevon Sq. G33 J22 38
Glendore St. G14 J12 33
Glendower Way O 3 45
*Spencer Dr.*
Glenduffhill Rd., Bail. L24 39
Gleneagles Av., Cumb. A 3 71
*Muirfield Rd.*
Gleneagles Cotts. G14 H11 19
*Dumbarton Rd.*
Gleneagles Dr., Bish. D19 11
Gleneagles Gdns., Bish. D19 11
Gleneagles La. N. G14 H11 19
*Dunglass Av.*
Gleneagles Pk., Both. R27 69
*Eden Pk.*
Gleneagles Ter. G14 H11 19
*Dumbarton Rd.*
Glenelg Quad. G34 J26 40
Glenetive Pl. G73 R21 66
Glenfarg Cres., Bear. D13 8
Glenfarg Rd. G73 Q19 65
Glenfarg St. G20 J16 35
Glenfield Cres., Pais. P 5 58
Glenfield Rd., Pais. P 5 58
Glenfinnan Dr. G20 G14 20
Glenfinnan Dr., Bear. D14 8
Glenfinnan Pl. G20 G14 20
Glenfinnan Rd. G20 G14 20
Glenfruin Dr., Pais. N 7 47
Glengarry Dr. G52 L10 33
*Wedderlea Dr.*
Glengavel Cres. G33 G21 24
Glengyre St. G34 J26 40
Glenhead Cres. G22 G17 22
Glenhead Rd., Dalm. C 7 5
Glenhead Rd., Lenz. D23 13
Glenhead St. G22 G17 22
Glenholme, Pais. N 4 45
Glenhove Rd., Cumb. C 3 71
Gleniffer Av. G13 G10 18
Gleniffer Dr., Barr. P 7 59
Gleniffer Rd., Pais. O 4 45
Gleniffer Rd., Renf. J 7 31
Gleniffer Ter., John. N 2 44
Gleniffer Vw., Clyde. D 8 5
*Kirkoswald Dr.*
Glenisa Av., Chr. D28 15
Glenisla St. G31 M20 53
Glenkirk Dr. G15 E10 6
Glenlee Cres. G52 M 9 48
Glenlora Dr. G53 O10 48
Glenlora Ter. G53 O10 48
Glenluce Dr. G32 M23 55
Glenlui Av. G73 P19 65
Glenlyon Pl. G73 Q20 65
Glenmanor Av., Chr. E27 15
Glenmore Av. G42 O18 52
Glenmuir Dr. G53 P10 60
Glenpark Rd. G31 L19 37
Glenpark St. G31 L19 37
Glenpark Ter. G72 O21 54
Glenpatrick Bldgs., John. N 2 44
Glenpatrick Rd., John. N 2 44
Glenraith Rd. G33 H22 24
Glenraith Sq. G33 H22 24
Glenraith Wk. G33 H23 25
Glenshee St. G31 M20 53
Glenshiel Av., Pais. N 7 47
Glenside Av. G53 N10 48
Glenside Dr. G73 P20 65
Glenspean Pl. G43 P14 62
*Glenspean St.*
Glenspean St. G43 P14 62
Glentanar Pl. G22 F16 21
Glentarbert Rd. G73 Q20 65
Glenturret St. G32 M22 54
Glentyan Av., Kilb. M07 42
Glentyan Dr. G53 P10 60
Glentyan Ter. G53 O10 48
Glenview Cres., Chr. D28 15
Glenview Pl., Blan. R26 68
Glenville Av., Giff. Q13 62
Glenwood Ct., Kirk. C22 12
Glenwood Dr., Thorn. R12 61
Glenwood Gdns., Kirk. C22 12
Glenwood Pl., Kirk. C22 12
Glenwood Rd., Kirk. C22 12
Gloucester Av. G73 P20 65
Gloucester St. G5 L16 35
Gockston Rd., Pais. K 5 30

| | | |
|---|---|---|
| Gogar Pl. G33 | K21 | 38 |
| Gogar St. G33 | K21 | 38 |
| Goldberry Av. G14 | G10 | 18 |
| Goldie Rd., Udd. | Q28 | 69 |
| Golf Ct. G44 | R15 | 63 |
| Golf Dr. G15 | E 9 | 6 |
| Golf Dr., Pais. | M 8 | 47 |
| Golf Rd. G73 | Q19 | 65 |
| Golf Vw., Bear. | C10 | 6 |
| Golf Vw., Dalm. | D 6 | 4 |
| Golfhill Dr. G31 | K19 | 37 |
| Golfhill La. G31 | K19 | 37 |
| *Whitehill St.* | | |
| Golfhill Ter. G31 | K18 | 36 |
| *Firpark St.* | | |
| Golspie St. G51 | K13 | 34 |
| Goosedubbs G1 | L17 | 36 |
| *Stockwell St.* | | |
| Gopher Av., Udd. | O28 | 57 |
| *Myrtle Rd.* | | |
| Gorbals Cross G5 | L17 | 36 |
| Gorbals La. G5 | L16 | 35 |
| *Oxford St.* | | |
| Gorbals St. G5 | L16 | 35 |
| Gordon Av. G44 | R15 | 63 |
| Gordon Av., Bail. | L24 | 39 |
| Gordon Dr. G44 | Q15 | 63 |
| Gordon La. G1 | K16 | 35 |
| *Gordon St.* | | |
| Gordon Rd. G44 | R15 | 63 |
| Gordon St. G1 | K16 | 35 |
| Gordon St., Pais. | M 6 | 46 |
| Gordon Ter., Blan. | R26 | 68 |
| Gorebridge St. G32 | K21 | 38 |
| Gorget Av. G13 | E11 | 7 |
| Gorget Pl. G13 | E11 | 7 |
| Gorget Quad. G15 | E10 | 6 |
| *Gorget Av.* | | |
| Gorse Dr., Barr. | Q 7 | 59 |
| Gorse Pl., Udd. | O28 | 57 |
| *Myrtle Rd.* | | |
| Gorsewood, Bish. | E18 | 10 |
| Gorstan Pl. G20 | G14 | 20 |
| *Wyndford Rd.* | | |
| Gorstan St. G23 | F14 | 20 |
| Gosford La. G14 | G 9 | 18 |
| *Dumbarton Rd.* | | |
| Goudie St., Pais. | K 5 | 30 |
| Gough St. G33 | K20 | 37 |
| Gourlay Path G21 | H17 | 22 |
| *Endrick St.* | | |
| Gourlay St. G21 | H17 | 22 |
| Gourlay St. G21 | H18 | 22 |
| *Millarbank St.* | | |
| Gourock Sq., Barr. | R 9 | 60 |
| Gourock St. G5 | M16 | 51 |
| Govan Cross G51 | K13 | 34 |
| Govan Rd. G51 | K12 | 33 |
| Govanhill St. G42 | N16 | 51 |
| Gowanbank Gdns., | N09 | 43 |
| John. | | |
| *Floors St.* | | |
| Gowanbrae, Lenz. | C23 | 13 |
| *Gallowhill Rd.* | | |
| Gowanlea Av. G15 | E10 | 6 |
| Gowanlea Dr., Giff. | Q14 | 62 |
| Gowanlea Ter., Udd. | O28 | 57 |
| Gower La. G51 | L14 | 34 |
| *Gower St.* | | |
| Gower St. G43 | M14 | 50 |
| Gower Ter. G41 | L14 | 34 |
| Goyle Av. G15 | D11 | 7 |
| Grace Av., Bail. | L27 | 41 |
| Grace St. G3 | K15 | 35 |
| Graffham Av., Giff. | Q14 | 62 |
| Grafton Pl. G4 | K17 | 36 |
| Graham Av. G72 | P23 | 67 |
| Graham Av., Clyde. | D 7 | 5 |
| Graham Sq. G31 | L18 | 36 |
| Graham St., Barr. | Q 7 | 59 |
| Graham St., John. | N09 | 43 |
| Graham Ter., Bish. | F19 | 23 |
| Grahamston Cres., Pais. | O 8 | 47 |
| Grahamston Ct., Pais. | O 8 | 47 |
| Grahamston Pl., Pais. | O 8 | 47 |
| *Grahamston Rd.* | | |
| Grahamston Rd., Barr. | P 7 | 59 |
| Graighead Av. G33 | H20 | 23 |
| Grainger Rd., Bish. | E20 | 11 |
| Grampian Av., Pais. | O 5 | 46 |
| Grampian Cres. G32 | M22 | 54 |
| Grampian Pl. G32 | M22 | 54 |

| | | |
|---|---|---|
| Grampian St. G32 | M22 | 54 |
| Grampian Way, Barr. | R 8 | 59 |
| Gran St., Clyde. | F 9 | 18 |
| Granby La. G12 | H14 | 20 |
| *Great George St.* | | |
| Granby Pl. G12 | H14 | 20 |
| *Great George St.* | | |
| Grandtully Dr. G12 | G14 | 20 |
| Grange Gdns. G71 | R28 | 69 |
| *Blairston Av.* | | |
| Grange Rd. G42 | O16 | 51 |
| Grange Rd., Bear. | C12 | 7 |
| Grangeneuk Gdnd., | C 1 | 70 |
| Cumb. | | |
| Grant St. G3 | J15 | 35 |
| Grantlea Gro. G32 | M23 | 55 |
| Grantlea Ter. G32 | M23 | 55 |
| Grantley Gdns. G41 | O14 | 50 |
| Grantley St. G41 | O14 | 50 |
| Granton St. G5 | N18 | 52 |
| Granville St. G3 | K15 | 35 |
| Granville St., Clyde. | D 7 | 5 |
| Gray Dr., Bear. | D12 | 7 |
| Gray St. G3 | J14 | 34 |
| Great Dovehill G1 | L17 | 36 |
| Great George La. G12 | H14 | 20 |
| *Great George St.* | | |
| Great George St. G12 | H14 | 20 |
| Great Kelvin La. G12 | H15 | 21 |
| *Glasgow St.* | | |
| Great Western Rd. G12 | H14 | 20 |
| Great Western Ter. G12 | H14 | 20 |
| Great Western Terrace | H14 | 20 |
| La. G12 | | |
| *Westbourne Gdns. W.* | | |
| Green Av., Lenz. | B23 | 13 |
| Green Farm Rd., Linw. | L 1 | 28 |
| Green Lodge Ter. G40 | M18 | 52 |
| *Greenhead St.* | | |
| Green Pk., Both. | R28 | 69 |
| *Green St.* | | |
| Green Rd. G73 | O19 | 53 |
| Green Rd., Pais. | M 4 | 45 |
| Green St. G40 | L18 | 36 |
| Green St., Both. | R28 | 69 |
| Green St., Clyde. | D 7 | 5 |
| Green, The, G40 | L18 | 36 |
| Greenan Av. G42 | O18 | 52 |
| Greenbank Dr., Pais. | O 5 | 46 |
| Greenbank Rd., Cumb. | C 1 | 70 |
| *Burnhead Rd.* | | |
| Greenbank St. G43 | P13 | 62 |
| *Harriet St.* | | |
| Greenbank St. G73 | O19 | 53 |
| Greendyke St. G1 | L17 | 36 |
| Greenend Av., John. | N08 | 43 |
| Greenend Pl. G32 | K23 | 39 |
| Greenfaulds Cres., | D 3 | 71 |
| Cumb. | | |
| Greenfaulds Rd., Cumb. | D 2 | 70 |
| Greenfield Av. G32 | K22 | 38 |
| Greenfield Pl. G32 | L22 | 38 |
| *Budhill Av.* | | |
| Greenfield Rd. G32 | L23 | 39 |
| Greenfield St. G51 | K12 | 33 |
| Greengairs Av. G51 | K11 | 33 |
| Greenhaugh St. G51 | K13 | 34 |
| Greenhead Rd., Bear. | D12 | 7 |
| Greenhead Rd., Renf. | F 5 | 16 |
| Greenhead St. G40 | M18 | 52 |
| Greenhill Av., Gart. | F27 | 27 |
| Greenhill Av., Giff. | R13 | 62 |
| Greenhill Cres., John. | N 2 | 44 |
| Greenhill Cres., Linw. | L 2 | 28 |
| Greenhill Ct. G73 | O19 | 53 |
| Greenhill Rd. G73 | O19 | 53 |
| Greenhill Rd., Pais. | L 5 | 30 |
| Greenhill St. G73 | O19 | 53 |
| Greenhill, Bish. | E19 | 11 |
| Greenholm Av., Udd. | O27 | 57 |
| Greenholme St. G40 | P16 | 63 |
| *Holmlea Rd.* | | |
| Greenknowe Rd. G43 | P13 | 62 |
| Greenlaw Av., Pais. | L 7 | 31 |
| Greenlaw Dr., Pais. | L 7 | 31 |
| Greenlaw Rd. G14 | G 9 | 18 |
| Greenlaw Ter., Pais. | L 7 | 31 |
| *Greenlaw Av.* | | |
| Greenlea Rd., Chr. | F25 | 26 |
| Greenlea St. G13 | G12 | 19 |
| Greenlees Gdns. G72 | Q21 | 66 |
| Greenlees Pk. G72 | Q22 | 66 |

| | | |
|---|---|---|
| Greenlees Rd. G72 | P22 | 66 |
| Greenloan Av. G51 | K11 | 33 |
| Greenloan Av. G51 | K11 | 33 |
| *Kenneth Dr.* | | |
| Greenmount G22 | F16 | 21 |
| Greenock Av. G44 | P16 | 63 |
| Greenock Rd., Pais. | K 5 | 30 |
| Greenock Rd., Renf. | G 5 | 16 |
| Greenrig St. G33 | H20 | 23 |
| Greenrig St., Udd. | P27 | 69 |
| Greenrigg Rd., Cumb. | C 3 | 71 |
| Greenshields Rd., Bail. | L25 | 40 |
| Greenside Cres. G33 | H21 | 24 |
| Greenside St. G33 | H21 | 24 |
| Greentree Dr., Bail. | M24 | 55 |
| Greenview St. G43 | O14 | 50 |
| Greenways Av., Pais. | N 4 | 45 |
| Greenways Ct., John. | N 4 | 45 |
| Greenwell Pl. G51 | K13 | 34 |
| Greenwell St. G51 | K13 | 34 |
| *Govan Rd.* | | |
| Greenwood Av. G72 | P24 | 67 |
| Greenwood Av., Chr. | E27 | 15 |
| Greenwood Dr., Bear. | D13 | 8 |
| Greenwood Quad., | E 8 | 5 |
| Clyde. | | |
| Greer Quad., Clyde. | D 7 | 5 |
| Grenville Dr. G72 | Q21 | 66 |
| Greran Dr., Renf. | H 7 | 17 |
| Gretna St. G40 | M19 | 53 |
| Greyfriars St. G32 | K21 | 38 |
| Greystone Av. G73 | P20 | 65 |
| Greywood St. G13 | F12 | 19 |
| Grier Path G31 | L20 | 37 |
| Grierson St. G33 | K20 | 37 |
| Grieve Rd., Cumb. | B 3 | 71 |
| Griqua Ter. G71 | R28 | 69 |
| Grogary Rd. G15 | D10 | 6 |
| *Springside Pl.* | | |
| Grosvenor Cres. G12 | H14 | 20 |
| *Observatory Rd.* | | |
| Grosvenor Cres. La. G12 | H14 | 20 |
| *Byers Rd.* | | |
| Grosvenor La. G12 | H14 | 20 |
| *Byers Rd.* | | |
| Grosvenor Mansions | H14 | 20 |
| G12 | | |
| *Observatory Rd.* | | |
| Grosvenor Ter. G12 | H14 | 20 |
| Grove Pk., Lenz. | D23 | 13 |
| Grove, The, Giff. | S13 | 62 |
| Grove, The, Kilb. | M07 | 42 |
| Groveburn Av., Thorn. | Q13 | 62 |
| Grovepark Pl. G20 | H16 | 21 |
| Grovepark St. G20 | H16 | 21 |
| Groves, The, Bish. | F20 | 23 |
| *Woodhill Rd.* | | |
| Grudie St. G34 | K25 | 40 |
| Gryffe Av., Renf. | H 7 | 17 |
| Gryffe Cres., Pais. | N 3 | 45 |
| Gryffe St. G44 | P16 | 63 |
| Guildford St. G33 | J23 | 39 |
| Gullane St. G11 | J13 | 34 |
| *Purdon St.* | | |
| Guthrie St. G20 | G14 | 20 |
| | | |
| Hagg Cres., John. | M09 | 43 |
| Hagg Pl., John. | M09 | 43 |
| Hagg Rd., John. | N09 | 43 |
| Haggs Rd. G41 | N14 | 50 |
| Haggs Wood Av. G41 | N14 | 50 |
| Haghill Rd. G31 | K20 | 37 |
| Haig Dr., Bail. | M24 | 55 |
| Haig St. G21 | H19 | 23 |
| Hailes Av. G32 | L23 | 39 |
| Haining Rd., Renf. | H 8 | 17 |
| Hairmyres St. G42 | N16 | 51 |
| *Govanhill St.* | | |
| Hairst St., Renf. | H 8 | 17 |
| Halbeath Av. G15 | D 9 | 6 |
| Halbert St. G41 | N15 | 51 |
| Haldane La. G14 | H11 | 19 |
| *Haldane St.* | | |
| Haldane St. G14 | H11 | 19 |
| Halgreen Av. G15 | D 9 | 6 |
| Halifax Way, Renf. | J 8 | 31 |
| *Britannia Way* | | |
| Hall St., Clyde. | E 7 | 5 |
| Hallbrae St. G33 | J21 | 38 |
| Halley Dr. G13 | F 9 | 18 |
| Halley Pl. G13 | F 9 | 18 |
| Halley Sq. G31 | G 9 | 18 |

|  | | |
|---|---|---|
| Halley St. G13 | F 9 | 18 |
| Halley Ter. G13 | G 9 | 18 |
| Hallhill Cres. G33 | L24 | 39 |
| Hallhill Rd. G32 | L22 | 38 |
| Hallhill Rd., John. | O08 | 43 |
| Hallidale Cres., Renf. | J 9 | 32 |
| Hallrule Dr. G52 | L11 | 33 |
| Hallside Av. G72 | P24 | 67 |
| Hallside Cres. G72 | P24 | 67 |
| Hallside Dr. G72 | P24 | 67 |
| Hallside Rd. G72 | Q24 | 67 |
| Hallside St. G5 | M17 | 52 |
| Hallydown Dr. G13 | G11 | 19 |
| Halton Gdns., Bail. | M24 | 55 |
| Hamilton Av. G41 | M13 | 50 |
| Hamilton Cres. G72 | Q23 | 67 |
| Hamilton Cres., Bear. | B12 | 7 |
| Hamilton Cres., Renf. | G 8 | 17 |
| Hamilton Dr. G12 | H15 | 21 |
| Hamilton Dr. G72 | P22 | 66 |
| Hamilton Dr., Both. | R28 | 69 |
| Hamilton Dr., Giff. | R14 | 62 |
| Hamilton Park Av. G12 | H15 | 21 |
| Hamilton Rd. G32 | N24 | 55 |
| Hamilton Rd. G72 & Blan. | P22 | 66 |
| Hamilton Rd. G73 | O19 | 53 |
| Hamilton Rd., Both. | R28 | 69 |
| Hamilton St. G42 | N17 | 52 |
| Hamilton St., Clyde. | F 8 | 17 |
| Hamilton St., Pais. | L 6 | 30 |
| Hamilton Ter., Clyde. | F 8 | 17 |
| Hamilton Vw., Udd. | O28 | 57 |
| Hamiltonhill Rd. G22 | H16 | 21 |
| Hampden Dr. G42 | O16 | 51 |
| *Cathcart Rd.* | | |
| Hampden La. G42 | O16 | 51 |
| *Cathcart Rd.* | | |
| Hampden Ter. G42 | O16 | 51 |
| *Cathcart Rd.* | | |
| Hampden Way, Renf. | J 8 | 31 |
| *Lewis Av.* | | |
| Hangingshaw Pl. G42 | O17 | 52 |
| Haning, The, Renf. | J 8 | 31 |
| Hanover St. G1 | K17 | 36 |
| Hanson St. G31 | K18 | 36 |
| Hapland Av. G53 | N11 | 49 |
| Hapland Rd. G53 | N11 | 49 |
| Harbour La., Pais. | L 6 | 30 |
| Harbour Rd., Pais. | K 6 | 30 |
| Harburn Pl. G23 | E15 | 9 |
| Harcourt Dr. G31 | K19 | 37 |
| Hardgate Rd. G51 | K11 | 33 |
| Hardie Av. G73 | O20 | 53 |
| Hardridge Av. G52 | N11 | 49 |
| *Hardridge Rd.* | | |
| Hardridge Pl. G52 | N12 | 49 |
| Hardridge Rd. G52 | N11 | 49 |
| Harefield Dr. G14 | G10 | 18 |
| Harelaw Av. G44 | Q15 | 63 |
| Harelaw Av., Barr. | R 8 | 59 |
| Harelaw Av., Pais. | O 5 | 46 |
| Harhill St. G51 | K12 | 33 |
| Harland Cotts. G14 | J11 | 33 |
| *South St.* | | |
| Harland St. G14 | H11 | 19 |
| Harlaw Gdns. G64 | E20 | 11 |
| Harley St. G51 | L14 | 34 |
| Harmetray St. G22 | G17 | 22 |
| Harmony Pl. G51 | K13 | 34 |
| Harmony Row G51 | K13 | 34 |
| Harmony Sq. G51 | K13 | 34 |
| Harmsworth St. G11 | J12 | 33 |
| Harport St. G46 | Q12 | 61 |
| Harriet St. G43 | P13 | 62 |
| Harriet St. G73 | O19 | 53 |
| Harrington St. G20 | G15 | 21 |
| *Maryhill Rd.* | | |
| Harris Rd. G23 | E15 | 9 |
| Harrison Dr. G51 | L13 | 34 |
| Harrow Ct. G15 | D 9 | 6 |
| *Linkwood Dr.* | | |
| Harrow Pl. G15 | D 9 | 6 |
| Hart St. G31 | L21 | 38 |
| Hart St., Linw. | L 1 | 28 |
| Hartfield Ter., Pais. | N 7 | 47 |
| Hartlaw Cres. G52 | L10 | 32 |
| Hartree Av. G13 | F 9 | 18 |
| Hartstone Pl. G53 | O10 | 48 |
| Hartstone Rd. G53 | O10 | 48 |
| Hartstone Ter. G53 | O10 | 48 |
| Harvey St. G4 | J17 | 36 |
| Harvey St. G4 | J17 | 36 |
| Harvie St. G51 | L14 | 34 |
| Harwood St. G32 | K21 | 38 |
| Hastie St. G3 | J14 | 34 |
| *Old Dumbarton Rd.* | | |
| Hatfield Dr. G12 | G12 | 19 |
| Hathaway Dr., Giff. | R13 | 62 |
| Hathaway St. G20 | G15 | 21 |
| Hathersage Av., Bail. | L25 | 40 |
| Hathersage Dr., Bail. | L25 | 40 |
| Hathersage Gdns., Bail. | L25 | 40 |
| Hatters Row G40 | M18 | 52 |
| *Dalmarnock Rd.* | | |
| Hatton Dr. G52 | M10 | 48 |
| Hatton Gdns. G52 | M10 | 48 |
| Haugh Rd. G3 | K14 | 34 |
| Haughburn Pl. G53 | O10 | 48 |
| Haughburn Rd. G53 | O10 | 48 |
| Haughburn Ter. G53 | O11 | 49 |
| Havelock La. G11 | J14 | 34 |
| *Dowanhill St.* | | |
| Havelock St. G11 | J14 | 34 |
| Hawick Av. G78 | N 4 | 45 |
| Hawick St. G13 | F 9 | 18 |
| Hawkhead Av., Pais. | N 7 | 47 |
| Hawkhead Rd., Pais. | M 7 | 47 |
| Hawthorn Av., Bish. | F19 | 23 |
| Hawthorn Av., Lenz. | C23 | 13 |
| Hawthorn Dr., Barr. | S 8 | 59 |
| Hawthorn Quad. G22 | G17 | 22 |
| Hawthorn St. G22 | G17 | 22 |
| Hawthorn St., Clyde. | D 7 | 5 |
| Hawthorn Wk. G72 | P20 | 65 |
| Hawthorn Wk., Bish. | F20 | 23 |
| *Letham Dr.* | | |
| Hawthornden Gdns. G23 | E15 | 9 |
| *Broughton Rd.* | | |
| Hawthorne Av., Bear. | B13 | 8 |
| Hawthorne Av., John. | N 1 | 44 |
| Hawthorne Ter., Udd. | O28 | 57 |
| *Douglas St.* | | |
| Hay Dr., John. | M 1 | 44 |
| Hayburn Cres. G11 | H13 | 20 |
| Hayburn La. G11 | J13 | 34 |
| *Rosevale St.* | | |
| Hayburn La. G12 | H13 | 20 |
| *Queensborough Gdns.* | | |
| Hayburn St. G11 | J13 | 34 |
| Hayfield St. G5 | M17 | 52 |
| Hayhill Cotts., Gart. | G28 | 27 |
| Hayle Gdns., Chr. | D27 | 15 |
| Haylynn St. G14 | J12 | 33 |
| Haymarket St. G32 | K21 | 38 |
| Haystack Pl., Lenz. | D23 | 13 |
| Hayston Cres. G22 | G16 | 21 |
| Hayston St. G22 | G16 | 21 |
| Haywood St. G22 | G16 | 21 |
| Hazel Av. G44 | Q15 | 63 |
| *Clarkston Rd.* | | |
| Hazel Av., John. | N 1 | 44 |
| Hazel Av., Lenz. | C23 | 13 |
| Hazel Dene, Bish. | E19 | 11 |
| Hazel Gro., Lenz. | C23 | 13 |
| Hazel Rd., Cumb. | B 4 | 71 |
| Hazel Ter., Udd. | O28 | 57 |
| *Douglas St.* | | |
| Hazelden Gdns. G44 | Q15 | 63 |
| Hazellea Dr., Giff. | Q14 | 62 |
| Hazelwood Av. G78 | O 3 | 45 |
| Hazelwood Dr., Blan. | S26 | 68 |
| Hazelwood Gdns. G73 | Q20 | 65 |
| Hazelwood Rd. G41 | M14 | 50 |
| Hazlitt St. G20 | G16 | 21 |
| Heath Av., Bish. | F19 | 23 |
| Heath Av., Lenz. | D23 | 13 |
| Heathcliffe Av., Blan. | R26 | 68 |
| Heathcot Av. G15 | E 9 | 6 |
| Heathcot Pl. G15 | E 9 | 6 |
| *Heathcot Av.* | | |
| Heather Av., Barr. | P 7 | 59 |
| Heather Dr., Lenz. | D22 | 12 |
| Heather Gdns., Lenz. | D22 | 12 |
| Heather Pl., John. | N 1 | 44 |
| Heather Pl., Lenz. | C22 | 12 |
| Heather St. G41 | L15 | 35 |
| *Scotland St.* | | |
| Heatherbrae, Bish. | E18 | 10 |
| Heatheryknowe Rd., Bail. | K27 | 41 |
| Heathfield Av., Chr. | E27 | 15 |
| Heathfield St. G33 | K23 | 39 |
| Heathfield Ter. G21 | G18 | 22 |
| *Broomfield Rd.* | | |
| Heathside Rd., Giff. | Q14 | 62 |
| Heathwood Dr., Thorn. | Q13 | 62 |
| Hecla Av. G15 | D 9 | 6 |
| Hecla Pl. G15 | D 9 | 6 |
| Hector Rd. G41 | O14 | 50 |
| Heggie Ter. G14 | H11 | 19 |
| *Dumbarton Rd.* | | |
| Helen St. G52 | L12 | 33 |
| Helenburgh Dr. G13 | G11 | 19 |
| Helenslea G72 | Q23 | 67 |
| Helenvale Ct. G31 | L20 | 37 |
| *Helenvale St.* | | |
| Helenvale St. G31 | M20 | 53 |
| Helmsdale Av., Blan. | Q26 | 68 |
| Helmsdale Ct. G72 | P23 | 67 |
| Hemlock St. G13 | F12 | 19 |
| Henderland Rd., Bear. | E12 | 7 |
| Henderson Av. G72 | P23 | 67 |
| Henderson St. G20 | H15 | 21 |
| Henderson St., Clyde. | F 9 | 18 |
| Henderson St., Pais. | L 5 | 30 |
| Henrietta St. G14 | H11 | 19 |
| Henry St., Barr. | Q 7 | 59 |
| Hepburn Rd. G52 | K10 | 32 |
| Herald Av. G13 | E11 | 7 |
| Herald Way, Renf. | J 8 | 31 |
| *Viscount Av.* | | |
| Herbert St. G20 | H15 | 21 |
| Herbertson St. G5 | L16 | 35 |
| *Eglinton St.* | | |
| Hercules Way, Renf. | J 8 | 31 |
| *Friendship Way* | | |
| Herichell St. G13 | G12 | 19 |
| *Foulis La.* | | |
| Heriot Av., Pais. | O 3 | 45 |
| Heriot Cres., Bish. | D19 | 11 |
| Heriot Rd., Lenz. | D23 | 13 |
| Herma St. G23 | F15 | 21 |
| Hermiston Av. G32 | L23 | 39 |
| Hermiston Pl. G32 | L23 | 39 |
| Hermiston Rd. G32 | K22 | 38 |
| Hermitage Av. G13 | G11 | 19 |
| Heron Ct., Clyde. | C 7 | 5 |
| Heron Pl., John. | O08 | 43 |
| Heron St. G40 | M18 | 52 |
| Heron Way, Renf. | J 8 | 31 |
| *Britannia Way* | | |
| Herries Rd. G41 | N14 | 50 |
| Herriet St. G41 | M15 | 51 |
| Herschell St. G13 | G12 | 19 |
| *Foulis La.* | | |
| Hertford Av. G12 | G13 | 20 |
| Hexham Gdns. G41 | N14 | 50 |
| Heys St., Barr. | R 8 | 59 |
| Hickman St. G42 | N16 | 51 |
| Hickory St. G22 | G18 | 22 |
| High Barholm, Kilb. | M07 | 42 |
| High Calside, Pais. | M 5 | 46 |
| High Craighall Rd. G4 | J16 | 35 |
| High Parksail, Renf. | F 5 | 16 |
| High Rd., Pais. | M 5 | 46 |
| High St. G1 | L17 | 36 |
| High St. G73 | O19 | 53 |
| High St., John. | M09 | 43 |
| High St., Pais. | M 5 | 46 |
| High St., Renf. | H 8 | 17 |
| Highburgh Dr. G73 | P19 | 65 |
| Highburgh Rd. G12 | J14 | 34 |
| Highburgh Ter. G12 | J14 | 34 |
| *Highburgh Rd.* | | |
| Highcraig Av., John. | N08 | 43 |
| Highcroft Av. G44 | P17 | 64 |
| Highfield Av., Pais. | O 5 | 46 |
| Highfield Cres., Pais. | O 5 | 46 |
| Highfield Dr. G12 | G13 | 20 |
| Highfield Dr. G73 | Q20 | 65 |
| Highfield Pl. G12 | G13 | 20 |
| Highkirk Vw., John. | N09 | 43 |
| Highland La. G51 | K14 | 34 |
| Hilary Av. G73 | P20 | 65 |
| Hilary Dr., Bail. | L24 | 39 |
| Hilda Cres. G33 | H21 | 24 |
| Hill Path G52 | L10 | 32 |
| Hill Pl. G52 | L10 | 32 |
| Hill St. G3 | J16 | 35 |
| Hillcrest Av. G32 | O22 | 54 |
| Hillcrest Av. G44 | Q15 | 63 |
| Hillcrest Av., Clyde. | B 7 | 5 |
| Hillcrest Av., Cumb. | D 2 | 70 |
| *North Carbrain Rd.* | | |

| Name | Ref | Pg |
|---|---|---|
| Hillcrest Av., Pais. | P 5 | 58 |
| Hillcrest Ct., Cumb. | D 2 | 70 |
| *North Carbrain Rd.* | | |
| Hillcrest Rd. G32 | O23 | 55 |
| Hillcrest Rd., Bear. | D12 | 7 |
| Hillcrest Rd., Udd. | O28 | 57 |
| Hillcrest Ter., Both. | Q28 | 69 |
| *Churchill Cres.* | | |
| Hillcrest, Chr. | F26 | 26 |
| Hillcroft Ter., Bish. | F18 | 22 |
| Hillend Cres., Clyde. | B 6 | 4 |
| Hillend Rd. G22 | F16 | 21 |
| Hillend Rd. G73 | P19 | 65 |
| Hillfoot Av. G73 | O19 | 53 |
| Hillfoot Av., Bear. | C12 | 7 |
| Hillfoot Dr., Bear. | C12 | 7 |
| Hillfoot Gdns., Udd. | O27 | 57 |
| Hillfoot St. G31 | K19 | 37 |
| Hillfoot Ter., Bear. | C13 | 8 |
| *Milngavie Rd.* | | |
| Hillhead Av. G73 | Q19 | 65 |
| Hillhead Av., Chr. | E27 | 15 |
| Hillhead Gdns. G12 | J14 | 34 |
| *Hillhead St.* | | |
| Hillhead Pl. G12 | J15 | 35 |
| *Bank St.* | | |
| Hillhead St. G12 | J14 | 34 |
| Hillhouse St. G21 | H19 | 23 |
| Hillington Gdns. G52 | M11 | 49 |
| Hillington Ind. Est. G52 | K 9 | 32 |
| Hillington Pk. Cres. G52 | L11 | 33 |
| Hillington Quad. G52 | L10 | 32 |
| Hillington Rd. G52 | J 9 | 32 |
| Hillington Rd. S., Renf. | L10 | 32 |
| Hillington Ter. G52 | L10 | 32 |
| Hillkirk Pl. G21 | H18 | 22 |
| Hillkirk St. G21 | H18 | 22 |
| Hillkirk Street La. G21 | H18 | 22 |
| *Hillkirk St.* | | |
| Hillneuk Av., Bear. | C12 | 7 |
| Hillneuk Dr., Bear. | C13 | 8 |
| Hillpark Av., Pais. | N 5 | 46 |
| Hillpark Dr. G43 | P14 | 62 |
| Hillsborough Rd., Bail. | L24 | 39 |
| Hillsborough Sq. G12 | J14 | 34 |
| *Hillhead St.* | | |
| Hillsborough Ter. G12 | H15 | 21 |
| *Bower St.* | | |
| Hillside Av., Bear. | C12 | 7 |
| Hillside Ct., Thorn. | Q12 | 61 |
| Hillside Dr., Barr. | Q 7 | 59 |
| Hillside Dr., Bear. | C13 | 8 |
| Hillside Dr., Bish. | E19 | 11 |
| Hillside Gardens La. G11 | H13 | 20 |
| *North Gardner St.* | | |
| Hillside Gdns. G11 | H13 | 20 |
| *Turnberry Rd.* | | |
| Hillside Gro., Barr. | Q 7 | 59 |
| Hillside Quad. G43 | P13 | 62 |
| Hillside Rd. G43 | P13 | 62 |
| Hillside Rd., Barr. | Q 7 | 59 |
| Hillside Rd., Pais. | N 7 | 47 |
| Hillswick Cres. G22 | F16 | 21 |
| Hilltop Rd., Chr. | E27 | 15 |
| *Eastwood Rd.* | | |
| Hillview Cres., Udd. | O27 | 57 |
| Hillview Dr., Blan. | R26 | 68 |
| Hillview Rd., John. | N 2 | 44 |
| Hillview St. G32 | L21 | 38 |
| Hilton Gardens La. G13 | F12 | 19 |
| *Fulton St.* | | |
| Hilton Gdns. G13 | F12 | 19 |
| Hilton Pk., Bish. | D18 | 10 |
| Hilton Rd., Bish. | D18 | 10 |
| Hilton Ter. G13 | F12 | 19 |
| Hilton Ter. G72 | Q21 | 66 |
| Hilton Ter., Bish. | D18 | 10 |
| Hinshaw St. G20 | H16 | 21 |
| Hinshelwood Dr. G51 | L13 | 34 |
| Hinshelwood Pl. G51 | L13 | 34 |
| *Edmiston Dr.* | | |
| Hirsel Pl., Bush. | R28 | 69 |
| *Lomond Dr.* | | |
| Hobart Cres., Dalm. | C 5 | 4 |
| Hobart St. G22 | H16 | 21 |
| Hobden St. G21 | H19 | 23 |
| Hoddam Av. G45 | Q19 | 65 |
| *Ardencraig Rd.* | | |
| Hoddam Av. G45 | Q19 | 65 |
| Hoddam Ter. G45 | Q19 | 65 |
| Hoey St. G51 | K14 | 34 |

| Name | Ref | Pg |
|---|---|---|
| Hogan Ct., Clyde. | C 6 | 4 |
| *Dalgleish Av.* | | |
| Hogarth Av. G32 | K20 | 37 |
| Hogarth Cres. G32 | K20 | 37 |
| Hogarth Dr. G32 | K20 | 37 |
| Hogarth Gdns. G32 | K20 | 37 |
| Hogg Av., John. | N09 | 43 |
| Hogganfield St. G33 | J20 | 37 |
| Holburn Av., Pais. | L 4 | 29 |
| Hole Brae, Cumb. | B 3 | 71 |
| Holeburn Rd. G43 | P14 | 62 |
| Holehouse Dr. G13 | G10 | 18 |
| Holland St. G2 | K16 | 35 |
| Hollinwell Rd. G23 | F15 | 21 |
| Hollowglen Rd. G32 | L22 | 38 |
| Hollows Av., Pais. | O 3 | 45 |
| Hollows Cres., Pais. | O 3 | 45 |
| Holly Pl., John. | O 1 | 44 |
| Holly St., Clyde. | D 7 | 5 |
| Hollybank Pl. G72 | Q22 | 66 |
| Hollybank St. G21 | J19 | 37 |
| Hollybrook St. G42 | N16 | 51 |
| Hollybush Av., Pais. | O 4 | 45 |
| Hollybush Rd. G52 | L 9 | 32 |
| Hollymount, Bear. | E12 | 7 |
| Holm Av., Pais. | N 6 | 46 |
| Holm Av., Udd. | O27 | 57 |
| Holm Pl., Linw. | K 1 | 28 |
| Holm St. G2 | K16 | 35 |
| Holmbank Av. G41 | O14 | 50 |
| Holmbrae Av., Udd. | O27 | 57 |
| Holmbrae Rd., Udd. | O27 | 57 |
| Holmbyre Rd. G45 | R17 | 64 |
| Holmbyre Ter. G45 | R17 | 64 |
| Holmes Av., Renf. | J 8 | 31 |
| Holmfauldhead Dr. G51 | K12 | 33 |
| Holmhead Cres. G44 | P16 | 63 |
| Holmhead Pl. G44 | P16 | 63 |
| Holmhead Rd. G44 | P16 | 63 |
| Holmhill Av. G72 | Q22 | 66 |
| Holmhills Dr. G72 | Q21 | 66 |
| Holmhills Gdns. G72 | Q21 | 66 |
| Holmhills Gro. G72 | Q21 | 66 |
| Holmhills Pl. G72 | Q21 | 66 |
| Holmhills Rd. G72 | Q21 | 66 |
| Holmhills Ter. G72 | Q21 | 66 |
| Holmlea Rd. G44 | O16 | 51 |
| Holms Pl., Gart. | F27 | 27 |
| Holmswood Av., Blan. | R26 | 68 |
| Holmwood Av., Udd. | O27 | 57 |
| Holmwood Gdns., Udd. | P27 | 69 |
| Holyrood Cres. G20 | J15 | 35 |
| Holyrood Quad. G20 | J15 | 35 |
| Holywell St. G31 | L19 | 37 |
| Homeston Av., Udd. | Q28 | 69 |
| Honeybog Rd. G52 | L 9 | 32 |
| Hood St., Clyde. | E 8 | 5 |
| Hope St. G2 | K16 | 35 |
| Hopefield Av. G12 | G14 | 20 |
| Hopehill Pl. G20 | H16 | 21 |
| *Hopehill Rd* | | |
| Hopehill Rd. G20 | H16 | 21 |
| Hopeman Av. G46 | Q12 | 61 |
| Hopeman Dr. G46 | Q12 | 61 |
| Hopeman Rd. G46 | Q12 | 61 |
| Hopeman St. G46 | Q12 | 61 |
| Hopetown Pl. G23 | E15 | 9 |
| *Broughton Rd.* | | |
| Hornal Rd., Udd. | Q28 | 69 |
| Hornbeam Dr., Dalm. | D 7 | 5 |
| Hornbeam Rd., Udd. | O28 | 57 |
| *Myrtle Rd.* | | |
| Horndean Cres. G33 | J23 | 39 |
| Horndean Ct., Bish. | D19 | 11 |
| Horne St. G22 | G18 | 22 |
| *Hawthorn St.* | | |
| Hornshill Rd. G33 | F24 | 25 |
| Hornshill St. G21 | H19 | 23 |
| Horsburgh St. G33 | J23 | 39 |
| Horse Shoe La., Bear. | D12 | 7 |
| Horse Shoe Rd., Bear. | C12 | 7 |
| Horslethill Rd. G12 | H14 | 20 |
| Hospital St. G5 | M16 | 51 |
| Hotspur St. G20 | H15 | 21 |
| Houldsworth La. G3 | K15 | 35 |
| *Finnieston St.* | | |
| Houldsworth St. G3 | K15 | 35 |
| *Hope St.* | | |
| Househillmuir Cres. G53 | O11 | 49 |
| Househillmuir La. G53 | O11 | 49 |
| Househillmuir Pl. G53 | O11 | 49 |
| Househillmuir Rd. G53 | P10 | 60 |

| Name | Ref | Pg |
|---|---|---|
| Househillwood Cres. G53 | O10 | 48 |
| Househillwood Rd. G53 | P10 | 60 |
| Housel Av. G13 | F10 | 18 |
| Houston Pl. G5 | L15 | 35 |
| Houston Pl., John. | N 2 | 44 |
| Houston Rd., Loanhead | H 1 | 28 |
| Houston Sq., John. | M09 | 43 |
| Houston St. G5 | L15 | 35 |
| Houston St., Renf. | H 8 | 17 |
| Howard St. G1 | L16 | 35 |
| Howard St., Pais. | M 7 | 47 |
| Howat St. G51 | K13 | 34 |
| Howden Dr., Linw. | L 1 | 28 |
| Howe St., Pais. | M 3 | 45 |
| Howford Rd. G52 | M10 | 48 |
| Howgate Av. G15 | D 9 | 6 |
| Howieshill Av. G72 | P22 | 66 |
| Howieshill Rd. G72 | Q22 | 66 |
| Howth Dr. G13 | F12 | 19 |
| Howth Ter. G13 | F12 | 19 |
| Howwood St. G41 | L15 | 35 |
| Hoylake Pl. G23 | E15 | 9 |
| Hoylake Pk., Both. | R27 | 69 |
| *Eden Pk.* | | |
| Hozier Cres., Udd. | O27 | 57 |
| Hozier St. G40 | M18 | 52 |
| Hubbard Dr. G11 | J12 | 33 |
| Hughenden Dr. G12 | H13 | 20 |
| Hughenden La. G12 | H13 | 20 |
| *Hughenden Rd.* | | |
| Hughenden Rd. G12 | H13 | 20 |
| Hughenden Ter. G12 | H13 | 20 |
| *Hughenden Rd.* | | |
| Hugo St. G20 | G15 | 21 |
| Humber St. G31 | L20 | 37 |
| Hume Dr., Udd. | O27 | 57 |
| Hume Dr., Udd. | Q28 | 69 |
| Hume Rd., Cumb. | B 3 | 71 |
| Hume St., Clyde. | E 7 | 5 |
| Hunter Pl. G78 | NO7 | 42 |
| Hunter Rd. G73 | N20 | 53 |
| Hunter St. G4 | L18 | 36 |
| Hunter St., Pais. | L 6 | 30 |
| Hunterfield Dr. G72 | P21 | 66 |
| Hunterhill Av., Pais. | M 6 | 46 |
| *Hunterhill Rd.* | | |
| Hunterhill Rd., Pais. | M 6 | 46 |
| Huntersfield Rd., John. | N08 | 43 |
| Huntershill Rd., Bish. | F18 | 22 |
| Huntershill St. G21 | G18 | 22 |
| Huntershill Way, Bish. | F18 | 22 |
| *Crowhill Rd.* | | |
| Huntingdon Sq. G21 | J18 | 36 |
| *Huntingdon Rd.* | | |
| Huntington Rd. G21 | J18 | 36 |
| Huntingtower Rd., Bail. | M25 | 56 |
| Huntley Dr., Bear. | B12 | 7 |
| *Tweedsmuir Dr.* | | |
| Huntley Rd. G52 | K 9 | 32 |
| Huntly Av., Giff. | R14 | 62 |
| Huntly Dr. G72 | Q22 | 66 |
| Huntly Gdns. G12 | H14 | 20 |
| Huntly Path, Chr. | E28 | 15 |
| *Burnbrae Av.* | | |
| Huntly Rd. G12 | H14 | 20 |
| Huntly Ter., Pais. | N 7 | 47 |
| Hurlet Rd., Pais.& G53 | N 8 | 47 |
| Hurley Hawkin, Bish. | F20 | 23 |
| Hurlford Av. G13 | F 9 | 18 |
| Hutcheson Rd., Thorn. | R13 | 62 |
| Hutcheson St. G1 | K17 | 36 |
| Hutchinson Ct. G2 | K16 | 35 |
| *Hope St.* | | |
| Hutchison Pl. G72 | Q24 | 67 |
| Hutchison Ct., Giff. | Q13 | 62 |
| *Berryhill Rd.* | | |
| Hutchison Dr., Bear. | E13 | 8 |
| Hutton Dr. G51 | K12 | 33 |
| Huxley St. G20 | G15 | 21 |
| Hydepark Pl. G21 | G18 | 22 |
| *Springburn Rd.* | | |
| Hydepark St. G3 | K15 | 35 |
| Hyndal Av. G53 | N11 | 49 |
| Hyndford St. G51 | K13 | 34 |
| Hyndland Av. G11 | J13 | 34 |
| Hyndland Rd. G12 | H13 | 20 |
| Hyndland St. G11 | J14 | 34 |
| Hyndlee Dr. G52 | L11 | 33 |
| Hyslop Pl., Clyde. | D 7 | 5 |
| *Albert Rd.* | | |

| | | |
|---|---|---|
| Iain Dr., Bear. | C11 | 7 |
| Iain Rd., Bear. | C11 | 7 |
| Ibrox St. G51 | L14 | 34 |
| Ibrox Ter. G51 | L13 | 34 |
| Ibrox Terrace La. G51 | L13 | 34 |
| Ibroxholm La. G51 | L14 | 34 |
| *Paisley Rd. W.* | | |
| Ibroxholm Oval G51 | L13 | 34 |
| Ibroxholm Pl. G51 | L14 | 34 |
| Ilay Av., Bear. | F12 | 19 |
| Ilay Ct., Bear. | F13 | 20 |
| Ilay Rd., Bear. | F13 | 20 |
| Inchbrae Rd. G52 | M11 | 49 |
| Inchfad Dr. G15 | D9 | 6 |
| Inchholm St. G11 | J12 | 33 |
| Inchinnan Rd., Pais. | K6 | 30 |
| Inchinnan Rd., Renf. | H7 | 17 |
| Inchkeith Pl. G32 | K22 | 38 |
| Inchlee St. G14 | J12 | 33 |
| Inchoch St. G33 | J24 | 39 |
| Inchrory Pl. G15 | D9 | 6 |
| Incle St., Pais. | L6 | 30 |
| India Dr., Renf. | G5 | 16 |
| India St. G2 | K16 | 35 |
| India St. G73 | O19 | 53 |
| Inga St. G20 | F15 | 21 |
| Ingerbreck Av. G73 | Q20 | 65 |
| Ingleby Dr. G31 | K19 | 37 |
| Inglefield St. G42 | N16 | 51 |
| Ingleneuk Av. G33 | G22 | 24 |
| Inglestone Av., Thorn. | R13 | 62 |
| Inglis St. G31 | L19 | 37 |
| Ingram St. G1 | K17 | 36 |
| Inishail Rd. G33 | J23 | 39 |
| Inkerman St. G52 | L9 | 32 |
| Innerwick Dr. G52 | L10 | 32 |
| Inver Rd. G33 | K24 | 39 |
| Inverary Dr., Bish. | D19 | 11 |
| Invercanny Dr. G15 | D9 | 6 |
| Invercanny Pl. G15 | D10 | 6 |
| Inverclyde Gdns. G11 | H12 | 19 |
| *Broomhill Dr.* | | |
| Inverclyde Gdns. G73 | Q21 | 66 |
| Inveresk Cres. G32 | L22 | 38 |
| Inveresk St. G32 | L22 | 38 |
| Inverewe Av. G46 | Q11 | 61 |
| Inverewe Dr. G46 | R11 | 61 |
| Inverewe Gdns. G46 | R11 | 61 |
| Inverewe Pl. G46 | Q11 | 61 |
| Invergarry Av. G46 | R11 | 61 |
| Invergarry Ct. G46 | R11 | 61 |
| Invergarry Dr. G46 | R11 | 61 |
| Invergarry Gdns. G46 | R11 | 61 |
| Invergarry Gro. G46 | R11 | 61 |
| Invergarry Pl. G46 | R11 | 61 |
| Invergarry Quad. G46 | R12 | 61 |
| Invergarry Vw. G46 | R12 | 61 |
| Inverglas Av., Renf. | J9 | 32 |
| *Morriston Cres.* | | |
| Invergordon Av. G43 | O15 | 51 |
| Invergyle Dr. G52 | L10 | 32 |
| Inverkar Dr., Pais. | N4 | 45 |
| *Brediland Rd.* | | |
| Inverkip St. G5 | L17 | 36 |
| Inverlair Av. G43 | P15 | 63 |
| Inverleith St. G32 | L20 | 37 |
| Inverlochy St. G33 | J23 | 39 |
| Invernairn St. G31 | L20 | 37 |
| Inverness St. G51 | L11 | 33 |
| Inveroran Dr., Bear. | D13 | 8 |
| Invershiel Rd. G23 | E14 | 8 |
| Invershin Dr. G20 | G14 | 20 |
| *Wyndford Rd.* | | |
| Inverurie St. G21 | H17 | 22 |
| Inzievar Ter. G32 | N22 | 54 |
| Iona Ct. G51 | K13 | 34 |
| Iona Dr., Pais. | O5 | 46 |
| Iona La., Chr. | E28 | 15 |
| *Heathfield Av.* | | |
| Iona Rd. G73 | Q21 | 66 |
| Iona Rd., Renf. | J8 | 31 |
| Iona St. G51 | K13 | 34 |
| Irongray St. G31 | K20 | 37 |
| Irvine Dr., Linw. | L1 | 28 |
| Irvine St. G40 | M19 | 53 |
| Irving Av., Clyde. | C7 | 5 |
| *Stewart Dr.* | | |
| Irving Quad., Clyde. | C7 | 5 |
| *Stewart Dr.* | | |
| Iser La. G41 | O15 | 51 |
| Island Rd., Cumb. | D1 | 70 |
| Islay Av. G73 | Q21 | 66 |
| Islay Cres., Pais. | O5 | 46 |
| Ivanhoe Rd. G13 | F11 | 19 |
| Ivanhoe Rd., Cumb. | D2 | 70 |
| Ivanhoe Rd., Pais. | N3 | 45 |
| Ivanhoe Way, Pais. | N3 | 45 |
| *Ivanhoe Rd.* | | |
| Ivybank Ave. G72 | Q23 | 67 |
| Jacks Rd., Udd. | P28 | 69 |
| Jagger Gdns., Bail. | M24 | 55 |
| Jamaica St. G1 | L16 | 35 |
| James Dunlop Gdns., Bish. | F19 | 23 |
| *Graham Ter.* | | |
| James Gray St. G41 | O15 | 51 |
| James Morrison St. G1 | L17 | 36 |
| *St. Andrews Sq.* | | |
| James Nisbet St. G21 | K18 | 36 |
| James St. G40 | M18 | 52 |
| James St. G42 | N16 | 51 |
| James Watt La. G2 | K16 | 35 |
| *James Watt St.* | | |
| James Watt St. G2 | K16 | 35 |
| Jamieson Ct., Clyde. | B7 | 5 |
| Jamieson St. G42 | N16 | 51 |
| Janebank Av. G72 | Q23 | 67 |
| Janefield Av., John. | N9 | 43 |
| Janefield St. G31 | L19 | 37 |
| Janes Brae, Cumb. | D2 | 70 |
| Janetta St., Clyde. | D7 | 5 |
| Jardine St. G20 | H15 | 21 |
| Jardine Ter., Gart. | G27 | 27 |
| Jasgray St. G42 | N15 | 51 |
| Jean Armour Dr., Clyde. | D8 | 5 |
| Jedburgh Av. G73 | O19 | 53 |
| Jedburgh Dr., Pais. | N4 | 45 |
| Jedburgh Gdns. G20 | H15 | 21 |
| Jedworth Av. G15 | D10 | 6 |
| Jellicoe St. Dalm. | D6 | 4 |
| Jennys Well Rd., Pais. | N7 | 47 |
| Jerviston Rd. G33 | J23 | 39 |
| Jessie St. G42 | N17 | 52 |
| Jessiman Sq., Renf. | J7 | 31 |
| John Brown Pl., Chr. | F26 | 26 |
| John Knox La. G4 | K18 | 36 |
| *Drygate* | | |
| John Knox St. G4 | K18 | 36 |
| John Knox St., Clyde. | F8 | 17 |
| John Lang St., John. | M1 | 44 |
| John St. G1 | K17 | 36 |
| John St., Barr. | Q7 | 59 |
| John St., Pais. | M5 | 46 |
| Johnshaven St. G43 | O14 | 50 |
| *Bengal St.* | | |
| Johnston Av., Clyde. | F8 | 17 |
| Johnston Rd., Gart. | G28 | 27 |
| Johnston St., Pais. | M6 | 46 |
| *Gordon St.* | | |
| Johnston St., Pais. | M6 | 46 |
| Johnstone Av. G52 | L10 | 32 |
| Johnstone Cotts., | B21 | 12 |
| Johnstone Dr. G72 | P22 | 66 |
| Johnstone Dr. G73 | O19 | 53 |
| Joppa St. G33 | K21 | 38 |
| Jordan St. G14 | J11 | 33 |
| Jordan Vale Av. G14 | J11 | 33 |
| Jordanhill Cres. G13 | G11 | 19 |
| *Jordanhill Dr.* | | |
| Jordanhill Dr. G13 | G11 | 19 |
| Jordanhill La. G13 | G12 | 19 |
| *Austen Rd.* | | |
| Jowitt Av., Clyde. | E8 | 5 |
| Joycelyn Sq. G1 | L17 | 36 |
| Jubilee Bank, Lenz. | D23 | 13 |
| *Heriot Rd.* | | |
| Jubilee Path, Bear. | D12 | 7 |
| Jubilee Ter. G78 | N08 | 43 |
| *Kilbarchan Rd.* | | |
| Jubilee Ter., John. | O08 | 43 |
| Julian Av. G12 | H14 | 20 |
| Julian La. G12 | H14 | 20 |
| *Julian Av.* | | |
| Juniper Ct., Lenz. | C22 | 12 |
| Juniper Pl. G32 | M24 | 55 |
| Juniper Pl., John. | O1 | 44 |
| Juniper Ter. G32 | M24 | 55 |
| Jura Av., Renf. | J8 | 31 |
| Jura Ct. G52 | L12 | 33 |
| Jura Dr., Blan. | Q26 | 68 |
| Jura Rd., Pais. | O5 | 46 |
| Jura St. G52 | L12 | 33 |
| Kaim Dr. G53 | P11 | 61 |
| Kames St. G5 | M16 | 51 |
| Karol Path G4 | J16 | 35 |
| *St. Peters St.* | | |
| Katewell Av. G15 | D9 | 6 |
| Katrine Av., Bish. | E19 | 11 |
| Katrine Dr., Pais. | N3 | 45 |
| Kay St. G21 | H18 | 22 |
| Kaystone Rd. G15 | E10 | 6 |
| Keal Av. G15 | F10 | 18 |
| Keal Cres. G15 | F10 | 18 |
| Keal Dr. G15 | F10 | 18 |
| Keal Pl. G15 | F10 | 18 |
| Kearn Av. G15 | E10 | 6 |
| Kearn Pl. G15 | E10 | 6 |
| Keats Pk., Udd. | Q28 | 69 |
| Keir Dr., Bish. | E18 | 10 |
| Keir St. G41 | M15 | 51 |
| Keirhill Rd, Cumb. | C1 | 70 |
| *Woodburn Rd.* | | |
| Keirs Wk. G72 | P22 | 66 |
| Keith Av., Giff. | Q14 | 62 |
| Keith Ct. G11 | J14 | 34 |
| *Keith St.* | | |
| Keith St. G11 | J14 | 34 |
| Kelbourne St. G20 | H15 | 21 |
| Kelburn St., Barr. | R7 | 59 |
| Kelburne Dr., Pais. | L7 | 31 |
| Kelburne Gdns., Bail. | M25 | 56 |
| Kelburne Gdns., Pais. | L7 | 31 |
| Kelburne Oval, Pais. | L7 | 31 |
| Kelhead Av. G52 | L9 | 32 |
| Kelhead Dr. G52 | L9 | 32 |
| Kelhead Path G52 | L10 | 32 |
| Kelhead Pl. G52 | L9 | 32 |
| Kellas St. G51 | L13 | 34 |
| Kells Pl. G15 | D9 | 6 |
| Kelso Av. G73 | O19 | 53 |
| Kelso Av., Pais. | N4 | 45 |
| Kelso St. G13 | G9 | 18 |
| Kelton St. G32 | M22 | 54 |
| Kelty Pl. G5 | L16 | 35 |
| *Bedford St.* | | |
| Kelty St. G5 | M16 | 51 |
| *Eglinton St.* | | |
| Kelvin Av. G52 | J9 | 32 |
| Kelvin Cres., Bear. | E12 | 7 |
| Kelvin Ct. G12 | G12 | 19 |
| Kelvin Dr. G20 | H14 | 20 |
| Kelvin Dr., Barr. | R8 | 59 |
| Kelvin Dr., Bish. | E19 | 11 |
| Kelvin Dr., Chr. | E27 | 15 |
| Kelvin Rd., Cumb. | D3 | 71 |
| Kelvin Rd., Udd. | O27 | 57 |
| Kelvin Way G3 | J14 | 34 |
| Kelvin Way, Udd. | Q28 | 69 |
| *Bracken Ter.* | | |
| Kelvindale Bldgs. G12 | G14 | 20 |
| *Kelvindale Rd.* | | |
| Kelvindale Cotts. G12 | G14 | 20 |
| *Kelvindale Rd.* | | |
| Kelvindale Glen G12 | G14 | 20 |
| *Kelvindale Rd.* | | |
| Kelvindale Pl. G20 | G14 | 20 |
| Kelvindale Rd. G12 | G14 | 20 |
| Kelvingrove St. G3 | K15 | 35 |
| Kelvingrove Ter. G3 | K15 | 35 |
| *Kelvingrove St.* | | |
| Kelvinhaugh Pl. G3 | K14 | 34 |
| *Kelvinhaugh St.* | | |
| Kelvinhaugh St. G3 | K14 | 34 |
| Kelvinside Av. G20 | H15 | 21 |
| *Queen Margaret Dr.* | | |
| Kelvinside Dr. G20 | H15 | 21 |
| Kelvinside Gdns. E. G20 | H15 | 21 |
| Kelvinside Gdns. G20 | H15 | 21 |
| Kelvinside Ter. S. G20 | H15 | 21 |
| Kelvinside Ter. W. G20 | H15 | 21 |
| Kemp Av., Renf. | J7 | 31 |
| Kemp St. G21 | H18 | 22 |
| Kempock St. G31 | M20 | 53 |
| Kempsthorn Cres. G53 | N10 | 48 |
| Kempsthorn Path G53 | N10 | 48 |
| Kempsthorn Rd. G53 | N10 | 48 |
| Kendal Av., Giff. | Q14 | 62 |
| Kendal Dr. G12 | G13 | 20 |
| Kendal Ter. G12 | G13 | 20 |
| Kendoon Av. G15 | D9 | 6 |
| Kenilworth Av. G41 | O14 | 50 |
| Kenilworth Cres., Bear. | C11 | 7 |
| Kenilworth, Pais. | O3 | 45 |
| Kenmar Gdns., Udd. | O26 | 56 |

| | | |
|---|---|---|
| Kenmore Gdns., Bear. | C13 | 8 |
| Kenmore Rd., Cumb. | C 3 | 71 |
| Kenmore St. G32 | L22 | 38 |
| Kenmuir Av. G32 | M24 | 55 |
| Kenmuir Rd. G32 | O23 | 55 |
| Kenmuirhill Rd. G32 | N23 | 55 |
| Kenmure Av., Bish. | E18 | 10 |
| Kenmure Cres., Bish. | E18 | 10 |
| Kenmure Dr., Bish. | E18 | 10 |
| Kenmure Gdns., Bish. | E18 | 10 |
| Kenmure Row G22 | E16 | 9 |
| Kenmure St. G41 | M15 | 51 |
| Kenmure Way G73 | Q19 | 65 |
| Kennedar Dr. G51 | K12 | 33 |
| Kennedy Ct., Giff. | Q14 | 62 |
| *Braidholm Cres.* | | |
| Kennedy St. G4 | K17 | 36 |
| Kennet St. G21 | J19 | 37 |
| Kennishead Av. G46 | P12 | 61 |
| Kennishead Pl. G46 | P12 | 61 |
| Kennishead Rd. G46 | Q12 | 61 |
| Kennishead Rd. G53 | Q11 | 61 |
| Kennisholm Av. G46 | P12 | 61 |
| Kennisholm Pl. G46 | P12 | 61 |
| Kennoway Dr. G11 | J12 | 33 |
| Kennoway La. G11 | J12 | 33 |
| *Thornwood Dr.* | | |
| Kennyhill Sq. G31 | K19 | 37 |
| Kensington Dr., Giff. | R14 | 62 |
| Kensington Gate G12 | H14 | 20 |
| *Kensington Rd.* | | |
| Kensington Rd. G12 | H14 | 20 |
| Kent Dr. G73 | P20 | 65 |
| Kent Rd. G3 | K15 | 35 |
| Kent St. G40 | L18 | 36 |
| Kentallen Rd. G33 | L24 | 39 |
| Kentigern Ter., Bish. | F19 | 23 |
| Keppel Dr. G44 | O18 | 52 |
| Keppoch St. G21 | H17 | 22 |
| Keppochhill Rd. G22 | H17 | 22 |
| Kerfield Pl. G15 | D 9 | 6 |
| Kerr St. G40 | L18 | 36 |
| Kerr St., Barr. | R 7 | 59 |
| Kerr St., Blan. | S27 | 69 |
| Kerr St., Pais. | L 5 | 30 |
| Kerrera Pl. G33 | L23 | 39 |
| Kerrera Rd. G33 | L23 | 39 |
| Kerry Pl. G15 | D 9 | 6 |
| Kerrycroy Av. G42 | O17 | 52 |
| Kerrycroy Pl. G42 | O17 | 52 |
| *Kerrycroy Av.* | | |
| Kerrycroy St. G42 | O17 | 52 |
| Kerrydale St. G40 | M19 | 53 |
| Kerrylamont Av. G42 | O18 | 52 |
| Kersland La. G12 | H14 | 20 |
| *Kersland St.* | | |
| Kersland St. G12 | H14 | 20 |
| Kessington Dr., Bear. | D13 | 8 |
| Kessington Rd., Bear. | D13 | 8 |
| Kestral Ct., Clyde. | C 7 | 5 |
| Kestrel Pl., John. | O08 | 43 |
| Kestrel Rd. G13 | G11 | 19 |
| Kew Gdns. G12 | H14 | 20 |
| *Ruthven St.* | | |
| Kew Gdns., Udd. | O28 | 57 |
| Kew La. G12 | H14 | 20 |
| *Saltoun St.* | | |
| Kew Ter. G12 | H14 | 20 |
| Keyden St. G41 | L15 | 35 |
| Kibbleston Rd., Kilb. | M07 | 42 |
| Kidston St. G5 | M17 | 52 |
| Kilbarchan Rd., John. | N08 | 43 |
| Kilbarchan St. G5 | L16 | 35 |
| *Bedford St.* | | |
| Kilbarchan St. G5 | L16 | 35 |
| *Bedford St.* | | |
| Kilbeg Ter. G46 | Q11 | 61 |
| Kilberry St. G21 | J19 | 37 |
| Kilbirnie St. G5 | M16 | 51 |
| Kilbowie Ct., Clyde. | D 7 | 5 |
| *Crown Av.* | | |
| Kilbowie Rd., Clyde. | C 7 | 5 |
| Kilbowie Rd., Cumb. | C 3 | 71 |
| Kilbrennan Rd., Linw. | L 1 | 28 |
| Kilbride St. G5 | N17 | 52 |
| Kilbride Vw., Udd. | O28 | 57 |
| *Hamilton Vw.* | | |
| Kilburn Gro., Blan. | R26 | 68 |
| Kilburn Pl. G13 | G10 | 18 |
| Kilchattan Dr. G44 | O17 | 52 |
| Kilchoan Rd. G33 | J23 | 39 |
| Kilcloy Av. G15 | D10 | 6 |

| | | |
|---|---|---|
| Kildale St. G73 | O18 | 52 |
| Kildale Way G73 | O18 | 52 |
| Kildary Av. G44 | P16 | 63 |
| Kildary Rd. G44 | P16 | 63 |
| Kildermorie Rd. G34 | K25 | 40 |
| Kildonan Dr. G11 | J13 | 34 |
| Kildonan Ter. G51 | L13 | 34 |
| *Copland Rd.* | | |
| Kildrostan St. G41 | N15 | 51 |
| *Terregles Av.* | | |
| Kildrum Rd., Cumb. | B 3 | 71 |
| Kilearn Rd., Pais. | K 7 | 31 |
| Kilfinan St. G22 | F16 | 21 |
| Kilkerran Dr. G33 | G21 | 24 |
| *Saughs Av.* | | |
| Killarn Way, Pais. | K 7 | 31 |
| Killearn Dr., Pais. | M 9 | 48 |
| Killearn St. G22 | H16 | 21 |
| Killermont Av., Bear. | E13 | 8 |
| Killermont Ct., Bear. | D13 | 8 |
| Killermont Rd., Bear. | D13 | 8 |
| Killermont St. G1 | K17 | 36 |
| Killermont Vw. G20 | E13 | 8 |
| Killiegrew Rd. G41 | N14 | 50 |
| Killin Dr., Linw. | L 1 | 28 |
| Killin St. G32 | M22 | 54 |
| Killoch Av., Pais. | L 4 | 29 |
| Killoch Dr. G13 | F10 | 18 |
| Killoch Dr., Barr. | R 8 | 59 |
| Killoch Rd., Pais. | L 4 | 29 |
| Kilmailing Rd. G44 | P16 | 63 |
| Kilmair Pl. G20 | G14 | 20 |
| *Wyndford Rd.* | | |
| Kilmaluag Ter. G46 | Q11 | 61 |
| Kilmany Dr. G32 | L21 | 38 |
| Kilmardinny Av., Bear. | C12 | 7 |
| Kilmardinny Cres., Bear. | C12 | 7 |
| Kilmardinny Dr., Bear. | C12 | 7 |
| Kilmardinny Gate, Bear. | C12 | 7 |
| *Kilmardinny Av.* | | |
| Kilmardinny Gro., Bear. | C12 | 7 |
| Kilmarnock Rd. G43 | P14 | 62 |
| Kilmartin Pl., Thorn. | Q12 | 61 |
| Kilmaurs Dr., Giff. | Q15 | 63 |
| Kilmaurs St. G51 | L12 | 33 |
| Kilmorie Dr. G73 | O18 | 52 |
| Kilmory Av., Udd. | O28 | 57 |
| *Spindlehow Rd.* | | |
| Kilmuir Cres. G46 | Q11 | 61 |
| Kilmuir Dr. G46 | Q12 | 61 |
| Kilmuir Rd. G46 | Q12 | 61 |
| Kilmuir Rd., Udd. | N27 | 57 |
| Kilmun La. G20 | F14 | 20 |
| *Kilmun St.* | | |
| Kilmun Pl. G20 | F14 | 20 |
| *Kilmun St.* | | |
| Kilmun St. G20 | F14 | 20 |
| Kilnside Rd., Pais. | L 6 | 30 |
| Kiloran St. G46 | Q12 | 61 |
| Kilpatrick Cres., Pais. | N 5 | 46 |
| Kiltearn Rd. G33 | K24 | 39 |
| Kilvaxter Dr. G46 | Q12 | 61 |
| Kimberley St., Dalm. | C 5 | 4 |
| Kinalty Rd. G44 | P16 | 63 |
| Kinarvie Cres. G53 | O 9 | 48 |
| Kinarvie Gdns. G53 | O 9 | 48 |
| *Kinarvie Rd.* | | |
| Kinarvie Gdns. G53 | O 9 | 48 |
| *Kinarvie Rd.* | | |
| Kinarvie Pl. G53 | O 9 | 48 |
| Kinarvie Rd. G53 | O 9 | 48 |
| Kinarvie Ter. G53 | O 9 | 48 |
| Kinbuck St. G22 | H17 | 22 |
| Kincardine Cres., Bish. | F19 | 23 |
| *Graham Ter.* | | |
| Kincardine Dr., Bish. | F19 | 23 |
| Kincardine Pl., Bish. | F20 | 23 |
| Kincardine Sq. G33 | J23 | 39 |
| Kincath Av. G73 | Q20 | 65 |
| Kinclaven Av. G15 | D10 | 6 |
| Kincraig St. G51 | L11 | 33 |
| Kinellan Rd., Bear. | E12 | 7 |
| Kinfauns Dr. G15 | D 9 | 6 |
| Kinfauns Ter. G51 | L13 | 34 |
| *Copland Rd.* | | |
| King Edward Rd. G13 | G12 | 19 |
| King George V Bridge G5 | L16 | 35 |
| King St. G1 | L17 | 36 |
| King St. G73 | O19 | 53 |
| King St., Clyde. | F 8 | 17 |
| King St., Pais. | L 5 | 30 |
| Kingarth St. G42 | N16 | 51 |

| | | |
|---|---|---|
| Kinghorn Dr. G44 | O17 | 52 |
| Kinglas Rd., Bear. | E11 | 7 |
| Kings Cres. G72 | P22 | 66 |
| Kings Cres., John. | M 2 | 44 |
| Kings Cross G31 | K18 | 36 |
| Kings Dr. G40 | M18 | 52 |
| Kings Inch Rd., Renf. | G 8 | 17 |
| Kings La. W., Renf. | H 8 | 17 |
| *Bell St.* | | |
| Kings Park Av. G44 | P17 | 64 |
| Kings Park Rd. G44 | O16 | 51 |
| Kings Pl. G22 | F16 | 21 |
| Kings Rd., John. | N 1 | 44 |
| Kingsacre Rd. G44 | O17 | 52 |
| Kingsbarns Dr. G44 | O16 | 51 |
| Kingsborough Gate G12 | H13 | 20 |
| *Prince Albert Rd.* | | |
| Kingsborough Gdns. | | H13 | 20 |
| G12 | | |
| Kingsborough Ter. G12 | H13 | 20 |
| *Hyndland Rd.* | | |
| Kingsbrae Dr. G44 | O17 | 52 |
| Kingsbridge Cres. G44 | P17 | 64 |
| Kingsbridge Dr. G44 | P17 | 64 |
| Kingsburgh Dr., Pais. | L 7 | 31 |
| Kingsburn Dr. G73 | P19 | 65 |
| Kingsburn Gro. G73 | P19 | 65 |
| Kingscliffe Av. G44 | P17 | 64 |
| Kingscourt Av. G44 | P17 | 64 |
| Kingsdale Av. G44 | O17 | 52 |
| Kingsdyke Av. G44 | O17 | 52 |
| Kingsford Av. G44 | Q15 | 63 |
| Kingshall Cotts., Gart. | H28 | 27 |
| Kingsheath Av. G73 | P18 | 64 |
| Kingshill Dr. G44 | P17 | 64 |
| Kingshouse Av. G44 | P17 | 64 |
| Kingshurst Av. G44 | O17 | 52 |
| Kingsknowe Dr. G73 | P18 | 64 |
| Kingsland Cres. G52 | L10 | 32 |
| Kingsland Dr. G52 | L10 | 32 |
| Kingsley Av. G42 | N16 | 51 |
| Kingsley Ct., Udd. | O28 | 57 |
| Kingslynn Dr. G44 | P17 | 64 |
| Kingslynn La. G44 | P17 | 64 |
| *Kingslynn Dr.* | | |
| Kingsmuir Dr. G73 | P18 | 64 |
| Kingston Bri. G3 | L15 | 34 |
| Kingston Pl., Dalm. | D 5 | 4 |
| Kingston St. G5 | L16 | 35 |
| Kingstone Av. G14 | G10 | 18 |
| Kingsway Ct. G14 | G10 | 18 |
| Kingsway G14 | G10 | 18 |
| Kingswood Dr. G44 | P17 | 64 |
| Kingussie Dr. G44 | P17 | 64 |
| Kiniver Dr. G15 | E10 | 6 |
| Kinloch Av. G72 | Q22 | 66 |
| Kinloch Av., Linw. | L 1 | 28 |
| *Pentland Dr.* | | |
| Kinloch Rd., Renf. | J 7 | 31 |
| Kinloch St. G40 | M20 | 53 |
| Kinmount Av. G44 | O16 | 51 |
| Kinmount La. G44 | O16 | 51 |
| *Kinmount Av.* | | |
| Kinnaird Cres., Bear. | D13 | 8 |
| Kinnaird Dr., Linw. | L 1 | 28 |
| Kinnaird Pl. G64 | F19 | 23 |
| Kinnear Rd. G40 | M19 | 53 |
| Kinnell Av. G52 | M11 | 49 |
| Kinnell Cres. G52 | M11 | 49 |
| Kinnell Pl. G52 | N12 | 49 |
| *Mosspark Dr.* | | |
| Kinnell Sq. G52 | M11 | 49 |
| Kinnellar Dr. G14 | G10 | 18 |
| Kinning St. G5 | L15 | 35 |
| Kinnoul Pl. G12 | H13 | 20 |
| *Crown Rd.* | | |
| Kinpurnie Rd., Pais. | L 8 | 31 |
| Kinross Av. G52 | M10 | 48 |
| Kinsail Dr. G52 | L 9 | 32 |
| Kintessack Pl., Bish. | E20 | 11 |
| Kintillo Dr. G13 | G10 | 18 |
| Kintore Rd. G43 | P15 | 63 |
| Kintra St. G51 | L13 | 34 |
| Kintyre Av., Linw. | L 1 | 28 |
| Kintyre St. G21 | J19 | 37 |
| Kippen St. G22 | G17 | 22 |
| Kippford St. G32 | M23 | 55 |
| Kirconnell Dr. G73 | P18 | 64 |
| Kirk La. G43 | O14 | 50 |
| *Riverbank St.* | | |
| Kirk Pl., Udd. | P27 | 69 |
| Kirk Rd., Bear. | C12 | 7 |

| Street | Ref | Pg |
|---|---|---|
| Kirkaig Av., Renf. | J 9 | 32 |
| Kirkbean Av. G73 | Q19 | 65 |
| Kirkburn Av. G72 | Q22 | 66 |
| Kirkcaldy Rd. G41 | N14 | 58 |
| Kirkconnel Av. G13 | G 9 | 18 |
| Kirkdale Dr. G52 | M12 | 49 |
| Kirkfield Rd., Udd. | Q28 | 69 |
| Kirkford Rd., Chr. | E27 | 15 |
| *Bridgeburn Dr.* | | |
| Kirkhill Av. G72 | Q22 | 66 |
| Kirkhill Dr. G20 | G14 | 20 |
| Kirkhill Gdns. G72 | Q22 | 66 |
| Kirkhill Gro. G72 | Q22 | 66 |
| Kirkhill Pl. G20 | G14 | 20 |
| Kirkhill Rd., Gart. | G27 | 27 |
| Kirkhill Rd., Udd. | O27 | 57 |
| Kirkhill Ter. G72 | Q22 | 66 |
| Kirkhope Dr. G15 | E10 | 6 |
| Kirkinner Rd. G32 | M23 | 55 |
| Kirkintilloch Rd., Bish. | F18 | 22 |
| Kirkintilloch Rd., Lenz. | C23 | 13 |
| Kirkland St. G20 | H15 | 21 |
| Kirklandneuk Rd., Renf. | H 7 | 17 |
| Kirklands Cres., Udd. | Q28 | 69 |
| Kirklea Av., Pais. | L 4 | 29 |
| Kirklee Circus G12 | H14 | 20 |
| Kirklee Gardens La. G12 | G14 | 20 |
| *Bellshaugh Rd.* | | |
| Kirklee Gdns. G12 | G14 | 20 |
| *Bellshaugh Rd.* | | |
| Kirklee Pl. G12 | H14 | 20 |
| Kirklee Quad. G12 | H14 | 20 |
| Kirklee Quad. La. G12 | H14 | 20 |
| *Kirklee Quad.* | | |
| Kirklee Rd. G12 | H14 | 20 |
| Kirklee Ter. G12 | H14 | 20 |
| Kirklee Terrace La. G12 | H14 | 20 |
| *Kirklee Ter.* | | |
| Kirkliston St. G32 | L21 | 38 |
| Kirkmuir Av., Renf. | J 7 | 31 |
| Kirkmuir Dr. G73 | Q19 | 65 |
| Kirknewton St. G32 | L22 | 38 |
| Kirkoswald Dr., Clyde. | D 8 | 5 |
| Kirkoswald Rd. G43 | P14 | 62 |
| Kirkpatrick St. G40 | L19 | 37 |
| Kirkriggs Av. G73 | P19 | 65 |
| Kirkriggs Gdns. G73 | P19 | 65 |
| Kirkriggs Way, Ruth. | P19 | 65 |
| Kirkstall Gdns., Bish. | D19 | 11 |
| Kirkstonside, Barr. | R 7 | 59 |
| Kirkton Av. G13 | G10 | 18 |
| Kirkton Cres. G13 | G10 | 18 |
| Kirkton Rd. G72 | P22 | 66 |
| Kirkview Gdns., Udd. | O27 | 57 |
| *Glencroft Av.* | | |
| Kirkville Pl. G15 | E10 | 6 |
| Kirkwall Av., Blan. | Q26 | 68 |
| Kirkwall, Cumb. | A 3 | 71 |
| Kirkwell Rd. G44 | P16 | 63 |
| Kirkwood Av., Clyde. | E 8 | 5 |
| Kirkwood Quad., Clyde. | E 8 | 5 |
| *Kirkwood Av.* | | |
| Kirkwood Rd., Udd. | N27 | 57 |
| *Newlands Rd.* | | |
| Kirkwood St. G51 | L14 | 34 |
| Kirkwood St. G73 | O19 | 53 |
| Kirn St. G20 | F14 | 20 |
| *Kilmun St.* | | |
| Kirriemuir Av. G52 | M11 | 49 |
| Kirriemuir Gdns., Bish. | E20 | 11 |
| Kirriemuir Rd., Bish. | E20 | 11 |
| Kirtle Dr., Renf. | J 9 | 32 |
| Kirton Av., Barr. | R 7 | 59 |
| Kishorn Pl. G32 | J23 | 39 |
| Knapdale St. G22 | F16 | 21 |
| Knightsbridge Rd. G13 | G11 | 19 |
| Knightscliffe Av. G13 | F11 | 19 |
| Knightswood Cross G13 | F11 | 19 |
| Knightswood Rd. G13 | E11 | 7 |
| Knightswood Ter., Blan. | R27 | 69 |
| Knock Way, Pais. | K 7 | 31 |
| Knockburnie Rd., Udd. | Q28 | 69 |
| Knockhall St. G33 | J23 | 39 |
| Knockhill Dr. G44 | O16 | 51 |
| Knockhill La. G44 | O16 | 51 |
| *Mount Annan Dr.* | | |
| Knockhill Rd., Renf. | J 7 | 31 |
| Knockside Av., Pais. | O 5 | 46 |
| Knowe Rd., Chr. | F26 | 26 |
| Knowe Rd., Pais. | K 7 | 31 |
| Knowe Ter. G22 | F16 | 21 |
| *Hillend Rd.* | | |

| Street | Ref | Pg |
|---|---|---|
| Knowehead Dr., Udd. | P27 | 69 |
| Knowehead Gdns., Udd. | P27 | 69 |
| Knowetap St. G20 | F15 | 21 |
| Knowhead Ter. G41 | M15 | 51 |
| *Albert Dr.* | | |
| Knox St., Pais. | M 4 | 45 |
| Kyle Dr., Giff. | Q14 | 62 |
| Kyle Rd., Cumb. | B 3 | 71 |
| Kyle Sq. G73 | P19 | 65 |
| Kyle St. G4 | J17 | 36 |
| Kyleakin Gdns., Blan. | R25 | 68 |
| Kyleakin Rd. G46 | Q11 | 61 |
| Kyleakin Ter. G46 | Q11 | 61 |
| Kylepark Av., Udd. | P26 | 68 |
| Kylepark Cres., Udd. | O26 | 56 |
| Kylepark Dr., Udd. | O26 | 56 |
| Kylerhea Rd. G46 | Q11 | 61 |
| La Belle Pl. G3 | J15 | 35 |
| Laburnum Gdns., Lenz. | C22 | 12 |
| *Laburnum Gro.* | | |
| Laburnum Gro., Lenz. | C22 | 12 |
| Laburnum Pl., John. | O 1 | 44 |
| Laburnum Rd. G41 | M14 | 50 |
| Laburnum Rd., Cumb. | C 4 | 71 |
| Lacrosse Ter. G12 | H15 | 21 |
| Lacy St., Pais. | L 7 | 31 |
| Lade Ter. G52 | M10 | 48 |
| Ladeside Dr., John. | N08 | 43 |
| Ladhope Pl. G13 | F 9 | 18 |
| Lady Anne St. G14 | G 9 | 18 |
| Lady Isle Cres., Udd. | P27 | 69 |
| Lady Jane Gate, Both. | Q27 | 69 |
| Lady La., Pais. | M 5 | 46 |
| Ladybank Dr. G52 | M12 | 49 |
| Ladyburn St., Pais. | M 7 | 47 |
| Ladyhill Dr., Bail. | M25 | 56 |
| Ladykirk Cres. G52 | L10 | 32 |
| Ladykirk Cres., Pais. | M 6 | 46 |
| Ladykirk Dr. G52 | L10 | 32 |
| Ladyloan Av. G15 | D 9 | 6 |
| Ladyloan Pl. G15 | D 9 | 6 |
| Ladymuir Cres. G53 | N11 | 49 |
| Ladysmith Av., Kilb. | N08 | 43 |
| Ladywell St. G4 | K18 | 36 |
| *Wishart St.* | | |
| Laggan Rd. G43 | P15 | 63 |
| Laggan Rd., Bish. | E19 | 11 |
| Laggan Ter., Renf. | H 7 | 17 |
| Laidlaw Gdns., Udd. | N27 | 57 |
| Laidlaw St. G5 | L16 | 35 |
| Laigh Kirk La., Pais. | M 6 | 46 |
| *Causeyside St.* | | |
| Laigh Possil Rd. G23 | F16 | 21 |
| *Balmore Rd.* | | |
| Laighcartside St., John. | M 1 | 44 |
| Laighlands Rd. G71 | R28 | 69 |
| Laighmuir St., Udd. | P27 | 69 |
| Laighpark Harbour, Pais. | K 6 | 30 |
| Lainshaw Dr. G45 | R16 | 63 |
| Laird Pl. G40 | M18 | 52 |
| Lairds Hill, Cumb. | C 2 | 70 |
| Lairg Dr., Blan. | R26 | 68 |
| Lamb St. G22 | G16 | 21 |
| Lambhill St. G41 | L14 | 34 |
| Lamerton Dr. G52 | L10 | 32 |
| Lamerton Rd., Cumb. | C 4 | 71 |
| Lamington Rd. G52 | M10 | 48 |
| Lamlash Cres. G33 | K22 | 38 |
| Lammermoor Av. G52 | M11 | 49 |
| Lammermoor Dr., Cumb. | D 2 | 70 |
| Lammermuir Dr., Pais. | O 6 | 46 |
| Lamont Rd. G21 | G19 | 23 |
| Lanark St. G1 | L17 | 36 |
| Lancaster Cres. G12 | H14 | 20 |
| Lancaster Cres. La. G12 | G13 | 20 |
| *Clevedon Rd.* | | |
| Lancaster Rd., Bish. | D19 | 11 |
| Lancaster Ter. G12 | H14 | 20 |
| *Westbourne Gdns. W.* | | |
| Lancaster Ter. La. G12 | H14 | 20 |
| *Westbourne Gdns. W.* | | |
| Lancefield Quay G3 | K15 | 35 |
| Lancefield St. G3 | K15 | 35 |
| Landemer Dr. G73 | P18 | 64 |
| Landressy St. G40 | M18 | 52 |
| Lanfine Rd., Pais. | M 7 | 47 |
| Lang Av., Renf. | J 8 | 31 |
| Lang St., Pais. | M 7 | 47 |
| Langa St. G20 | F15 | 21 |
| Langbank St. G5 | M16 | 51 |
| *Eglinton St.* | | |

| Street | Ref | Pg |
|---|---|---|
| Langbar Cres. G33 | K24 | 39 |
| Langbar Path G33 | K23 | 39 |
| Langcraigs Cres., Pais. | P 5 | 58 |
| Langcraigs Ter., Pais. | P 5 | 58 |
| Langcroft Dr. G72 | Q23 | 67 |
| Langcroft Pl. G51 | K11 | 33 |
| Langcroft Rd. G51 | K11 | 33 |
| Langcroft Ter. G51 | K11 | 33 |
| Langdale Av. G33 | H21 | 24 |
| Langdale Av., Cumb. | C 1 | 70 |
| Langdale St. G33 | H21 | 24 |
| Langfaulds Cres., Clyde. | C 8 | 5 |
| Langford Av. G53 | Q10 | 60 |
| Langford Dr. G53 | Q10 | 60 |
| Langford Pl. G53 | Q10 | 60 |
| *Langford Dr.* | | |
| Langhill Dr., Cumb. | B 1 | 70 |
| *Redhill Rd.* | | |
| Langholm Ct., Chr. | E28 | 15 |
| *Heathfield Av.* | | |
| Langholm Dr., Linw. | L 2 | 28 |
| Langholm St. G14 | G 9 | 18 |
| Langlands Av. G51 | K11 | 33 |
| Langlands Dr. G51 | K11 | 33 |
| Langlands Path G51 | K12 | 33 |
| Langlands Rd. G51 | K11 | 33 |
| Langlands Rd. G51 | K13 | 34 |
| Langlea Av. G72 | Q20 | 65 |
| Langlea Gro. G72 | Q21 | 66 |
| Langlea Rd. G72 | Q21 | 66 |
| Langley Av. G13 | F10 | 18 |
| Langmuir Rd. G21 | H19 | 23 |
| Langmuir Rd., Bail. | L28 | 41 |
| Langmuirhead Rd., Lenz. | C22 | 12 |
| Langness Rd. G33 | K22 | 38 |
| Langrig Rd. G21 | H19 | 23 |
| Langshot St. G51 | L14 | 34 |
| Langside Av. G41 | N15 | 51 |
| Langside Av., Udd. | P29 | 69 |
| Langside Dr. G43 | P15 | 63 |
| Langside Dr. G78 | N07 | 42 |
| Langside La. G42 | N16 | 51 |
| Langside Pk. G78 | N07 | 42 |
| Langside Pl. G41 | O15 | 51 |
| Langside Rd. G42 | O16 | 51 |
| Langside Rd., Both. | R28 | 69 |
| Langside St., Clyde. | C 9 | 6 |
| Langstile Pl. G52 | L 9 | 32 |
| Langstile Rd. G52 | L 9 | 32 |
| Langton Cres. G53 | N11 | 49 |
| Langton Cres., Barr. | R 8 | 59 |
| Langton Gdns., Bail. | M24 | 55 |
| Langton Rd. G53 | N11 | 49 |
| Langtree Av., Giff. | R13 | 62 |
| Lanrig Pl., Chr. | F26 | 26 |
| Lanrig Rd., Chr. | F26 | 26 |
| Lansbury Gdns., Pais. | K 5 | 30 |
| *Cowdie St.* | | |
| Lansdowne Cres. G20 | J15 | 35 |
| Lansdowne Cres. La. G12 | H15 | 21 |
| *Great Western Rd.* | | |
| Lanton Dr. G52 | L10 | 32 |
| Lanton Rd. G43 | P15 | 63 |
| Lappin St., Clyde. | F 8 | 17 |
| Larch Av., Bish. | F19 | 23 |
| Larch Av., Lenz. | C23 | 13 |
| Larch Cres., Lenz. | C23 | 13 |
| Larch Ct., Cumb. | B 4 | 71 |
| Larch Gro. G67 | B 5 | 71 |
| Larch Pl., John. | O 1 | 44 |
| Larch Rd. G41 | M13 | 50 |
| Larch Rd., Cumb. | B 4 | 71 |
| Larches, The, Chr. | D28 | 15 |
| Larchfield Av. G14 | H10 | 18 |
| Larchfield Dr. G73 | Q19 | 65 |
| Larchfield Pl. G14 | H10 | 18 |
| Larchfield Rd. G69 | E27 | 15 |
| Larchfield Rd., Bear. | E12 | 7 |
| Larchgrove Av. G32 | L23 | 39 |
| Larchgrove Pl. G32 | K23 | 39 |
| *Larchgrove Rd.* | | |
| Larchgrove Rd. G32 | K23 | 39 |
| Larchwood Ter., Barr. | R 9 | 60 |
| Largie Rd. G43 | P15 | 63 |
| Largo Pl. G51 | K12 | 33 |
| Largs St. G31 | K19 | 37 |
| Larkfield Rd., Lenz. | C24 | 13 |
| Larkfield St. G42 | N16 | 51 |
| *Cathcart Rd.* | | |
| Larkin Gdns., Pais. | K 5 | 30 |
| Lasswade St. G14 | G 9 | 18 |
| Latherton Dr. G20 | G14 | 20 |

| | | |
|---|---|---|
| Latherton Pl. G20 | G14 | 20 |
| *Latherton Dr.* | | |
| Latimer Gdns. G52 | M10 | 48 |
| Lauder Dr. G73 | O20 | 53 |
| Lauder Dr., Linw. | L 1 | 28 |
| Lauder Gdns., Blan. | R26 | 68 |
| Lauder St. G5 | M16 | 51 |
| *Eglinton St.* | | |
| Lauderdale Gdns. G12 | H13 | 20 |
| Laundry La. G33 | G23 | 25 |
| Laurel Av., Dalm. | D 5 | 4 |
| Laurel Av., Lenz. | C23 | 13 |
| Laurel Bank Rd., Chr. | F25 | 26 |
| Laurel Pl. G11 | J13 | 34 |
| Laurel St. G11 | J13 | 34 |
| Laurel Way, Barr. | Q 7 | 59 |
| *Graham St.* | | |
| Laurel Wk. G73 | Q20 | 65 |
| Laurence Dr., Bear. | C11 | 7 |
| Laurie Ct., Udd. | O28 | 57 |
| *Hillcrest Rd.* | | |
| Laurieston La. G51 | L14 | 34 |
| *Paisley Rd.* | | |
| Laurieston Way G73 | Q19 | 65 |
| Laverock Ter., Chr. | E27 | 15 |
| Laverockhall St. G21 | H18 | 22 |
| Law St. G40 | L19 | 37 |
| Lawers Rd. G43 | P13 | 62 |
| Lawers Rd., Bear. | C11 | 7 |
| Lawers Rd., Renf. | J 8 | 31 |
| Lawhill Av. G44 | Q17 | 64 |
| Lawmoor Av. G5 | M17 | 52 |
| Lawmoor La. G5 | L17 | 36 |
| *Ballater St.* | | |
| Lawmoor Rd. G5 | M17 | 52 |
| Lawmoor St. G5 | M17 | 52 |
| Lawn St., Pais. | L 6 | 30 |
| Lawrence Av., Giff. | R14 | 62 |
| Lawrence St. G11 | J14 | 34 |
| Lawrie St. G11 | J13 | 34 |
| Lawside Dr. G53 | O11 | 49 |
| Laxford Av. G44 | Q16 | 63 |
| Laxton Dr., Lenz. | D24 | 13 |
| Leabank Av., Pais. | O 6 | 46 |
| Leadburn Rd. G21 | H20 | 23 |
| *Rye Rd.* | | |
| Leadburn St. G32 | K21 | 38 |
| Leader St. G33 | J20 | 37 |
| Leander Cres., Renf. | J 9 | 32 |
| Leckethill St. G21 | H18 | 22 |
| *Springburn Rd.* | | |
| Leckie St. G43 | O14 | 50 |
| Ledaig Pl. G31 | K20 | 37 |
| Ledaig St. G31 | K20 | 37 |
| Ledard Rd. G42 | O15 | 51 |
| Ledcameroch Cres., Bear. | D11 | 7 |
| Ledcameroch Pk., Bear. | D11 | 7 |
| *Ledcameroch Rd.* | | |
| Ledcameroch Rd., Bear. | D11 | 7 |
| Ledgowan Pl. G20 | F14 | 20 |
| Ledi Dr., Bear. | B10 | 6 |
| Ledi Rd. G43 | P14 | 62 |
| Ledmore Dr. G15 | D 9 | 6 |
| Lednock Rd. G33 | G23 | 25 |
| Lednock Rd. G52 | L10 | 32 |
| Lee Av. G33 | J21 | 38 |
| Lee Cres., Bish. | F18 | 22 |
| Leebank Dr. G44 | R15 | 63 |
| Leefield Av. G44 | R15 | 63 |
| Leehill Rd. G21 | F18 | 22 |
| Leeside Rd. G21 | F18 | 22 |
| Leewood Dr. G44 | R15 | 63 |
| Leicester Av. G12 | G13 | 20 |
| Leighton St. G20 | G15 | 21 |
| Leitchland Rd. G78 | O 2 | 44 |
| Leitchs Ct. G1 | L17 | 36 |
| *Trongate* | | |
| Leith St. G33 | K20 | 37 |
| Leithland Av. G53 | O10 | 48 |
| Leithland Rd. G53 | N10 | 48 |
| Lendale La., Bish. | D19 | 11 |
| Lendel Pl. G51 | L15 | 35 |
| *Paisley Rd. W.* | | |
| Lenhall Dr. G45 | R18 | 64 |
| Lenhall Ter. G45 | R18 | 64 |
| Lennox Av. G14 | H11 | 19 |
| Lennox Cres., Bish. | F18 | 22 |
| Lennox Ct., Pais. | B12 | 7 |
| Lennox Dr., Bear. | C12 | 7 |
| Lennox Dr., Clyde. | B 8 | 5 |

| | | |
|---|---|---|
| Lennox La. W. G14 | H11 | 19 |
| *Lennox Av.* | | |
| Lennox La. W. G14 | H11 | 19 |
| *Lennox Av.* | | |
| Lennox Pl. G14 | H11 | 19 |
| *Scotstoun St.* | | |
| Lennox Pl., Dalm. | D 6 | 4 |
| *Swindon St.* | | |
| Lennox Rd., Cumb. | C 2 | 70 |
| Lennox Ter., Pais. | K 7 | 31 |
| Lennox Vw., Clyde. | D 7 | 5 |
| *Granville St.* | | |
| Lentran St. G34 | K26 | 40 |
| Leny St. G20 | H16 | 21 |
| Lenzie Dr. G21 | G18 | 22 |
| Lenzie Rd. G33 | G23 | 25 |
| Lenzie St. G21 | G18 | 22 |
| Lenziemill Rd., Cumb. | D 3 | 71 |
| Lerwick St. G4 | J16 | 35 |
| *Dobbies Loan* | | |
| Leslie Rd. G41 | N15 | 51 |
| Leslie St. G41 | M15 | 51 |
| Lesmuir Dr. G14 | G10 | 18 |
| Lesmuir Pl. G14 | G 9 | 18 |
| Letham Ct. G43 | P15 | 63 |
| Letham Dr. G43 | P15 | 63 |
| Letham Dr. G64 | F20 | 23 |
| Lethamhill Cres. G33 | J21 | 38 |
| Lethamhill Pl. G33 | J21 | 38 |
| Lethamhill Rd. G33 | J21 | 38 |
| Letherby Dr. G44 | O16 | 51 |
| Lethington Av. G41 | O15 | 51 |
| Letterickhills Cres. G72 | Q24 | 67 |
| Lettoch St. G51 | L13 | 34 |
| Leven Av., Bish. | E19 | 11 |
| Leven Ct., Barr. | P 7 | 59 |
| Leven Dr., Bear. | D12 | 7 |
| Leven Sq., Renf. | H 7 | 17 |
| Leven St. G41 | M15 | 51 |
| Leven Vw., Clyde. | D 7 | 5 |
| *Radnor St.* | | |
| Leven Way, Pais. | N 3 | 45 |
| Levern Cres., Barr. | R 7 | 59 |
| Levern Gdns., Barr. | Q 7 | 59 |
| *Chappel St.* | | |
| Levernside Av., Barr. | R 7 | 59 |
| Levernside Cres. G53 | N10 | 48 |
| Levernside Rd. G53 | N10 | 48 |
| Lewis Av., Renf. | J 8 | 31 |
| Lewis Gdns., Bear. | C10 | 6 |
| Lewiston Dr. G23 | E14 | 8 |
| *Lewiston Rd.* | | |
| Lewiston Pl. G23 | E14 | 8 |
| *Lewiston Rd.* | | |
| Lewiston Rd. G23 | E14 | 8 |
| Lexwell Av., John. | M 2 | 44 |
| Lexwell Rd., Pais. | N 3 | 45 |
| Leyden Ct. G20 | G15 | 21 |
| *Leyden St.* | | |
| Leyden Gdns. G20 | G15 | 21 |
| *Leyden St.* | | |
| Leyden St. G20 | G15 | 21 |
| Leys, The, Bish. | E19 | 11 |
| Liberton St. G33 | K20 | 37 |
| Liberty Av., Bail. | L28 | 41 |
| Libo Av. G53 | N11 | 49 |
| Liddale Way G73 | O18 | 52 |
| Liddel Rd., Cumb. | C 2 | 70 |
| Liddell St. G32 | N23 | 55 |
| Liddesdale Av. | O 2 | 44 |
| Liddesdale Pl. G22 | F17 | 22 |
| *Liddesdale Sq.* | | |
| Liddesdale Rd. G22 | F17 | 22 |
| Liddesdale Sq. G22 | F17 | 22 |
| Liddesdale Ter. G22 | F18 | 22 |
| Liff Gdns., Bish. | F20 | 23 |
| Liff Pl. G34 | J26 | 40 |
| Lightburn Pl. G32 | K22 | 38 |
| Lightburn Rd. G72 | Q23 | 67 |
| Lilac Av., Dalm. | D 6 | 4 |
| Lilac Gdns., Bish. | F19 | 23 |
| Lilac Pl., John. | N 1 | 44 |
| Lily St. G40 | M19 | 53 |
| Lilybank Av. G72 | Q23 | 67 |
| Lilybank Av., Chr. | F26 | 26 |
| Lilybank Gardens La. G12 | H14 | 20 |
| *Great George St.* | | |
| Lilybank Gdns. G12 | J14 | 34 |
| Lilybank Ter. G12 | H14 | 20 |
| *Great George St.* | | |

| | | |
|---|---|---|
| Lilybank Terrace La. G12 | H14 | 20 |
| *Great George St.* | | |
| Lilyburn Pl. G15 | C 9 | 6 |
| Lime Gro., Blan. | R26 | 68 |
| Lime Gro., Lenz. | C23 | 13 |
| Lime St. G14 | H11 | 19 |
| Limecraigs Cres., Pais. | O 5 | 46 |
| Limecraigs Rd., Pais. | O 5 | 46 |
| Limekiln St., Clyde. | B 8 | 5 |
| Limeside Av. G73 | O19 | 53 |
| Limeside Gdns. G73 | O20 | 53 |
| *Calderwood Rd.* | | |
| Limetree Av., Udd. | O28 | 57 |
| Limetree Dr., Dalm. | D 7 | 5 |
| Linacre Dr. G32 | L23 | 39 |
| Linacre Gdns. G32 | L23 | 39 |
| Linbank Av. G53 | O11 | 49 |
| Linburn Pl. G52 | L10 | 32 |
| Linburn Rd. G52 | K 9 | 32 |
| Linclive Link Rd., Linw. | L 3 | 29 |
| Linclive Ter., Linw. | L 2 | 28 |
| Lincoln Av. G13 | G10 | 18 |
| Lincoln Av., Udd. | N27 | 57 |
| Lincuan Av., Giff. | S14 | 62 |
| Lindams, Udd. | P27 | 69 |
| Linden St. G13 | F12 | 19 |
| Lindores Av. G73 | O19 | 53 |
| Lindores St. G42 | O16 | 51 |
| *Somerville Dr.* | | |
| Lindrick Dr. G23 | E15 | 9 |
| Lindsay Dr. G12 | G13 | 20 |
| Lindsay Pl. G12 | G13 | 20 |
| Lindsay Pl., Lenz. | D23 | 13 |
| Lindsaybeg Rd., Lenz.& Chr. | D24 | 13 |
| Linfern Rd. G12 | H14 | 20 |
| Links Rd. G32 | M23 | 55 |
| Links Rd. G44 | Q17 | 64 |
| Linkwood Av. G15 | D 9 | 6 |
| *Kinfauns Dr.* | | |
| Linkwood Cres. G15 | D 9 | 6 |
| Linkwood Dr. G15 | D 9 | 6 |
| Linkwood Pl. G15 | D 9 | 6 |
| *Kinfauns Dr.* | | |
| Linlithgow Gdns. G32 | L23 | 39 |
| *Hailes Av.* | | |
| Linn Cres., Pais. | O 5 | 46 |
| Linn Dr. G44 | Q15 | 63 |
| Linnet Av., John. | O08 | 43 |
| Linnhe Av. G44 | Q16 | 63 |
| Linnhe Av., Bish. | E19 | 11 |
| Linnhe Dr., Barr. | P 7 | 59 |
| Linnhe Pl., Blan. | R26 | 68 |
| Linnhead Dr. G53 | P10 | 60 |
| Linnhead Pl. G14 | H10 | 18 |
| Linnpark Av. G44 | R15 | 63 |
| Linnpark Ct. G44 | R15 | 63 |
| Linnpark Gdns., John. | N 1 | 44 |
| *Lunn Brae* | | |
| Linside Av., Pais. | M 7 | 47 |
| Lintfield Loan, Udd. | P28 | 69 |
| *Myers Cres.* | | |
| Linthaugh Rd. G53 | N10 | 48 |
| Linthouse Bldgs. G51 | K12 | 33 |
| Lintlaw Dr. G52 | L11 | 33 |
| Lintlaw, Blan. | R26 | 68 |
| Linton St. G33 | K21 | 38 |
| Linwell Cres., Pais. | O 5 | 46 |
| Linwood Ct. G44 | P16 | 63 |
| *Clarkston Rd.* | | |
| Linwood Moss Rd., Linw. | L 2 | 28 |
| Linwood Rd., John. | L 2 | 28 |
| Linwood Ter. G12 | H15 | 21 |
| *Glasgow St.* | | |
| Lismore Av., Renf. | J 8 | 31 |
| Lismore Dr., Pais. | O 5 | 46 |
| Lismore Dr., Chr. | D28 | 15 |
| *Altnacreag Gdns.* | | |
| Lismore Rd. G12 | H13 | 20 |
| Lister Rd. G52 | K10 | 32 |
| Lister St. G4 | J17 | 36 |
| Lithgow Cres., Pais. | N 7 | 47 |
| Little Dovehill G1 | L17 | 36 |
| Little Holm, Dalm. | D 6 | 4 |
| Little St. G3 | K15 | 35 |
| Littlehill St. G21 | H18 | 22 |
| *Edgefauld Rd.* | | |
| Littleton Dr. G23 | E14 | 8 |
| *Rothes Dr.* | | |
| Littleton St. G23 | E14 | 8 |
| *Rothes Dr.* | | |
| Livingstone Av. G52 | K10 | 32 |

| Street | Grid | Page |
|---|---|---|
| Maclehose Rd., Cumb. | B 4 | 71 |
| Maclellan St. G41 | L14 | 34 |
| Madison Av. G44 | P16 | 63 |
| Madison La. G44 | P16 | 63 |
| *Carmunnock Rd.* | | |
| Madras Pl. G40 | M18 | 52 |
| *Madras St.* | | |
| Madras St. G40 | M18 | 52 |
| Mafeking St. G51 | L13 | 34 |
| Magdalen Way, Pais. | O 2 | 44 |
| Magnus Cres. G44 | Q16 | 63 |
| Mahon Ct., Chr. | E27 | 15 |
| Maida St. G43 | O13 | 50 |
| Maidland Rd. G53 | O11 | 49 |
| Mailerbeg Gdns., Chr. | D27 | 15 |
| Mailing Av., Bish. | E19 | 11 |
| Main Rd., John. | M 2 | 44 |
| Main St. G40 | M18 | 52 |
| Main St. G72 | P22 | 66 |
| Main St. G73 | O19 | 53 |
| Main St., Bail. | M25 | 56 |
| Main St., Barr. | R 7 | 59 |
| Main St., Both. | R28 | 69 |
| Main St., Chr. | E26 | 14 |
| Main St., Cumb. | A 3 | 71 |
| Main St., Thorn. | Q12 | 61 |
| Main St., Udd. | P27 | 69 |
| Mainhead Ter., Cumb. | A 3 | 71 |
| *Roadside* | | |
| Mainhill Av., Bail. | L26 | 40 |
| Mainhill Pl., Bail. | L26 | 40 |
| Mainhill Rd., Bail. | L27 | 41 |
| Mains Av., Giff. | R13 | 62 |
| Mains Dr., Renf. | E 5 | 4 |
| Mains Hill, Renf. | E 5 | 4 |
| Mains Holm, Renf. | E 5 | 4 |
| Mains River, Renf. | E 5 | 4 |
| Mains Wood, Renf. | E 5 | 4 |
| Mainscroft, Renf. | E 5 | 4 |
| Mair St. G51 | L15 | 35 |
| Maitland Pl., Renf. | J 7 | 31 |
| Maitland St. G4 | J16 | 35 |
| Malcolm St. G31 | L20 | 37 |
| Malin Pl. G33 | K21 | 38 |
| Mallaig Path G51 | K11 | 33 |
| Mallaig Pl. G51 | K11 | 33 |
| Mallaig Rd. G51 | K11 | 33 |
| Mallard Rd., Clyde. | C 7 | 5 |
| Malloch Cres., John. | N 1 | 44 |
| Malloch St. G20 | G15 | 21 |
| Malta St., Clyde. | F 8 | 17 |
| Maltbarns St. G20 | H16 | 21 |
| Malvern Ct. G31 | L19 | 37 |
| Malvern Way, Pais. | K 5 | 30 |
| Mambeg Dr. G51 | K12 | 33 |
| Mamore Pl. G43 | P14 | 62 |
| Mamore St. G43 | P14 | 62 |
| Manchester Dr. G12 | G13 | 20 |
| Manitoba Pl. G31 | L19 | 37 |
| *Janefield St.* | | |
| Mannering Ct. G41 | O14 | 50 |
| *Pollokshaws Rd.* | | |
| Mannering Rd. G31 | O14 | 50 |
| Mannering Rd., Pais. | O 3 | 45 |
| Mannofield, Bear. | D11 | 7 |
| *Chesters Rd.* | | |
| Manor Rd. G14 | H12 | 19 |
| Manor Rd. G15 | E 9 | 6 |
| Manor Rd., Gart. | G27 | 27 |
| Manor Rd., Pais. | N 3 | 45 |
| Manor Way G73 | Q19 | 65 |
| Manse Av., Bear. | C12 | 7 |
| Manse Brae G44 | P16 | 63 |
| Manse Ct., Barr. | Q 8 | 59 |
| Manse Rd. G32 | M23 | 55 |
| Manse Rd., Bail. | L27 | 41 |
| Manse Rd., Bear. | C12 | 7 |
| Manse St., Renf. | H 8 | 17 |
| Mansefield Av. G72 | Q22 | 66 |
| Mansefield Dr., Udd. | P28 | 69 |
| Mansefield St. G11 | J14 | 34 |
| Mansel St. G21 | G18 | 22 |
| Mansewood Rd. G43 | P13 | 62 |
| Mansfield Rd. G52 | K 9 | 32 |
| Mansion St. G72 | P22 | 66 |
| Mansion St. G22 | G17 | 22 |
| Mansion St. G72 | P22 | 66 |
| Mansionhouse Av. G32 | O23 | 55 |
| Mansionhouse Dr. G32 | L23 | 39 |
| Mansionhouse Gdns. G41 | O15 | 51 |
| *Mansionhouse Rd.* | | |
| Mansionhouse Rd. G32 | M24 | 55 |
| Mansionhouse Rd. G42 | O15 | 51 |
| Mansionhouse Rd., Pais. | L 7 | 31 |
| Maple Ct., Barr. | S 8 | 59 |
| *Oakbank Dr.* | | |
| Maple Dr., Dalm. | C 6 | 4 |
| Maple Dr., John. | O 1 | 44 |
| Maple Dr., Lenz. | C22 | 12 |
| Maple Rd. G41 | M13 | 50 |
| Mar Gdns. G73 | Q20 | 65 |
| March La. G41 | N15 | 51 |
| *Nithsdale Dr.* | | |
| March St. G41 | N15 | 51 |
| Marchfield Av., Pais. | K 5 | 30 |
| Marchfield, Bish. | D18 | 10 |
| Marchfield, Bish. | D18 | 10 |
| *Westlands* | | |
| Marchglen Pl. G51 | K11 | 33 |
| *Mallaig Rd.* | | |
| Marchmont Gdns., Bish. | D18 | 10 |
| Marchmont Ter. G12 | H14 | 20 |
| *Observatory Rd.* | | |
| Maree Dr. G52 | M12 | 49 |
| Maree Gdns., Bish. | E19 | 11 |
| Maree Rd., Pais. | N 4 | 45 |
| Marfield St. G32 | L21 | 38 |
| Margaret St. G41 | K17 | 36 |
| *Martha St.* | | |
| Margarette Bldgs. G44 | P16 | 63 |
| *Clarkston Rd.* | | |
| Marguerite Av., Lenz. | C23 | 13 |
| Marguerite Dr., Lenz. | C23 | 13 |
| Marguerite Gdns., Lenz. | C23 | 13 |
| Marguerite Gdns., Udd. | Q28 | 69 |
| Marguerite Gro., Lenz. | C23 | 13 |
| Mariscat Rd. G41 | N15 | 51 |
| Marjory Dr., Pais. | K 7 | 31 |
| Marjory Rd., Renf. | J 7 | 31 |
| Market Rd., Lenz. | B25 | 14 |
| Market St. G40 | L18 | 36 |
| Markinch St. G5 | L16 | 35 |
| *West St.* | | |
| Marlborough Av. G11 | H12 | 19 |
| Marlinford Rd., Renf. | H10 | 18 |
| Marlow St. G41 | M15 | 51 |
| Marlow Ter. G41 | L15 | 35 |
| *Seaward St.* | | |
| Marmion Pl., Cumb. | D 2 | 70 |
| Marmion Rd., Cumb. | D 2 | 70 |
| Marmion Rd., Pais. | O 3 | 45 |
| Marmion St. G20 | H15 | 21 |
| Marne St. G31 | K19 | 37 |
| Marnock Ter., Pais. | N 7 | 47 |
| Marnock Way, Chr. | E27 | 15 |
| *Braeside Av.* | | |
| Marr St. G51 | K13 | 34 |
| Marshalls La., Pais. | M 6 | 46 |
| Mart St. G1 | L17 | 36 |
| Martha St. G1 | K17 | 36 |
| Martin Cres., Bail. | L26 | 40 |
| Martin St. G40 | M18 | 52 |
| Martlet Dr., John. | O08 | 43 |
| Martyr St. G4 | K18 | 36 |
| Martyrs Pl. G64 | F19 | 23 |
| Marwick St. G31 | K19 | 37 |
| Marwood Av., Chr. & | C25 | 14 |
| Waterside | | |
| Mary St. G4 | J16 | 35 |
| Mary St., John. | M 1 | 44 |
| Mary St., Pais. | N 6 | 46 |
| Maryhill Rd., Bear.& G20 | E13 | 8 |
| Maryland Dr. G52 | L12 | 33 |
| Maryland Gdns. G52 | L12 | 33 |
| Marys La., Renf. | H 8 | 17 |
| Maryston Pl. G33 | J20 | 37 |
| Maryston St. G33 | J20 | 37 |
| Maryview Gdns., Udd. | N26 | 56 |
| *Edinburgh Rd.* | | |
| Maryville Av., Giff. | R14 | 62 |
| Marywood Sq. G41 | N15 | 51 |
| Masonfield Av., Cumb. | C 1 | 70 |
| *Middlerigg Rd.* | | |
| Masterton St. G21 | H17 | 22 |
| Mathieson La. G5 | M17 | 52 |
| *Mathieson St.* | | |
| Mathieson Rd. G73 | N20 | 53 |
| Mathieson St. G5 | M17 | 52 |
| Mathieson St., Pais. | L 7 | 31 |
| Matilda Rd. G41 | M15 | 51 |
| Mauchline St. G5 | M16 | 51 |
| Maukinfauld Ct. G31 | M21 | 54 |
| Maukinfauld Rd. G32 | M21 | 54 |
| Mauldslie St. G40 | M19 | 53 |
| Maule Dr. G11 | J13 | 34 |
| Mause Av., Both. | R28 | 69 |
| Mavis Bank, Bish. | F18 | 22 |
| Mavisbank Rd. G51 | K13 | 34 |
| *Govan Rd.* | | |
| Mavisbank Ter., Pais. | M 6 | 46 |
| Maxton Ter. G72 | Q21 | 66 |
| Maxwell Av. G41 | M15 | 51 |
| Maxwell Av., Bail. | M25 | 56 |
| Maxwell Av., Barr. | Q 7 | 59 |
| Maxwell Av., Bear. | E12 | 7 |
| Maxwell Dr. G41 | M14 | 50 |
| Maxwell Dr., Bail. | L25 | 40 |
| Maxwell Gdns. G41 | M14 | 50 |
| Maxwell Gro. G41 | M14 | 50 |
| Maxwell Oval G41 | M15 | 51 |
| Maxwell Pl. G41 | M16 | 51 |
| Maxwell Rd. G41 | M15 | 51 |
| Maxwell Sq. G41 | M15 | 51 |
| Maxwell St. G18 | L17 | 36 |
| Maxwell St., Bail. | M25 | 56 |
| Maxwell St., Dalm. | D 6 | 4 |
| Maxwell St., Pais. | L 6 | 30 |
| Maxwellton Rd. G78 | M 4 | 45 |
| Maxwellton St., Pais. | M 5 | 46 |
| Maxwelton Rd. G33 | J20 | 37 |
| May Rd., Pais. | O 6 | 46 |
| May Ter. G42 | O16 | 51 |
| *Prospecthill Rd.* | | |
| May Ter., Giff. | Q14 | 62 |
| Maybank La. G42 | N16 | 51 |
| *Victoria Rd.* | | |
| Maybank St. G42 | N16 | 51 |
| Mayberry Cres. G32 | L23 | 39 |
| Mayberry Gdns. G32 | L23 | 39 |
| Maybole St. G53 | P 9 | 60 |
| Mayfield St. G20 | G15 | 21 |
| McAlpine St. G2 | L16 | 35 |
| McArthur St. G43 | O14 | 50 |
| *Pleasance St.* | | |
| McArthur St., Clyde. | G 8 | 17 |
| McAslin Ct. G4 | K17 | 36 |
| McAslin St. G4 | K18 | 36 |
| McCallum Av. G73 | O19 | 53 |
| McClue Rd., Renf. | H 7 | 17 |
| McClue Rd., Renf. | H 7 | 17 |
| McCracken Av., Renf. | J 7 | 31 |
| McCreery St., Clyde. | F 8 | 17 |
| McCulloch St. G41 | M15 | 51 |
| McDonald Av., John. | N09 | 43 |
| McDonald Cres., Clyde. | F 8 | 17 |
| McEwan St. G31 | L20 | 37 |
| McFarlane St. G4 | L18 | 36 |
| McFarlane St., Pais. | K 5 | 30 |
| McGhee St., Clyde. | D 7 | 5 |
| McGown St., Pais. | L 5 | 30 |
| McGregor Av., Renf. | J 7 | 31 |
| *Porterfield Rd.* | | |
| McGregor Rd., Cumb. | C 2 | 70 |
| McGregor St. G51 | L12 | 33 |
| McGregor St., Clyde. | F 8 | 17 |
| McIntoch Ct. G31 | K18 | 36 |
| *McIntoch St.* | | |
| McIntosh St. G31 | K18 | 36 |
| McIntyre Pl., Pais. | N 5 | 46 |
| McIntyre St. G72 | K15 | 35 |
| McIntyre Ter. G72 | P22 | 66 |
| McIver St. G72 | P23 | 67 |
| McKay Cres., John. | N 1 | 44 |
| McKean St., Pais. | L 5 | 30 |
| McKenzie Av., Clyde. | D 7 | 5 |
| McKenzie St., Pais. | L 5 | 30 |
| McKerrel St., Pais. | L 7 | 31 |
| McLaren Av., Renf. | J 8 | 31 |
| *Newmains Rd.* | | |
| McLaurin Cres., John. | N08 | 43 |
| McLean Pl., Pais. | K 5 | 30 |
| McLean Sq. G51 | L14 | 34 |
| McLean St., Clyde. | F 9 | 18 |
| *Wood Quad.* | | |
| McLennan St. G42 | O16 | 51 |
| McNair St. G32 | L22 | 38 |
| McNeil St. G5 | M17 | 52 |
| McNeill Av., Clyde. | E 9 | 6 |
| McPhail St. G40 | M18 | 52 |
| McPhater St. G4 | J16 | 35 |
| *Dunblane St.* | | |
| McPherson Dr., Udd. | Q28 | 69 |
| *Wordsworth Way* | | |

| Name | Ref | Pg |
|---|---|---|
| McPherson St. G1 | L17 | 36 |
| *High St.* | | |
| McTaggart Rd., Cumb. | D 2 | 70 |
| Meadow La., Renf. | G 8 | 17 |
| Meadow Rd. G11 | J13 | 34 |
| Meadow Vw., Cumb. | B 4 | 71 |
| Meadowbank La., Udd. | P26 | 68 |
| Meadowbank La., Udd. | P27 | 69 |
| Meadowburn Av. G66 | C24 | 13 |
| Meadowburn, Bish. | D19 | 11 |
| Meadowhead Av., Chr. | E27 | 15 |
| Meadowpark St. G31 | K19 | 37 |
| Meadowside Av., John. | N 2 | 44 |
| Meadowside St. G11 | J13 | 34 |
| Meadowside St., Renf. | G 8 | 17 |
| Meadowwell St. G32 | L22 | 38 |
| Meadside Av. G78 | M07 | 42 |
| Meadside Rd., Kilb. | M07 | 42 |
| Mears Way, Bish. | E20 | 11 |
| Medlar Rd., Cumb. | C 4 | 71 |
| Medwin St. G72 | P24 | 67 |
| *Mill Rd.* | | |
| Medwyn St. G14 | H11 | 19 |
| Meek Pl. G72 | P22 | 66 |
| Meetinghouse La., Pais. | L 6 | 30 |
| *Moss St.* | | |
| Megan Gate G40 | M18 | 52 |
| *Megan St.* | | |
| Megan St. G40 | M18 | 52 |
| Meikle Av., Renf. | J 8 | 31 |
| Meikle Rd. G53 | O11 | 49 |
| Meiklerig Cres. G53 | N11 | 49 |
| Meikleriggs Dr., Pais. | N 4 | 45 |
| Meiklewood Rd. G51 | L11 | 33 |
| Melbourne Av., Dalm. | C 5 | 4 |
| Melbourne St. G31 | L18 | 36 |
| Meldon Pl. G51 | K12 | 33 |
| Meldrum Gdns. G41 | N14 | 50 |
| Meldrum St., Clyde. | F 9 | 18 |
| Melford Av., Giff. | R14 | 62 |
| Melford Way, Pais. | K 7 | 31 |
| *Knock Way* | | |
| Melfort Av., Clyde. | D 7 | 5 |
| Melfort Av., G41 | M13 | 50 |
| Melfort Gdns., John. | N08 | 43 |
| *Milliken Park Rd.* | | |
| Melness Pl. G51 | K11 | 33 |
| *Mallaig Rd.* | | |
| Melville Ct. G1 | K17 | 36 |
| *Brunswick St.* | | |
| Melville Gdns., Bish. | E19 | 11 |
| Melville St. G41 | M15 | 51 |
| Memel St. G21 | G18 | 22 |
| Memus Av. G52 | M11 | 49 |
| Mennock Dr., Bish. | D19 | 11 |
| Menock Rd. G44 | P16 | 63 |
| Menteith Av., Bish. | E19 | 11 |
| Menteith Dr. G73 | R20 | 65 |
| Menteith Pl. G73 | R20 | 65 |
| Menzies Dr. G21 | G19 | 23 |
| Menzies Pl. G21 | G19 | 23 |
| Menzies Rd. G21 | G19 | 23 |
| Merchant La. G1 | L17 | 36 |
| *Clyde St.* | | |
| Merchants Clo., Pais. | M07 | 42 |
| *Church St.* | | |
| Merchiston Av., Linw. | L 1 | 28 |
| Merchiston St. G32 | K21 | 38 |
| Merkland St. G11 | J13 | 34 |
| *Vine St.* | | |
| Merkland St. G11 | J13 | 34 |
| Merksworth Way, Pais. | K 5 | 30 |
| *Mosslands Rd.* | | |
| Merlewood Av. G71 | Q28 | 69 |
| Merlin Way, Pais. | K 7 | 31 |
| Merrick Gdns. G51 | L13 | 34 |
| Merrick Ter., Udd. | O28 | 57 |
| Merrick Way G73 | Q19 | 65 |
| Merryburn Av., Giff. | P14 | 62 |
| Merrycrest Av., Giff. | Q14 | 62 |
| Merrycroft Av., Giff. | Q14 | 62 |
| Merryland Pl. G51 | K14 | 34 |
| Merryland St. G51 | K13 | 34 |
| Merrylea Cres., Giff. | P14 | 62 |
| Merrylee Park Av., Giff. | Q14 | 62 |
| Merrylee Park La., Giff. | Q14 | 62 |
| Merrylee Park Ms., Giff. | Q14 | 62 |
| Merrylee Rd. G43 | P14 | 62 |
| Merryton Av. G15 | D10 | 6 |
| Merryton Av., Giff. | Q14 | 62 |
| Merryton Pl. G15 | D10 | 6 |
| Merryvale Av., Giff. | Q14 | 62 |
| Merryvale Pl., Giff. | P14 | 62 |
| Merton Dr. G52 | L10 | 32 |
| Meryon Gdns. G32 | N23 | 55 |
| Meryon Rd. G32 | N23 | 55 |
| Methil St. G14 | H11 | 19 |
| Methuen Rd., Renf. | J 7 | 31 |
| Methven Av., Bear. | C13 | 8 |
| Methven St. G31 | M20 | 53 |
| Methven St., Dalm. | D 6 | 4 |
| Metropole La. G1 | L16 | 35 |
| *Howard St.* | | |
| Michillen Rd., Bear. & G23 | C14 | 8 |
| Mid Cotts, Gart. | H26 | 26 |
| Midcroft Av. G44 | P17 | 64 |
| *Westlands* | | |
| Midcroft, Bish. | D18 | 10 |
| Middle Hard St., Clyde. | B 8 | 5 |
| Middlemuir Av., Lenz. | C23 | 13 |
| Middlemuir Rd., Lenz. | C23 | 13 |
| Middlerigg Rd., Cumb. | C 1 | 70 |
| Middlesex St. G41 | L15 | 35 |
| Middleton Cres., Pais. | L 5 | 30 |
| Middleton Rd., Linw. | K 2 | 28 |
| Middleton St. G51 | L14 | 34 |
| Midland St. G1 | L16 | 35 |
| Midlem Dr. G52 | L11 | 33 |
| Midlem Oval G52 | L11 | 33 |
| Midlock St. G51 | L14 | 34 |
| Midlothian Dr. G41 | N14 | 50 |
| Midton Cotts., Chr. | E28 | 15 |
| Midton St. G21 | H18 | 22 |
| Midwharf St. G4 | J17 | 36 |
| Migvie Pl. G20 | G14 | 20 |
| *Wyndford Rd.* | | |
| Milan St. G41 | M16 | 51 |
| Milford St. G33 | K22 | 38 |
| Mill Cres. G40 | M18 | 52 |
| Mill Pl., Linw. | L 1 | 28 |
| Mill Rd. G72 | Q23 | 67 |
| Mill Rd., Barr. | Q 7 | 59 |
| Mill Rd., Both. | R28 | 69 |
| Mill Rd., Clyde. | F 8 | 17 |
| Mill River, Lenz. | D23 | 13 |
| Mill Road Gdns. G40 | L18 | 36 |
| Mill St. G40 | M18 | 52 |
| Mill St. G73 | O19 | 53 |
| Mill St., Pais. | M 6 | 46 |
| Mill Vennel, Renf. | H 9 | 18 |
| *High St.* | | |
| Mill Way, Lenz. | C25 | 14 |
| Millands Av., Blan. | R26 | 68 |
| Millar St., Pais. | L 6 | 30 |
| Millar Ter. G73 | N19 | 53 |
| Millarbank St. G21 | H18 | 22 |
| Millarston Av., Pais. | M 4 | 45 |
| Millarston Dr., Pais. | M 4 | 45 |
| Millbeg Cres. G33 | L24 | 39 |
| Millbeg Pl. G33 | L24 | 39 |
| Millbrae Cres. G13 | F 8 | 17 |
| Millbrae Cres. G42 | O15 | 51 |
| Millbrae Ct. G42 | O15 | 51 |
| *Millbrae Rd.* | | |
| Millbrae Rd. G42 | O15 | 51 |
| Millbrix Av. G14 | G10 | 18 |
| Millburn Av. G73 | P19 | 65 |
| Millburn Av., Clyde. | F 9 | 18 |
| Millburn Av., Renf. | H 9 | 18 |
| Millburn Dr., Renf. | H 8 | 17 |
| Millburn Rd., Renf. | H 8 | 17 |
| Millburn St. G21 | J19 | 37 |
| Millburn Way, Renf. | H 9 | 18 |
| Millcroft Rd. G73 | N18 | 52 |
| Millcroft Rd., Cumb. | C 3 | 71 |
| Miller St. G1 | K17 | 36 |
| Miller St., Bail. | M25 | 56 |
| Miller St., Clyde. | E 7 | 5 |
| Miller St., John. | M 1 | 44 |
| Millerfield Pl. G40 | M19 | 53 |
| Millerfield Rd. G40 | M19 | 53 |
| Millers Pl., Lenz. | D23 | 13 |
| Millersneuk Av., Lenz. | D23 | 13 |
| Millersneuk Cres. G33 | G22 | 24 |
| Millersneuk Dr., Lenz. | D23 | 13 |
| Millerston St. G31 | L19 | 37 |
| Millford Dr., Linw. | L 1 | 28 |
| Millgate Av., Udd. | O27 | 57 |
| Millgate, Udd. | O27 | 57 |
| Millholm Rd. G44 | Q16 | 63 |
| Milliken Dr., Kilb. | N08 | 43 |
| Milliken Park Rd., Kilb. | N07 | 42 |
| Millpond Dr. G40 | L18 | 36 |
| Millport Av. G44 | O17 | 52 |
| Millroad Dr. G40 | L18 | 36 |
| Millroad St. G40 | L18 | 36 |
| Millwood St. G41 | O15 | 51 |
| Milnbank St. G31 | K19 | 37 |
| Milncroft Rd. G33 | J22 | 38 |
| Milner Rd. G13 | G12 | 19 |
| Milngavie Rd., Bear. | D12 | 7 |
| Milnpark St. G41 | L15 | 35 |
| Milovaig St. G23 | E14 | 8 |
| Milrig Rd. G73 | O18 | 52 |
| Milton Av. G72 | P21 | 66 |
| Milton Douglas Rd., Clyde. | C 7 | 5 |
| Milton Dr., Bish. | F18 | 22 |
| Milton Gdns., Udd. | O27 | 57 |
| Milton Mains Rd., Dalm. | C 7 | 5 |
| Milton St. G4 | J17 | 35 |
| Milverton Av., Bear. | C11 | 7 |
| Milverton Rd., Giff. | R13 | 62 |
| Minard Rd. G41 | N15 | 51 |
| Minard Way, Udd. | O28 | 57 |
| *Newton Dr.* | | |
| Minerva St. G3 | K15 | 35 |
| Minerva Way G3 | K15 | 35 |
| Mingarry La. G20 | H14 | 20 |
| *Clouston St.* | | |
| Mingary St. G20 | H15 | 21 |
| Mingulay Cres. G22 | F17 | 22 |
| Mingulay Pl. G22 | F18 | 22 |
| Mingulay St. G22 | F17 | 22 |
| Minmoir Rd. G53 | O 9 | 48 |
| Minstrel Rd. G13 | E11 | 7 |
| Minto Av. G73 | Q20 | 65 |
| Minto Cres. G52 | L12 | 33 |
| Minto St. G52 | L12 | 33 |
| Mireton St. G22 | G16 | 21 |
| Mirrlees Dr. G12 | H14 | 20 |
| Mirrlees La. G12 | H14 | 20 |
| *Redlands Rd.* | | |
| Mitchell Av. G72 | P24 | 67 |
| Mitchell Av., Renf. | J 7 | 31 |
| Mitchell Dr. G73 | P19 | 65 |
| Mitchell La. G1 | K16 | 35 |
| *Buchanan St.* | | |
| Mitchell Rd., Cumb. | C 3 | 71 |
| Mitchell St. G1 | K16 | 35 |
| Mitchell St., Coat. | M28 | 57 |
| Mitchellhill Rd. G42 | R18 | 64 |
| Mitchison Rd., Cumb. | B 3 | 71 |
| Mitre Ct. G14 | H11 | 19 |
| *Mitre Rd.* | | |
| Mitre La. G14 | H12 | 19 |
| Mitre La. W. G14 | H12 | 19 |
| *Mitre Rd.* | | |
| Mitre Rd. G14 | H12 | 19 |
| Moat Av. G13 | F11 | 19 |
| Mochrum Rd. G43 | P15 | 63 |
| Moffat Pl., Blan. | R26 | 68 |
| Moffat St. G5 | M17 | 52 |
| Mogarth Av., Pais. | O 4 | 45 |
| *Amochrie Rd.* | | |
| Moidart Av., Renf. | H 7 | 17 |
| Moidart Cres. G52 | L12 | 33 |
| *Moidart Rd.* | | |
| Moidart Ct., Barr. | P 8 | 59 |
| Moidart Pl. G52 | L12 | 33 |
| *Moidart Rd.* | | |
| Moidart Rd. G52 | L12 | 33 |
| Moir La. G1 | L17 | 36 |
| *Moir St.* | | |
| Moir St. G1 | L17 | 36 |
| Molendinar St. G1 | L17 | 36 |
| Mollinsburn St. G21 | H18 | 22 |
| Monach Rd. G33 | K23 | 39 |
| Monachie Gdns. | E20 | 11 |
| *Muirhead Way* | | |
| Moncrieff Av., Lenz. | C23 | 13 |

Moncrieff Gdns., Lenz. C23 13
Moncrieff Pl. G4 J16 35
*North Woodside Rd.*
Moncrieff St. G4 J16 35
*Balnain St.*
Moncur St. G40 L18 36
Moness Dr. G52 M12 49
Monifieth Av. G52 M11 49
Monikie Gdns., Bish. E20 11
*Muirhead Way*
Monkcastle Dr. G73 P22 66
Monkland Av., Lenz. C23 13
Monkland View Cres., L28 41
Bail.
Monkland Vw, Udd. N28 57
*Lincoln Av.*
Monksbridge Av. G13 E11 7
Monkscroft Av. G11 H13 20
Monkscroft Gdns. G11 H13 20
*Monkscroft Av.*
Monkscroft Gdns. G11 H13 20
*Kirkmichael Av.*
Monkton Dr. G15 E10 6
Monmouth Av. G12 G13 20
Monreith Av., Bear. E11 7
Monreith Rd. E. G44 P16 63
Monreith Rd. G43 P14 62
Monroe Dr., Udd. N27 57
Monroe Pl., Udd. N27 57
Montague La. G12 H13 20
Montague St. G4 J15 35
Montague Ter. G12 H13 20
*Hyndland Rd.*
Montclair Pl., Linw. L1 28
Monteith Dr., Clark. S15 63
Monteith Gdns., Clark. S15 63
Monteith Pl. G40 L18 36
Monteith Pl., Blan. R27 69
Monteith Row G40 L18 36
Monteith Row La. G40 L18 36
*Monteith Pl.*
Montford Av. G44 O17 52
Montgomerie Gdns. G14 H11 19
*Lennox Av.*
Montgomery Av., Pais. K7 31
Montgomery Dr., Giff. R14 62
Montgomery Dr., Kilb. M07 42
*Meadside Av.*
Montgomery La. G42 O16 51
*Somerville Dr.*
Montgomery Rd., Pais. K7 31
Montgomery St. G42 M18 52
*London Rd.*
Montgomery St. G72 P24 67
*Mill Rd.*
Montrave St. G52 M11 49
Montrave St. G73 N19 53
Montreal Ho., Dalm. C5 4
*Perth Cres.*
Montron Dr. G15 E10 6
*Moraine Av.*
Montrose Av. G32 N22 54
Montrose Av. G52 K9 32
Montrose Dr., Bear. B12 7
Montrose Gdns., Blan. R26 68
Montrose Pl., Linw. L1 28
Montrose Rd., Pais. O3 45
Montrose St. G4 K17 36
Montrose St., Clyde. E7 5
Montrose Ter., Bish. F20 23
Monymusk Gdns., Bish. E20 11
Monymusk Pl. G15 C9 6
Moodies Ct. G2 K16 35
*Argyle St.*
Moodiesburn St. G33 J20 37
Moorburn Av., Giff. Q13 62
Moore Dr., Bear. D12 7
Moore St. G31 L19 37
*Gallowgate*
Moorfoot Av., Pais. N4 45
Moorfoot Av. G46 Q13 62
Moorfoot Av., Pais. N5 46
Moorfoot St. G32 L21 38
Moorfoot, Bish. E20 11
Moorhouse Av. G13 G9 18
Moorhouse St., Barr. R8 59
Moorpark Av. G52 L9 32
Moorpark Av., Chr. F26 26
Moorpark Dr. G52 L10 32
Moorpark Pl. G52 L9 32
Moorpark Sq., Renf. J7 31
Morag Av., Blan. R26 68

Moraine Av. G15 E10 6
Moraine Circus G15 E10 6
Moraine Dr. G15 E10 6
Moraine Pl. G15 E10 6
*Moraine Dr.*
Morar Cres., Bish. E18 10
Morar Ct., Cumb. DO 70
Morar Dr. G73 Q19 65
Morar Dr., Bear. D13 8
Morar Dr., Cumb. DO 70
Morar Dr., Linw. L1 28
Morar Dr., Pais. N4 45
Morar Pl., Renf. H7 17
Morar Rd. G52 L12 33
Morar Ter., Udd. O28 57
Moravia Av., Both. Q28 69
Moray Gate, Both. Q27 69
Moray Gdns., Udd. O27 57
Moray Pl. G41 N15 51
Moray Pl., Bish. E20 11
Moray Pl., Linw. L1 28
Mordaunt St. G40 M19 53
Moredun Cres. G32 K23 39
Moredun Dr., Pais. N4 45
Moredun Rd., Pais. N4 45
Moredun St. G32 K23 39
Morefield Rd. G51 K11 33
Morgan Ms. G42 M16 51
Morion Rd. G13 F11 19
Morley St. G42 O16 51
Morna Pl. G41 J12 33
*Victoria Park Dr. S.*
Morningside St. G33 K20 37
Morrin Path G21 H18 22
*Crichton St.*
Morrin Sq. G4 K18 36
*Collins St.*
Morrin St. G21 H18 22
Morris Pl. G40 L18 36
Morrison Quad., Clyde. E9 6
Morrison St. G5 L16 35
Morrison St., Clyde. C6 4
Morrisons Ct. G2 K16 35
*Argyle St.*
Morriston Cres., Renf. J9 32
Morriston St. G72 P22 66
Mortimer St. G20 H15 21
*Hotspur St.*
Morton Gdns. G41 N14 50
Morven Av., Bish. E20 11
Morven Av., Blan. R26 68
Morven Av., Pais. O5 46
Morven Dr., Linw. L1 28
Morven Gdns., Udd. O27 57
Morven Rd. G72 Q21 66
Morven Rd., Bear. C12 7
Morven St. G52 L12 33
Mosesfield St. G21 G18 22
Mosesfield Ter. G21 G18 22
*Balgray Hill Rd.*
Moss Av., Linw. L1 28
Moss Dr., Barr. P7 59
Moss Heights G52 L11 33
Moss Knowe, Cumb. C4 71
Moss Rd. G51 K11 33
Moss Rd., Chr. F26 26
Moss Rd., Cumb. B4 71
Moss Rd., Lenz. C23 13
Moss Sq. G33 J22 38
Moss St., Pais. L6 30
Moss-side Rd. G41 N15 51
Mossbank Dr. G33 H21 24
Mosscastle Rd. G33 J23 39
Mossend La. G33 K23 39
Mossend Rd., Pais. K5 30
*Mosslands Rd.*
Mossend St. G33 K23 39
Mossgiel Av. G73 P19 65
Mossgiel Dr., Clyde. D8 5
Mossgiel Gdns., Udd. O27 57
Mossgiel Pl. G73 P19 65
Mossgiel Rd. G43 P14 62
Mossgiel Rd., Cumb. C3 71
Mossgiel Ter., Blan. R26 68
Mosshead Rd., Bear. B13 8
Mossland Rd. G52 K9 32
Mosslands Rd. G52 J9 32
Mosslands Rd., Pais. K5 30
Mossneuk Dr., Pais. O5 46
Mosspark Av. G52 M12 49
Mosspark Boulevard G52 M12 49

Mosspark Dr. G52 M11 49
Mosspark La. G52 N12 49
*Mosspark Dr.*
Mosspark Oval G52 M12 49
Mosspark Sq. G52 M12 49
Mossvale Cres. G33 J23 39
Mossvale La., Pais. L5 30
Mossvale Path G33 H23 25
Mossvale Rd. G33 H22 24
Mossvale Rd. G33 J24 39
Mossvale Sq. G33 J23 39
Mossvale St., Pais. K5 30
Mossvale Ter., Chr. D28 15
Mossvale Way G33 J23 39
Mossvale Wk. G33 J23 39
Mossview Cotts., Chr. G26 26
Mossview Quad. G52 L11 33
Mossview Rd. G33 G24 25
Mote Hill Rd., Pais. L7 31
Moulin Circus G52 M10 48
Moulin Pl. G52 M10 48
Moulin Rd. G52 M10 48
Moulin Ter. G52 M10 48
Mount Annan Dr. G44 O16 51
Mount Harriet Av. G33 G24 25
Mount Harriet Dr. G33 G23 25
Mount St. G20 H15 21
Mount Stuart St. G41 O15 51
Mount Vernon Av. G32 M24 55
Mountainblue St. G31 L19 37
Mountblow Ho., Dalm. C5 4
*Melbourne Av.*
Mountblow Rd., Dalm. C6 4
Mountgarrie Path G51 K11 33
*Mountgarrie Rd.*
Mountgarrie Rd. G51 K11 33
Mowbray Av., Gart. G27 27
Mowcraigs Ct., Clyde. F8 17
*Yokerburn Ter.*
Moy St. G11 J14 34
*Church St.*
Moyne Rd. G53 N10 48
Muckcroft Rd., Chr. D25 14
Muir Park Ter. G64 F18 22
Muir St. G21 H18 22
Muir St., Bish. E19 11
Muir St., Renf. H8 17
Muir Ter., Pais. K7 31
Muirbank Av. G73 O18 52
Muirbank Gdns. G73 O18 52
*Cathcart Rd.*
Muirbrae Rd. G73 Q19 65
Muirbrae Way G73 Q19 65
Muirburn Av. G44 Q15 63
Muirdrum Av. G52 M11 49
Muirdykes Av. G52 L10 32
Muirdykes Cres., Pais. L4 29
Muirdykes Rd. G52 L10 32
Muirdykes Rd., Pais. L4 29
Muiredge Ct., Udd. P27 69
*Watson St.*
Muiredge Ter., Bail. M25 56
Muirend Av. G44 Q15 63
Muirend Rd. G44 Q15 63
Muirfield Cres. G23 E15 9
Muirfield Rd., Cumb. A3 71
Muirhead Ct., Bail. M26 56
Muirhead Dr., Linw. L1 28
Muirhead Gdns., Bail. M26 56
Muirhead Rd., Udd. & M25 56
Bail.
Muirhead St. G11 J13 34
*Purdon St.*
Muirhead Way, Bish. E20 11
Muirhill Av., G44 Q15 63
Muirhill Cres., G13 F10 18
Muirhouse St. G41 N15 51
*Pollokshaws Rd.*
Muirkirk Dr. G13 F12 19
Muirpark Av., Renf. J8 31
Muirpark Dr., Bish. F19 23
Muirpark St. G11 J13 34
Muirpark Ter., Bish. F18 22
*Crowhill Rd.*
Muirshiel Av. G53 P11 61
Muirshiel Cres. G53 P11 61
Muirside Av. G32 M24 55
Muirside Rd., Bail. M25 56
Muirside St., Bail. M25 56
Muirskeith Cres. G43 P15 63
Muirskeith Pl. G43 P15 63
Muirskeith Rd. G43 P15 63

| Street | Ref | Pg |
|---|---|---|
| Muirton Dr., Bish. | D18 | 10 |
| Muirton Gdns., Bish. | D18 | 10 |
| Muiryfauld Dr. G31 | M21 | 54 |
| Mulben Cres. G53 | O9 | 48 |
| Mulben Pl. G53 | O9 | 48 |
| Mulben Ter. G53 | O9 | 48 |
| Mulberry Rd. G43 | P14 | 62 |
| Mull Av., Pais. | O6 | 46 |
| Mull Av., Renf. | J8 | 31 |
| Mull St. G21 | J19 | 37 |
| Mullardoch St. G23 | E14 | 8 |
| *Rothes Dr.* | | |
| Mungo Pl., Udd. | N28 | 57 |
| *Lincoln Av.* | | |
| Munlochy Rd. G51 | K11 | 33 |
| Munro Ct., Clyde. | C6 | 4 |
| *Gentle Row* | | |
| Munro La. G13 | G12 | 19 |
| Munro Pl. G13 | G12 | 19 |
| Munro Pl., Udd. | N28 | 57 |
| *Kirkwood Rd.* | | |
| Munro Rd. G13 | G12 | 19 |
| Munro Vw., Udd. | N28 | 57 |
| *Kirkwood Rd.* | | |
| Murano St. G20 | H15 | 21 |
| Murdoch St. G21 | G18 | 22 |
| *Lenzie St.* | | |
| Muriel St., Barr. | Q8 | 59 |
| Murray Pl., Barr. | Q8 | 59 |
| Murray Rd., Both. | Q28 | 69 |
| Murray St., Pais. | L5 | 30 |
| Murray St., Renf. | H8 | 17 |
| Murrayfield Dr., Bear. | E12 | 7 |
| Murrayfield St. G32 | K21 | 38 |
| Murrayfield, Bish. | D19 | 11 |
| *Ashfield* | | |
| Murrin Av., Bish. | E20 | 11 |
| Murroes Rd. G51 | K11 | 33 |
| Muslin St. G40 | M18 | 52 |
| Mybster Pl. G51 | K11 | 33 |
| Mybster Rd. G51 | K11 | 33 |
| Myers Cres., Udd. | P28 | 69 |
| Myres Rd. G53 | O11 | 49 |
| Myreside Pl. G32 | L20 | 37 |
| Myreside St. G32 | L20 | 37 |
| Myrie Gdns., Bish. | E19 | 11 |
| Myroch Pl. G34 | J26 | 40 |
| Myrtle Av., Lenz. | C23 | 13 |
| Myrtle Hill La. G42 | O17 | 52 |
| Myrtle Hill Vw. G42 | O17 | 52 |
| Myrtle Pk. G42 | N17 | 52 |
| Myrtle Pl. G42 | O17 | 52 |
| Myrtle Rd., Dalm. | D5 | 4 |
| Myrtle Rd., Udd. | O28 | 57 |
| Myrtle Sq., Bish. | F19 | 23 |
| Myrtle St., Blan. | R26 | 68 |
| Myrtle Wk. G72 | P21 | 66 |
| Naburn St. G5 | M17 | 52 |
| Nairn Av., Blan. | R26 | 68 |
| Nairn Gdns., Bear. | D11 | 7 |
| Nairn Pl., Dalm. | D6 | 4 |
| *Dumbarton Rd.* | | |
| Nairn St. G3 | J14 | 34 |
| Nairn St., Dalm. | D6 | 4 |
| Nairnside Rd. G21 | F20 | 23 |
| Naismith St. G32 | O23 | 55 |
| Nansen St. G20 | H16 | 21 |
| Napier Ct., Old.K. | C5 | 4 |
| *Freelands Rd.* | | |
| Napier Dr. G51 | K13 | 34 |
| Napier Gdns., Linw. | L2 | 28 |
| Napier Gdns., Linw. | L2 | 28 |
| Napier Pl. G51 | K13 | 34 |
| Napier Pl., Old.K. | C5 | 4 |
| *Old Dalnottar Rd.* | | |
| Napier Rd. G52 | J9 | 32 |
| Napier Rd. G63 | K13 | 34 |
| Napier St. G51 | K14 | 34 |
| Napier St., Clyde. | F8 | 17 |
| Napier St., Linw. | L2 | 28 |
| Napier Ter. G51 | K13 | 34 |
| Napiershall La. G20 | J15 | 35 |
| *Napiershall St.* | | |
| Napiershall Pl. G20 | J15 | 35 |
| *Napiershall St.* | | |
| Napiershall St. G20 | J15 | 35 |
| Naseby Av. G11 | H12 | 19 |
| Nasmyth Rd. G52 | K10 | 32 |
| Nasmyth Rd. N. G52 | K10 | 32 |
| Nasmyth Rd. S. G52 | K10 | 32 |
| Navar Pl., Pais. | N7 | 47 |
| Naver St. G33 | J21 | 38 |
| Neilsland Oval G53 | O11 | 49 |
| Neilsland Sq. G53 | N11 | 49 |
| Neilston Av. G53 | P11 | 61 |
| Neilston Rd., Barr. | R7 | 59 |
| Neilston Rd., Pais. | M6 | 46 |
| Neilvaig Dr. G73 | Q20 | 65 |
| Nelson Mandela Pl. G2 | K17 | 36 |
| Nelson Pl., Bail. | M25 | 56 |
| Nelson St. G5 | L16 | 35 |
| Nelson St., Bail. | M25 | 56 |
| Nelson Ter. G12 | H15 | 21 |
| *Glasgow St.* | | |
| Neptune St. G51 | K13 | 34 |
| Nerston Av. G53 | O11 | 49 |
| Ness Av., John. | O08 | 43 |
| Ness Dr., Blan. | R27 | 69 |
| Ness Gdns., Bish. | E19 | 11 |
| Ness Rd., Renf. | H7 | 17 |
| Ness St. G33 | J21 | 38 |
| Netham St. G51 | K13 | 34 |
| Nether Auldhouse Rd. G43 | P13 | 62 |
| Netherburn Av. G44 | R15 | 63 |
| Netherby Dr. G41 | M14 | 50 |
| Nethercairn Rd. G43 | Q14 | 62 |
| Nethercliffe Av. G44 | R15 | 63 |
| Nethercommon Harbour, Pais. | K6 | 30 |
| Nethercraig Cotts., Pais. | P5 | 58 |
| *Glenfield Rd.* | | |
| Nethercraigs Dr., Pais. | O5 | 46 |
| Nethercraigs Rd., Pais. | O4 | 45 |
| Netherdale Dr., Pais. | M9 | 48 |
| Netherfield St. G31 | L20 | 37 |
| Netherhill Av. G44 | R15 | 63 |
| Netherhill Cres., Pais. | L7 | 31 |
| Netherhill Rd., Chr. | E27 | 15 |
| Netherhill Rd., Pais. | L6 | 30 |
| Netherhouse Av., Lenz. | D24 | 13 |
| Netherhouse Pl., Bail. | K27 | 41 |
| *Netherhouse Rd.* | | |
| Netherhouse Rd., Bail. | K26 | 40 |
| Netherlee Rd., G44 | Q15 | 63 |
| Netherpark Av. G44 | R15 | 63 |
| Netherplace Cres. G53 | O10 | 48 |
| Netherplace Rd. G53 | O10 | 48 |
| Netherton Ct. G42 | R18 | 64 |
| Netherton Dr., Barr. | R9 | 60 |
| Netherton Rd. G13 | F12 | 19 |
| Netherton St. G13 | F12 | 19 |
| *Crow Rd.* | | |
| Nethervale Av. G44 | R15 | 63 |
| Netherview Rd. G44 | R16 | 63 |
| Netherway G44 | R15 | 63 |
| Nethy Way, Renf. | J9 | 32 |
| *Teith Av.* | | |
| Neuk Way G32 | O23 | 55 |
| Nevis Rd. G43 | P13 | 62 |
| Nevis Rd., Bear. | B10 | 6 |
| Nevis Rd., Renf. | J7 | 31 |
| New City Rd. G4 | J16 | 35 |
| New Edinburgh Rd., Udd. | O27 | 57 |
| New Inchinnan Rd., Pais. | K6 | 30 |
| New Kirk Pl., Bear. | C12 | 7 |
| *New Kirk Rd.* | | |
| New Kirk Rd., Bear. | C12 | 7 |
| New Rd. G72 | Q24 | 67 |
| New Sneddon St., Pais. | L6 | 30 |
| New St., Clyde. | C7 | 5 |
| New St., Kilb. | M07 | 42 |
| New St., Pais. | M6 | 46 |
| New Wynd G1 | L17 | 36 |
| Newark Dr. G41 | M14 | 50 |
| Newark Dr., Pais. | O5 | 46 |
| Newbattle Ct. G32 | N22 | 54 |
| Newbattle Gdns. G32 | N22 | 54 |
| Newbattle Pl. G32 | N22 | 54 |
| Newbattle Rd. G32 | N22 | 54 |
| Newbold Av. G21 | F18 | 22 |
| Newburgh St. G43 | O14 | 50 |
| Newcastleton Dr. | E15 | 9 |
| Newcroft Dr. G44 | P17 | 64 |
| Newfield Pl. G73 | O18 | 52 |
| Newfield Pl., Thorn. | R12 | 61 |
| *Rouken Glen Rd.* | | |
| Newfield Sq. G53 | P10 | 60 |
| Newhall St. G40 | M18 | 52 |
| Newhaven Rd. G33 | K22 | 38 |
| Newhaven St. G32 | K22 | 38 |
| Newhills Rd. G33 | K24 | 39 |
| Newington St. G32 | L21 | 38 |
| Newlands Gdns., John. | N2 | 44 |
| *Renshaw Rd.* | | |
| Newlands Rd. G43 | P15 | 63 |
| Newlands Rd., Udd. | O27 | 57 |
| Newlandsfield Rd. G43 | O14 | 50 |
| Newluce Dr. G32 | M23 | 55 |
| Newmains Rd., Renf. | J7 | 31 |
| Newmill Rd. G21 | G20 | 23 |
| Newnham Rd., Pais. | M9 | 48 |
| Newshot Ct., Clyde. | F8 | 17 |
| *Clydeholm Ter.* | | |
| Newshot Dr., Renf. | E5 | 4 |
| Newton Av. G72 | P23 | 67 |
| Newton Av., Barr. | R8 | 59 |
| Newton Av., John. | M3 | 45 |
| Newton Av., Pais. | K7 | 31 |
| Newton Brae G72 | P24 | 67 |
| Newton Dr., John. | M3 | 45 |
| Newton Dr., Udd. | O28 | 57 |
| Newton Farm Rd. G72 | O24 | 55 |
| Newton Pl. G3 | J15 | 35 |
| Newton Rd., Lenz. | D24 | 13 |
| Newton St., Pais. | M5 | 46 |
| Newton Station Rd. G72 | P24 | 67 |
| Newton Ter. G3 | K15 | 35 |
| *Sauchiehall St.* | | |
| Newton Terrace La. G3 | J15 | 35 |
| *Elderslie St.* | | |
| Newtongrange Av. G32 | N22 | 54 |
| Newtongrange Gdns. G32 | N22 | 54 |
| Newtyle Pl., Bish. | E20 | 11 |
| Newtyle Rd., Pais. | M8 | 47 |
| Nicholas St. G1 | K17 | 36 |
| Nicholson La. G5 | L16 | 35 |
| *Nicholson St.* | | |
| Nicholson St. G5 | L16 | 35 |
| Nicholson St. G5 | L16 | 35 |
| Niddrie Rd. G42 | N15 | 51 |
| Niddrie Sq. G42 | N15 | 51 |
| Niddry St., Pais. | L6 | 30 |
| Nigel Gdns. G41 | N14 | 50 |
| Nigg Pl. G34 | K25 | 40 |
| Nightingale Pl., John. | O08 | 43 |
| Nimmo Dr. G51 | K12 | 33 |
| Nisbet St. G31 | L20 | 37 |
| Nith Av., Pais. | N3 | 45 |
| Nith Dr., Renf. | J9 | 32 |
| Nith Pl., John. | O08 | 43 |
| Nith St. G33 | J20 | 37 |
| Nithsdale Cres., Bear. | C11 | 7 |
| Nithsdale Dr. G41 | N15 | 51 |
| Nithsdale Pl. G41 | M15 | 51 |
| *Shields Rd.* | | |
| Nithsdale Rd. G41 | M13 | 50 |
| Nithsdale Rd. G41 | N15 | 51 |
| Nitshill Rd. G53 | P9 | 60 |
| Niven St. G20 | G14 | 20 |
| Noldrum Av. G32 | O23 | 55 |
| Noldrum Gdns. G32 | O23 | 55 |
| Norbreck Dr., Giff. | Q14 | 62 |
| Norby Rd. G11 | H12 | 19 |
| Norfield Dr. G44 | O16 | 51 |
| Norfolk Cres., Bish. | D18 | 10 |
| Norfolk Ct. G5 | L16 | 35 |
| Norfolk La. G5 | L16 | 35 |
| *Norfolk St.* | | |
| Norfolk St. G5 | L16 | 35 |
| Norham St. G41 | N15 | 51 |
| Norman St. G40 | M18 | 52 |
| Norse La. N. G14 | H11 | 19 |
| *Ormiston Av.* | | |
| Norse La. S. G14 | H11 | 19 |
| *Verona Av.* | | |
| Norse La. S. G14 | H11 | 19 |
| *Duncan Av.* | | |
| Norse Rd. G14 | H11 | 19 |
| North Av. G72 | P21 | 66 |
| North Av., Clyde. | E7 | 5 |
| North Bank Pl., Clyde. | F8 | 17 |
| *North Bank St.* | | |
| North Bank St., Clyde. | F8 | 17 |
| North Brae Pl., G13 | F10 | 18 |
| North British Rd., Udd. | P27 | 69 |
| North Canalbank St. G4 | J17 | 36 |
| North Carbrain Rd., Cumb. | D2 | 70 |
| North Claremont St. G3 | J15 | 35 |
| North Corsebar Av., Pais. | N5 | 46 |

| Name | Ref | Page |
|---|---|---|
| North Court La. G1 | K17 | 36 |
| *Buchanan St.* | | |
| North Croft St., Pais. | L 6 | 30 |
| North Deanpark Av., | Q28 | 69 |
| Udd. | | |
| *Fallside Rd.* | | |
| North Douglas St., | F 8 | 17 |
| Clyde. | | |
| North Dr. G1 | L17 | 36 |
| North Dr., Linw. | L 1 | 28 |
| North Elgin St., Clyde. | F 8 | 17 |
| North Erskine Pk., Bear. | C11 | 7 |
| North Gardner St. G11 | H13 | 20 |
| North Grange Rd., Bear. | C12 | 7 |
| North Greenhill Rd., | K 5 | 30 |
| Pais. | | |
| North Hanover Pl. G4 | J17 | 36 |
| North Hanover St. G1 | K17 | 36 |
| North Iverton Park Rd., | M 1 | 44 |
| John. | | |
| North Lodge Rd., Renf. | H 8 | 17 |
| North Moraine La. G15 | E11 | 7 |
| *Moraine Av.* | | |
| North Park Av., Thorn. | Q12 | 61 |
| North Park St. G20 | H15 | 21 |
| North Pl. G3 | K15 | 35 |
| *North St.* | | |
| North Portland St. G1 | K17 | 36 |
| North Queen St. G2 | K17 | 36 |
| *George Sq.* | | |
| North Rd., John. | N09 | 43 |
| North St. G3 | K15 | 35 |
| North St., Clyde. | E 7 | 5 |
| *Dumbarton Rd.* | | |
| North St., Pais | L 6 | 30 |
| North Vw., Bear. | E11 | 7 |
| North Wallace St. G4 | J17 | 36 |
| North Way, Blan. | R26 | 68 |
| North Woodside Rd. | H15 | 21 |
| G20 | | |
| Northampton Dr. G12 | G13 | 20 |
| Northampton La. G12 | G13 | 20 |
| *Northampton Dr.* | | |
| Northbank Av. G72 | P23 | 67 |
| Northbank St. G72 | P23 | 67 |
| Northcroft Rd. G21 | H18 | 22 |
| Northcroft Rd., Chr. | E27 | 15 |
| Northgate Quad. G21 | F20 | 23 |
| Northgate Rd. G21 | F20 | 23 |
| Northinch St. G14 | J11 | 33 |
| Northland Dr. G14 | G11 | 19 |
| Northland La. G14 | H11 | 19 |
| *Northland Dr.* | | |
| Northmuir Rd. G15 | D10 | 6 |
| Northpark Ter. G12 | H15 | 21 |
| *Hamilton Dr.* | | |
| Northumberland St. | H15 | 21 |
| G20 | | |
| Norval St. G11 | J13 | 34 |
| Norwich Dr. G12 | G13 | 20 |
| Norwood Dr., Giff. | R13 | 62 |
| Norwood Ter. G12 | J15 | 35 |
| *Southpark Av.* | | |
| Norwood, Bear. | D12 | 7 |
| Nottingham Av. G12 | G13 | 20 |
| Nottingham La. G12 | G13 | 20 |
| *Northampton Dr.* | | |
| Novar Dr. G12 | H13 | 20 |
| Novar Gdns., Bish. | E18 | 10 |
| Numrow Ct., Clyde. | C 6 | 4 |
| Nuneaton St. G40 | M19 | 53 |
| Nurseries Rd., Bail. | L24 | 39 |
| Nursery La. G41 | N15 | 51 |
| Nursery St. G41 | N15 | 51 |
| *Pollokshaws Rd.* | | |
| Nursery Street La. G41 | N15 | 51 |
| *Nithsdale Dr.* | | |
| | | |
| Oak Cres., Bail. | M25 | 56 |
| Oak Dr. G72 | Q23 | 67 |
| Oak Dr., Lenz. | C22 | 12 |
| Oak Pl., Bish. | E19 | 11 |
| Oak Rd., Dalm. | C 6 | 4 |
| Oak Rd., Pais. | N 7 | 47 |
| Oakbank Dr., Barr. | S 8 | 59 |
| Oakbank La. G20 | H16 | 21 |
| Oakbank Ter. G20 | H16 | 21 |
| Oakdene Av., Udd. | O28 | 57 |
| Oakfield Av. G12 | J15 | 35 |
| Oakfield Ter. G12 | J15 | 35 |
| *Oakfield Av.* | | |
| Oakhill Av., Bail. | M24 | 55 |
| Oakley Dr. G44 | Q15 | 63 |
| Oakley Ter. G31 | K18 | 36 |
| Oaks, The, John. | N08 | 43 |
| Oakshaw School Brae, | L 5 | 30 |
| Pais. | | |
| Oakshaw St., Pais. | L 5 | 30 |
| Oakshawhead, Pais. | L 5 | 30 |
| Oakwood Av., Pais. | N 4 | 45 |
| Oatfield St. G21 | H19 | 23 |
| Oban Ct. G22 | H15 | 21 |
| Oban Dr. G20 | H15 | 21 |
| Observatory La. G12 | H14 | 20 |
| *Observatory Rd.* | | |
| Observatory Rd. G12 | H14 | 20 |
| Ochil Dr., Barr. | R 8 | 59 |
| Ochil Dr., Pais. | O 6 | 46 |
| Ochil Pl. G32 | M22 | 54 |
| Ochil Rd., Bish. | E20 | 11 |
| Ochil Rd., Renf. | J 7 | 31 |
| Ochil St. G32 | M22 | 54 |
| OchiltreeAv. G13 | F12 | 19 |
| Ogilvie Pl. G31 | M21 | 54 |
| Ogilvie St. G31 | M20 | 53 |
| Old Bothwell Rd., Both. | R28 | 69 |
| Old Castle Rd. G44 | P16 | 63 |
| Old Dalmarnock Rd. | M18 | 52 |
| G40 | | |
| Old Dalnottar Rd., | C 5 | 4 |
| Old K. | | |
| Old Dumbarton Rd. G3 | J14 | 34 |
| Old Edinburgh Rd., Udd. | N27 | 57 |
| Old Gartcosh Rd., Gart. | G27 | 27 |
| Old Glasgow Rd., Udd. | O26 | 56 |
| Old Govan Rd., Renf. | H 9 | 18 |
| Old Greenock Rd., Renf. | F 5 | 16 |
| Old Manse Rd. G32 | L23 | 39 |
| Old Mill Rd. G72 | P23 | 67 |
| Old Mill Rd., Both. | R28 | 69 |
| Old Mill Rd., Clyde. | C 7 | 5 |
| Old Mill Rd., Udd. | P27 | 69 |
| Old Rd., John. | M 2 | 44 |
| Old Renfrew Rd., Renf. | J10 | 32 |
| Old Roundknowe Rd., | N26 | 56 |
| Udd. | | |
| Old Rutherglen Rd. G5 | M17 | 52 |
| Old Shettleston Rd. G32 | L21 | 38 |
| Old Sneddon St., Pais. | L 6 | 30 |
| Old St., Clyde. | C 6 | 4 |
| Old Wood Rd., Bail. | M25 | 56 |
| Old Wynd G1 | L17 | 36 |
| Oldhall Rd., Pais. | L 8 | 31 |
| Olifard Av., Udd. | Q28 | 69 |
| Oliphant Cres., Pais. | O 3 | 45 |
| Olive St. G33 | H20 | 23 |
| Olrig Ter. G41 | M15 | 51 |
| *Shields Rd.* | | |
| Olympia St. G40 | L18 | 36 |
| Onslow Dr. G31 | K19 | 37 |
| Onslow Rd., Clyde. | E 8 | 5 |
| Onslow Sq. G31 | K19 | 37 |
| *Onslow Dr.* | | |
| Oran Gate G20 | H15 | 21 |
| Oran Gdns. G20 | G15 | 21 |
| Oran Pl. G20 | G15 | 21 |
| Oran St. G20 | G15 | 21 |
| Oransay Cres., Bear. | D13 | 8 |
| Orcades Dr. G44 | Q16 | 63 |
| Orchard Av. G17 | R28 | 69 |
| Orchard Ct. G32 | O22 | 54 |
| Orchard Ct., Thorn. | Q13 | 62 |
| Orchard Dr. G73 | O18 | 52 |
| Orchard Dr., Giff. | Q13 | 62 |
| Orchard Gro., Giff. | Q13 | 62 |
| Orchard Park Av., | Q13 | 62 |
| Thorn. & Giff. | | |
| Orchard Pk., Giff. | Q14 | 62 |
| Orchard Pl., Lenz. | B24 | 13 |
| Orchard Sq., Pais. | M 6 | 46 |
| Orchard St., Pais. | M 6 | 46 |
| Orchard St., Renf. | H 8 | 17 |
| Orchardfield, Lenz. | D23 | 13 |
| Orchy Cres., Bear. | E11 | 7 |
| Orchy Cres., Pais. | N 3 | 45 |
| Orchy Dr., Clyde. | C 8 | 5 |
| Orchy Dr., Clark. | R15 | 63 |
| Orchy Gdns., Clark. | R15 | 63 |
| Orchy St. G44 | P16 | 63 |
| Oregon Pl. G5 | M17 | 52 |
| Orkney Pl. G51 | K13 | 34 |
| *Orkney St.* | | |
| Orkney St. G51 | K13 | 34 |
| Orleans Av. G14 | H12 | 19 |
| Orleans La. G14 | H12 | 19 |
| Ormiston Av. G14 | H11 | 19 |
| Ormiston La. G14 | H11 | 19 |
| *Ormiston Av.* | | |
| Ormiston La. S. G14 | H11 | 19 |
| *Ormiston Av.* | | |
| Ormonde Av. G44 | Q15 | 63 |
| Ormonde Cres. G44 | Q15 | 63 |
| Ormonde Ct. G44 | Q15 | 63 |
| Ormonde Dr. G44 | Q15 | 63 |
| Ornsay St. G22 | F17 | 22 |
| Orr Pl. G40 | L18 | 36 |
| Orr Sq. , Pais. | L 6 | 30 |
| Orr St. G40 | L18 | 36 |
| Orr St., Pais. | L 6 | 30 |
| Orr St., Pais. | M 6 | 46 |
| Orton St. G51 | L13 | 34 |
| Orwell St. G21 | H18 | 22 |
| Osborn Ter. G51 | L13 | 34 |
| *Copland St.* | | |
| Osborne St. G1 | L17 | 36 |
| Osborne St., Clyde. | D 7 | 5 |
| Osborne Vill. G44 | P16 | 63 |
| *Holmhead Rd.* | | |
| Osprey Dr., Udd. | O28 | 57 |
| Ossian Av., Pais. | L 9 | 32 |
| *Auchmannoch Av.* | | |
| Ossian Rd. G43 | P15 | 63 |
| Oswald La. G1 | L16 | 35 |
| *Oswald St.* | | |
| Oswald St. G1 | L16 | 35 |
| Otago La. G12 | J15 | 35 |
| *Otago St.* | | |
| Otago La. N. G12 | J15 | 35 |
| *Otago St.* | | |
| Otago St. G12 | J15 | 35 |
| Ottawa Cres., Dalm. | D 5 | 4 |
| Otter La. G11 | J13 | 34 |
| *Castlebank St.* | | |
| Otterburn Dr., Giff. | R14 | 62 |
| Otterswick Pl. G33 | J23 | 39 |
| Oulnain St. G72 | P24 | 67 |
| Oval, The, Clark. | R15 | 63 |
| Overbrae Pl. G15 | C 9 | 6 |
| Overdale Av. G42 | O15 | 51 |
| Overdale Gdns. G42 | O15 | 51 |
| Overdale St. G42 | O15 | 51 |
| Overdale Vills. G42 | O15 | 51 |
| *Overdale St.* | | |
| Overlea Av. G73 | P20 | 65 |
| Overnewton Pl. G3 | K14 | 34 |
| *Kelvinhaugh St.* | | |
| Overnewton Sq. G3 | K14 | 34 |
| Overnewton St. G3 | J14 | 34 |
| Overton Cres., John. | M 1 | 44 |
| Overton Rd. G72 | Q23 | 67 |
| Overton Rd., John. | N 1 | 44 |
| Overton St. G72 | Q23 | 67 |
| Overtoun Ct., Dalm. | D 6 | 4 |
| *Dunswin Av.* | | |
| Overtoun Dr. G73 | O19 | 53 |
| Overtoun Dr., Dalm. | D 6 | 4 |
| Overtoun Rd., | D 6 | 4 |
| Dalm. & Clyde. | | |
| Overtown Av. G53 | P10 | 60 |
| Overtown St. G31 | L19 | 37 |
| Overwood Dr. G44 | P17 | 64 |
| Oxford Dr., Linw. | L 1 | 28 |
| Oxford La. G5 | L16 | 35 |
| Oxford Rd., Renf. | H 8 | 17 |
| Oxford St. G5 | L16 | 35 |
| Oxgang Pl., Lenz. | B24 | 13 |
| Oxton Dr. G52 | L10 | 32 |
| | | |
| Paisley Ct., Barr. | Q 7 | 59 |
| *Paisley Rd.* | | |
| Paisley Rd. G5 | L15 | 35 |
| Paisley Rd. W. G5 | M10 | 48 |
| Paisley Rd., Barr. | Q 7 | 59 |
| Paisley Rd., Renf. | J 7 | 31 |
| Palace St. G31 | M20 | 53 |
| Paladin Av. G13 | F11 | 19 |
| Palermo St. G21 | H18 | 22 |
| Palmer Av. G13 | E11 | 7 |
| Palmerston Pl. G3 | K14 | 34 |
| *Kelvinhaugh St.* | | |
| Palmerston Pl., John. | O08 | 43 |
| Pandora Way, Udd. | O28 | 57 |
| *Hillcrest Rd.* | | |
| Panmure St. G20 | H16 | 21 |
| Park Av. G3 | J15 | 35 |
| Park Av., Bar. | R 7 | 59 |

| Name | Grid | Pg | Name | Grid | Pg | Name | Grid | Pg |
|---|---|---|---|---|---|---|---|---|
| Park Av., Bish. | D19 | 11 | Partick Bridge St. G11 | J14 | 34 | Pilrig St. G32 | K21 | 38 |
| Park Av., John. | N 2 | 44 | Partickhill Av. G11 | H13 | 20 | Pilton Rd. G15 | D10 | 6 |
| Park Av., Pais. | N 5 | 46 | Partickhill Ct. G11 | H13 | 20 | Pine Cres., John. | N 1 | 44 |
| Park Bank, Renf. | E 4 | 4 | *Partickhill Av.* | | | Pine Gro., Udd. | O28 | 57 |
| Park Brae, Renf. | F 5 | 16 | Partickhill Rd. G11 | H13 | 20 | *Douglas Cres.* | | |
| *Park Dr.* | | | Paterson St. G5 | L16 | 35 | Pine Pl. G5 | M17 | 52 |
| Park Burn Av., Lenz. | B23 | 13 | Pathead Gdns. G33 | G21 | 24 | Pine Pl., Cumb. | B 5 | 71 |
| Park Circus C3 | J15 | 35 | Patna St. G40 | M19 | 53 | Pine Rd., Cumb. | B 5 | 71 |
| Park Circus La. G3 | J15 | 35 | Paton St. G31 | K19 | 37 | Pine Rd., Dalm. | D 5 | 4 |
| *Lynedoch Pl.* | | | Patrick St., Pais. | M 6 | 46 | Pine St., Pais. | N 7 | 47 |
| Park Circus Pl. G3 | J15 | 35 | Patterton Dr., Barr. | R 8 | 59 | Pinelands, Bish. | D19 | 11 |
| Park Cres., Bear. | C10 | 6 | Pattison St., Dalm. | D 6 | 4 | Pinewood Av., Lenz. | C22 | 12 |
| Park Cres., Bish. | D19 | 11 | Payne St. G4 | J17 | 36 | Pinewood Ct., Lenz. | C22 | 12 |
| Park Cres., Renf. | F 5 | 16 | Pearce La. G51 | K13 | 34 | Pinewood Pl., Kirk. | C22 | 12 |
| Park Ct., Bish. | D19 | 11 | Pearson Dr., Renf. | J 8 | 31 | Pinewood Pl., Lenz. | C22 | 12 |
| Park Ct., Dalm. | D 6 | 4 | Pearson Pl., Linw. | L 1 | 28 | Pinkerton Av. G73 | O18 | 52 |
| *Little Holm* | | | Peat Pl. G53 | P10 | 60 | Pinkston Dr. G21 | J17 | 36 |
| Park Ct., Giff. | Q13 | 62 | Peat Rd. G53 | P10 | 60 | Pinkston Rd. G21 | H17 | 22 |
| *Belmont Dr.* | | | Peathill Av., Chr. | F25 | 26 | Pinmore Path G53 | P 9 | 60 |
| Park Ct., Giff. | R13 | 62 | Peathill St. G21 | H17 | 22 | Pinmore Pl. G53 | P 9 | 60 |
| Park Dr. G3 | J15 | 35 | Peebles Dr. G73 | O20 | 53 | Pinmore St. G53 | P 9 | 60 |
| Park Dr. G73 | O19 | 53 | Peebles Dr. G73 | P20 | 65 | Pinwherry Pl., Udd. | Q28 | 69 |
| Park Dr., Renf. | F 5 | 16 | Peel Glen Rd., | | | *Hume Dr.* | | |
| Park Gardens La. G3 | J15 | 35 | Bear. & G15 | C10 | 6 | Pirn St. G40 | M18 | 52 |
| *Clifton St.* | | | Peel La. G11 | J13 | 34 | Pitcairn St. G31 | M21 | 54 |
| Park Gate G3 | J15 | 35 | *Burgh Hall St.* | | | Pitcaple Dr. G43 | P13 | 62 |
| Park Gdns. G3 | J15 | 35 | Peel Pl., Both. | Q28 | 69 | Pitlochry Dr. G52 | M10 | 48 |
| Park Gdns., Kilb. | M07 | 42 | Peel St. G11 | J13 | 34 | Pitmedden Rd., Bish. | E20 | 11 |
| Park Gro., Renf. | F 5 | 16 | Peel Vw., Clyde. | D 8 | 5 | Pitmilly Rd. G15 | D11 | 7 |
| Park La. G40 | L18 | 36 | *Kirkoswald Dr.* | | | Pitreavie Pl. G33 | J23 | 39 |
| Park La., Blan. | S26 | 69 | Peirshill St. G32 | K21 | 38 | Pitt St. G2 | K16 | 35 |
| Park La., Pais. | L 6 | 30 | Pembroke St. G3 | K15 | 35 | Pladda Rd., Renf. | J 8 | 31 |
| *Netherhill Rd.* | | | Pencaitland Dr. G32 | M22 | 54 | Plane Tree Pl., John. | N 1 | 44 |
| Park Pl. G20 | F14 | 20 | *Falside Rd.* | | | Planetree Rd., Dalm. | C 7 | 5 |
| *Fingal St.* | | | Pencaitland Gro. G32 | M22 | 54 | Planetrees Av., Pais. | N 6 | 46 |
| Park Quad. G3 | J15 | 35 | *Falside Rd.* | | | *Carriagehill Dr.* | | |
| Park Rd. G4 | J15 | 35 | Pendeen Cres. G33 | L24 | 39 | Plant St. G31 | L20 | 37 |
| Park Rd., Bail. | L27 | 41 | Pendeen Pl. G33 | L24 | 39 | Plantation Pl. G51 | L15 | 35 |
| Park Rd., Bish. | E19 | 11 | Pendeen Rd. G33 | L24 | 39 | *Govan Rd.* | | |
| Park Rd., Chr. | F26 | 26 | Pendicle Cres., Bear. | D11 | 7 | Plantation Sq. G51 | L15 | 35 |
| Park Rd., Dalm. | D 6 | 4 | Pendicle Rd., Bear. | D11 | 7 | Playfair St. G40 | M19 | 53 |
| Park Rd., Giff. | R14 | 62 | Penicuik St. G32 | L20 | 37 | Pleaknowe Cres., Chr. | E27 | 15 |
| Park Rd., John. | N09 | 43 | Penilee Rd., Pais. | L 9 | 32 | Pleamuir Pl., Cumb. | C 1 | 70 |
| Park Rd., Pais. | N 5 | 46 | Penilee Ter. G52 | K 9 | 32 | Plean St. G14 | G10 | 18 |
| Park Rd., Renf. | F 5 | 16 | Peninver Dr. G51 | K12 | 33 | Pleasance La. G43 | O14 | 50 |
| Park Ridge, Renf. | F 5 | 16 | Penman Av. G73 | O18 | 52 | Pleasance St. G43 | O14 | 50 |
| *Park Dr.* | | | Pennan Pl. G14 | G10 | 18 | Plover Pl., John. | O08 | 43 |
| Park St. S. G3 | J15 | 35 | Penneld Rd. G52 | L 9 | 32 | Pollock Dr., Bish. | E18 | 10 |
| Park Ter. G3 | J15 | 35 | Penrith Av., Giff. | R14 | 62 | Pollock Rd., Bear. | D13 | 8 |
| Park Ter. G42 | N15 | 51 | Penrith Dr. G12 | G13 | 20 | Pollokshaws Rd. | O13 | 50 |
| *Queens Dr.* | | | Penryn Gdns. G32 | M23 | 55 | Polmadie Av. G42 | N17 | 52 |
| Park Ter., Giff. | R14 | 62 | Penston Rd. G33 | K23 | 39 | Polmadie Rd. G5 | N17 | 52 |
| Park Top, Renf. | F 5 | 16 | Pentland Cres., Pais. | O 5 | 46 | Polmadie St. G42 | N17 | 52 |
| Park Way, Cumb. | B 3 | 71 | Pentland Ct., Barr. | R 7 | 59 | Polnoon Av. G13 | G10 | 18 |
| Park Winding, Renf. | F 5 | 16 | Pentland Dr., Barr. | R 8 | 59 | Polson Dr., John. | N09 | 43 |
| Park Wood, Renf. | E 4 | 4 | Pentland Dr., Bish. | E20 | 11 | Polwarth Gdns. G12 | H13 | 20 |
| Parkburn Av., Lenz. | C23 | 13 | Pentland Dr., Linw. | L 1 | 28 | *Novar Dr.* | | |
| Parker St. G14 | J12 | 33 | Pentland Dr., Renf. | K 7 | 31 | Polwarth La. G12 | H13 | 20 |
| Parkglade, Renf. | F 4 | 16 | Pentland Pl. G40 | M18 | 52 | *Novar Dr.* | | |
| Parkgrove Av., Giff. | Q14 | 62 | Pentland Pl., Bear. | B10 | 6 | Polwarth St. G12 | H13 | 20 |
| Parkgrove Ct., Giff. | Q14 | 62 | Pentland Rd. G43 | P14 | 62 | Poplar Av. G11 | H12 | 19 |
| Parkgrove Ter. G3 | J15 | 35 | Pentland Rd., Chr. | F26 | 26 | Poplar Av., John. | N 1 | 44 |
| Parkgrove Ter. La. G3 | K15 | 35 | Penzance Way, Chr. | D27 | 15 | Poplar Cotts. G14 | G 9 | 18 |
| *Derby St.* | | | Peockland Gdns. | M 1 | 44 | *Dumbarton Rd.* | | |
| Parkhall Rd., Dalm. | D 6 | 4 | Peockland Pl., John. | M 1 | 44 | Poplar Dr., Dalm. | C 6 | 4 |
| Parkhall Ter., Dalm. | C 6 | 4 | Percy Dr., Giff. | R14 | 62 | Poplar Dr., Lenz. | C22 | 12 |
| Parkhead Cross G31 | L20 | 37 | Percy Rd., Renf. | K 7 | 31 | Poplar Pl., Blan. | R26 | 68 |
| Parkhill Dr. G73 | O19 | 53 | Percy St. G51 | L14 | 34 | Poplar Rd. G41 | L13 | 34 |
| Parkhill Rd. G43 | O14 | 50 | Perran Gdns., Chr. | E27 | 15 | *Urrdale Rd.* | | |
| Parkholm La. G5 | L15 | 35 | Perth Cres., Dalm. | C 5 | 4 | Poplin St. G40 | M18 | 52 |
| *Paisley Rd.* | | | Peters Ct. G20 | F14 | 20 | Porchester St. G33 | J23 | 39 |
| Parkhouse La. G4 | K18 | 36 | *Maryhill Rd.* | | | Port Dundas Rd. G4 | J17 | 36 |
| Parkhouse Path G53 | Q10 | 60 | Petershill Ct. G21 | H19 | 23 | Port St. G3 | K15 | 35 |
| Parkhouse Rd. G53 | Q 9 | 60 | Petershill Dr. G21 | H19 | 23 | Portal Rd. G13 | F11 | 19 |
| Parklands Rd. G44 | Q15 | 63 | Petershill Pl. G21 | H19 | 23 | Porterfield Rd., Renf. | J 7 | 31 |
| Parklea, Bish. | D18 | 10 | Petershill Rd. G21 | H18 | 22 | Portland Rd., Pais. | M 7 | 47 |
| *Westlands* | | | Petition Pl., Udd. | P28 | 69 | Portman Pl. G12 | J15 | 35 |
| Parklea, Bish. | D18 | 10 | Pettigrew St. G32 | L22 | 38 | *Cowan St.* | | |
| *Midcroft* | | | Peveril Av. G41 | N14 | 50 | Portman St. G41 | L15 | 35 |
| Parkmoor, Renf. | F 4 | 16 | Peveril Av. G73 | P20 | 65 | Portmarnock Dr. G23 | F14 | 20 |
| Parkneuk Rd. G43 | Q14 | 62 | Pharonhill St. G31 | L21 | 38 | Portreath Rd., Chr. | D27 | 15 |
| Parksail Dr., Renf. | F 5 | 16 | *Quarrybrae St.* | | | Portsoy Av. G13 | F 9 | 18 |
| Parksail, Renf. | F 5 | 16 | Phoenix Park Ter. G4 | J16 | 35 | Portsoy Pl. G13 | F 9 | 18 |
| Parkview Av., Lenz. | C23 | 13 | *Corn St.* | | | Portugal La. G5 | L16 | 35 |
| Parkview Ct., Lenz. | B23 | 13 | Phoenix Pl., John. | M 2 | 44 | *Bedford St.* | | |
| Parkview Dr. G33 | G24 | 25 | *Glenpatrick Rd.* | | | Portugal St. G5 | L16 | 35 |
| Parkview G78 | M07 | 42 | Phoenix Rd. G4 | J16 | 35 | *Norfolk St.* | | |
| Parkview, Pais. | N 5 | 46 | *Great Western Rd.* | | | Possil Cross G22 | H16 | 21 |
| Parliament Rd. G21 | K18 | 36 | Piccadilly St. G3 | K15 | 35 | Possil Rd. G4 | H16 | 21 |
| Parliamentary Rd. G4 | K17 | 36 | Pikeman Av. G13 | G11 | 19 | Post La., Renf. | H 8 | 17 |
| Parnie St. G1 | L17 | 36 | Pikeman Rd. G13 | G11 | 19 | Potassels Rd., Chr. | F26 | 26 |
| Parson St. G4 | K18 | 36 | Pilmuir Av. G44 | Q15 | 63 | Potter Pl. G32 | M21 | 54 |

|  | | |
|---|---|---|
| Potter St. G32 | M21 | 54 |
| Potterhill Av., Pais. | O 6 | 46 |
| Potterhill Rd. G53 | N10 | 48 |
| Powburn Cres., Udd. | O26 | 56 |
| Powfoot St. G31 | L20 | 37 |
| Powrie St. G33 | H23 | 25 |
| Preston Pl. G42 | N16 | 51 |
| Prestwick St. G53 | P10 | 60 |
| Priesthill Av. G53 | P11 | 61 |
| Priesthill Cres. G53 | P11 | 61 |
| Priesthill Rd. G53 | P10 | 60 |
| Primrose St. G14 | H11 | 19 |
| Prince Albert Rd. G12 | H13 | 20 |
| Prince Edward St. G42 | N16 | 51 |
| Prince of Wales Gdns. | F14 | 20 |
| G20 | | |
| Prince of Wales Ter. G12 | H14 | 20 |
| *Byres Rd.* | | |
| Princes Gate G73 | O19 | 53 |
| *Greenbank St.* | | |
| Princes Gdns. G12 | H13 | 20 |
| Princes Pl. G12 | H14 | 20 |
| Princes Sq., Barr. | Q 8 | 59 |
| Princes St. G73 | O19 | 53 |
| Princes Ter. G12 | H14 | 20 |
| Princess Cres., Pais. | L 7 | 31 |
| Priory Av., Pais. | K 7 | 31 |
| Priory Cotts., Blan. | R26 | 68 |
| Priory Dr., Udd. | O26 | 56 |
| Priory Pl. G13 | F11 | 19 |
| Priory Rd. G13 | F11 | 19 |
| Prosen St. G32 | M21 | 54 |
| Prospect Av. G72 | P21 | 66 |
| Prospect Av., Udd. | O27 | 57 |
| Prospect Rd. G43 | O14 | 50 |
| Prospecthill Circus G42 | N17 | 52 |
| Prospecthill Cres. G42 | O18 | 52 |
| Prospecthill Dr. G42 | O17 | 52 |
| Prospecthill Pl. G42 | O18 | 52 |
| Prospecthill Rd. G42 | O16 | 51 |
| Prospecthill Sq. G42 | O17 | 52 |
| Provan Rd. G33 | J20 | 37 |
| Provand Hall Cres., Bail. | M25 | 56 |
| Provanhill Pl. G21 | J18 | 36 |
| Provanmill Pl. G33 | H20 | 23 |
| *Provanmill Rd.* | | |
| Provanmill Rd. G33 | H20 | 23 |
| Purdon St. G11 | J13 | 34 |
| Pykestone Rd. G33 | J23 | 39 |
| | | |
| Quadrant Rd. G43 | P15 | 63 |
| Quadrant, The, Clark. | S15 | 63 |
| Quarrelton Rd., John. | N09 | 43 |
| Quarry Av. G72 | Q24 | 67 |
| Quarry Pl. G72 | P21 | 66 |
| Quarry Rd., Barr. | Q 7 | 59 |
| Quarry Rd., Pais. | N 6 | 46 |
| Quarry St., John. | M09 | 43 |
| Quarrybank, John. | N08 | 43 |
| Quarrybrae St. G31 | L21 | 38 |
| Quarryknowe G73 | O18 | 52 |
| Quarryknowe St. G31 | L21 | 38 |
| Quarrywood Av. G21 | H20 | 23 |
| Quarrywood Rd. G21 | H20 | 23 |
| Quay Rd. G73 | N19 | 53 |
| Quay Rd. N. G73 | N19 | 53 |
| Quebec Ho., Dalm. | C 5 | 4 |
| *Perth Cres.* | | |
| Queen Arc. G2 | K16 | 5 |
| *Renfrew St.* | | |
| Queen Elizabeth Av. G52 | K 9 | 32 |
| Queen Margaret Cres. | H15 | 21 |
| G12 | | |
| *Hamilton Dr.* | | |
| Queen Margaret Ct. G20 | H15 | 21 |
| Queen Margaret Dr. G12 | H14 | 20 |
| Queen Margaret Dr. G20 | H15 | 21 |
| Queen Mary Av. G42 | N16 | 51 |
| Queen Mary Av., Clyde. | E 8 | 5 |
| Queen Mary St. G40 | M18 | 52 |
| Queen Sq. G41 | N15 | 51 |
| Queen St. G1 | K17 | 36 |
| Queen St. G73 | O19 | 53 |
| Queen St., Pais. | M 5 | 46 |
| Queen St., Renf. | H 8 | 17 |
| Queen Victoria Dr. G14 | H11 | 19 |
| Queen Victoria Gate | G11 | 19 |
| G13 | | |
| Queenbank Av., Gart. | F27 | 27 |
| Queens Av. G72 | P22 | 66 |
| Queens Cres. G4 | J16 | 35 |
| Queens Cres., Bail. | L27 | 41 |
| Queens Cross G20 | H15 | 21 |
| Queens Dr. G42 | N15 | 51 |
| Queens Drive La. G42 | N16 | 51 |
| Queens Gdns. G12 | H14 | 20 |
| *Victoria Crescent Rd.* | | |
| Queens Park Av. G42 | N16 | 51 |
| Queens Pl. G12 | H14 | 20 |
| Queens Rd., John. | N 2 | 44 |
| Queensborough Gdns. | H13 | 20 |
| G12 | | |
| Queensferry St. G5 | N18 | 52 |
| *Rosebery St.* | | |
| Queenshill St. G21 | H18 | 22 |
| Queensland Ct. G52 | L11 | 33 |
| Queensland Dr. G52 | L11 | 33 |
| Queensland Gdns. G52 | L11 | 33 |
| Queensland La. E. G52 | L10 | 32 |
| *Kingsland Dr.* | | |
| Queensland La. W. G52 | L11 | 33 |
| *Queensland Dr.* | | |
| Queenslie Ind. Est. G33 | K23 | 39 |
| Queenslie St. G33 | J20 | 37 |
| Quentin St. G41 | N15 | 51 |
| Quinton Gdns., Bail. | L25 | 40 |
| | | |
| Raasay Dr., Pais. | O 5 | 46 |
| Raasay Pl. G22 | F17 | 22 |
| Raasay St. G22 | F17 | 22 |
| Rachan St. G34 | J26 | 40 |
| Radnor St. G3 | K15 | 35 |
| *Argyle St.* | | |
| Radnor St., Clyde. | D 7 | 5 |
| Raeberry St. G20 | H15 | 21 |
| Raeswood Gdns. G53 | D 9 | 48 |
| Raeswood Pl. G53 | D 9 | 48 |
| *Raeswood Dr.* | | |
| Raeswood Rd. G53 | D 9 | 48 |
| Raglan St. G4 | J16 | 35 |
| Raith Av. G44 | Q17 | 64 |
| Raithburn Av. G45 | Q17 | 64 |
| Raithburn Rd. G45 | Q17 | 64 |
| Ralston Av., Pais.& G52 | M 9 | 48 |
| Ralston Ct. G52 | M 9 | 48 |
| Ralston Dr. G52 | M 9 | 48 |
| Ralston Path G52 | M 9 | 48 |
| *Ralston Dr.* | | |
| Ralston Pl. G52 | M 9 | 48 |
| Ralston Rd., Bear. | C12 | 7 |
| Ralston St., Barr. | R 8 | 59 |
| Ralston St., Pais. | M 7 | 47 |
| *Seedhill Rd.* | | |
| Ram St. G32 | L21 | 38 |
| Rampart Av. G13 | F10 | 18 |
| Ramsay Av., John. | N09 | 43 |
| Ramsay Cres., John. | O07 | 42 |
| Ramsay Pl., John. | N09 | 43 |
| Ramsay St., Dalm. | D 6 | 4 |
| Ranald Gdns. G73 | Q20 | 65 |
| Randolph Av., Clark. | R15 | 63 |
| Randolph Dr., Clark. | R15 | 63 |
| Randolph Gdns., Clark. | R15 | 63 |
| Randolph Rd. G11 | H12 | 19 |
| Randolph Ter. G72 | P22 | 66 |
| *Hamilton Dr.* | | |
| Ranfurley Rd. G52 | L 9 | 32 |
| Rankine Pl., John. | M09 | 43 |
| *Rankine St.* | | |
| Rankine St., John. | M09 | 43 |
| Rankines La., Renf. | H 8 | 17 |
| *Manse St.* | | |
| Rannoch Av., Bish. | E19 | 11 |
| Rannoch Dr., Bear. | E13 | 8 |
| Rannoch Dr., Renf. | H 8 | 17 |
| Rannoch Gdns., Bish. | E19 | 11 |
| Rannoch Pl., Pais. | M 7 | 47 |
| Rannoch Rd., John. | N09 | 43 |
| Rannoch Rd., Udd. | N27 | 57 |
| Rannoch St. G44 | P16 | 63 |
| Ranza Pl. G33 | H20 | 23 |
| Raploch Av. G14 | H10 | 18 |
| Ratford St. G51 | K13 | 34 |
| Rathlin St. G51 | K13 | 34 |
| Ratho Dr. G21 | G18 | 22 |
| Rattray St. G32 | M21 | 54 |
| Ravel Row G31 | L20 | 37 |
| Ravelston Rd., Bear. | E12 | 7 |
| Ravelston St. G32 | L20 | 37 |
| Ravens Ct., Bish. | F18 | 22 |
| *Lennox Cres.* | | |
| Ravenscliffe Dr., Giff. | Q13 | 62 |
| Ravenscraig Av., Pais. | N 5 | 46 |
| Ravenscraig Dr. G53 | P10 | 60 |
| Ravenscraig Ter. G53 | P11 | 61 |
| Ravenshall Rd. G41 | O14 | 50 |
| Ravenstone Rd., Giff. | Q14 | 62 |
| Ravenswood Av. | O 3 | 45 |
| Ravenswood Av. G78 | O 3 | 45 |
| *Crosbie Dr.* | | |
| Ravenswood Dr. G41 | N14 | 50 |
| Ravenswood Rd., Bail. | L26 | 40 |
| Rayne Pl. G15 | D10 | 6 |
| Red Rd. G21 | H19 | 23 |
| Red Road Ct. G21 | H19 | 23 |
| Redan St. G40 | L18 | 36 |
| Redcastle Sq. G33 | J23 | 39 |
| Redford St. G33 | K20 | 37 |
| Redgate Pl. G14 | H10 | 18 |
| Redhill Rd., Cumb. | B 1 | 70 |
| Redlands La. G12 | H14 | 20 |
| *Kirklee Rd.* | | |
| Redlands Rd. G12 | H14 | 20 |
| Redlands Ter. G12 | H14 | 20 |
| Redlands Terrace La. | H14 | 20 |
| G12 | | |
| *Julian Av.* | | |
| Redlawood Pl., G72 | P25 | 68 |
| *Redlawood Rd.* | | |
| Redlawood Rd. G72 | P25 | 68 |
| Redmoss Rd., Clyde. | C 6 | 4 |
| Redmoss St. G22 | G16 | 21 |
| Rednock St. G22 | H17 | 22 |
| Redpath Dr. G52 | L10 | 32 |
| Redwood Pl., Lenz. | C22 | 12 |
| Redwood Rd., Cumb. | C 4 | 71 |
| Reelick Av. G13 | F 9 | 18 |
| Reelick Quad. G13 | F 9 | 18 |
| Regent Moray St. G3 | J14 | 34 |
| Regent Park Sq. G41 | N15 | 51 |
| Regent Park Ter. G41 | N15 | 51 |
| *Pollokshaws Rd.* | | |
| Regent Pl., Dalm. | D 6 | 4 |
| Regent Sq., Lenz. | D23 | 13 |
| Regent St., Dalm. | D 6 | 4 |
| Regent St., Pais. | L 7 | 31 |
| Regents Gate, Both. | Q27 | 69 |
| Regwood St. G41 | O14 | 50 |
| Reid Av., Bear. | C13 | 8 |
| Reid Av., Linw. | L 1 | 28 |
| Reid Pl. G40 | M18 | 52 |
| *Muslin St.* | | |
| Reid St. G40 | M18 | 52 |
| Reid St. G73 | O19 | 53 |
| Reidhouse St. G21 | H18 | 22 |
| *Muir St.* | | |
| Reids Row, Bail. | M26 | 56 |
| Reidvale St. G31 | L18 | 36 |
| Renfield St. G2 | K16 | 35 |
| Renfield St., Renf. | H 8 | 17 |
| Renfrew Ct. G2 | K16 | 35 |
| *Renfrew St.* | | |
| Renfrew La. G2 | K16 | 35 |
| *Renfield St.* | | |
| Renfrew Rd. G51 | J10 | 32 |
| Renfrew Rd., Pais. | L 6 | 30 |
| Renfrew Rd., Renf. | J10 | 32 |
| Renfrew St. G3 | J16 | 35 |
| Rennies Rd., Renf. | F 5 | 16 |
| Renshaw Dr. G52 | L10 | 32 |
| Renshaw Rd., John. | N 2 | 44 |
| Renton St. G4 | J17 | 36 |
| Renwick St. G41 | L15 | 35 |
| *Scotland St.* | | |
| Residdl Rd. G33 | G24 | 25 |
| Reston Dr. G52 | L10 | 32 |
| Revoch Dr. G13 | F10 | 18 |
| Rhannan Rd. G44 | P16 | 63 |
| Rhannan Ter. G44 | P16 | 63 |
| Rhindmuir Av., Bail. | L26 | 40 |
| Rhindmuir Rd., Bail. | L26 | 40 |
| Rhinds St., Coat. | M28 | 57 |
| Rhinsdale Cres., Bail. | L26 | 40 |
| Rhumor Gdns. G78 | N08 | 43 |
| *Ladysmith Av.* | | |
| Rhumor Gdns., John. | O08 | 43 |
| Rhymer St. G21 | J18 | 36 |
| Rhymie Rd. G32 | M23 | 55 |
| Rhynie Pl. G51 | L13 | 34 |
| Riccarton St. G42 | N15 | 51 |
| Riccartsbar Av., Pais. | M 5 | 46 |
| Richard St., Renf. | H 8 | 17 |
| Richmond Ct. G73 | O20 | 53 |
| Richmond Dr. G72 | O20 | 53 |
| *Main St.* | | |
| Richmond Dr. G73 | O20 | 53 |

| Name | Grid | Page |
|---|---|---|
| Richmond Dr., Bish. G64 | D19 | 11 |
| Richmond Dr., G73 | P21 | 66 |
| Richmond Dr., Linw. | K 1 | 28 |
| Richmond Gdns., Chr. | E25 | 14 |
| Richmond Pl. G73 | O20 | 53 |
| Richmond St. G1 | K17 | 36 |
| Richmond St., Clyde. | E 8 | 5 |
| Riddell St., Clyde. | D 8 | 5 |
| Riddon Av. G13 | F 9 | 18 |
| Riddrie Cres. G33 | K21 | 38 |
| Riddrie Knowes G33 | K21 | 38 |
| Riddrie Ter. G33 | H20 | 23 |
| *Provamill Rd.* | | |
| Riddrievale Ct. G33 | J21 | 38 |
| Riddrievale St. G33 | J21 | 38 |
| Rigby St. G32 | L20 | 37 |
| Rigg Pl. G33 | K24 | 39 |
| Rigghead Av. G67 | A 3 | 71 |
| *Roadside* | | |
| Riggside Rd. G33 | J23 | 39 |
| Riggside St. G33 | J23 | 39 |
| Riglands Way, Renf. | H 8 | 17 |
| Riglaw Pl. G13 | F10 | 18 |
| Rigmuir Rd. G51 | L11 | 33 |
| Rimsdale St. G40 | L19 | 37 |
| Ringford St. G21 | H18 | 22 |
| Ripon Dr. G12 | G13 | 20 |
| Risk St. G40 | L18 | 36 |
| Risk St., Dalm. | D 6 | 4 |
| Ristol Rd. G13 | G11 | 19 |
| *Anniesland Rd.* | | |
| Ritchie Cres., John. | M 2 | 44 |
| Ritchie St. G5 | M16 | 51 |
| River Rd. G32 | O22 | 54 |
| River Rd. Mansion-house Rd. G32 | O15 | 51 |
| Riverbank St. G43 | O14 | 50 |
| Riverford Rd. G43 | O14 | 50 |
| Riverford Rd. G73 | N20 | 53 |
| Riversdale Cotts G14 | G 9 | 18 |
| *Dumbarton Rd.* | | |
| Riversdale La. G14 | G 9 | 18 |
| *Dumbarton Rd.* | | |
| Riverside Pl. G72 | P24 | 67 |
| Riverside Rd. G43 | O15 | 51 |
| Riverview Av. G5 | L16 | 35 |
| *West St.* | | |
| Riverview Dr. G5 | L16 | 35 |
| Riverview Pl. G5 | L16 | 35 |
| *Riverview Dr.* | | |
| Roadside, Cumb. | A 3 | 71 |
| Robb St. G21 | H18 | 22 |
| Robert Burns Av., Clyde. | D 8 | 5 |
| Robert St. G51 | K13 | 34 |
| Roberton Av. G41 | N14 | 50 |
| Roberts St., Dalm. | D 6 | 4 |
| Robertson La. G2 | K16 | 35 |
| *Robertson St.* | | |
| Robertson St. G2 | K16 | 35 |
| Robertson St., Barr. | Q 7 | 59 |
| Robertson Ter., Bail. | L26 | 40 |
| *Edinburgh Rd.* | | |
| Robin Way G32 | O23 | 55 |
| Robroyston Av. G33 | H21 | 24 |
| Robroyston Rd. G33 | G21 | 24 |
| Robslee Cres., Thorn. | Q13 | 62 |
| Robslee Dr., Giff. | Q13 | 62 |
| Robslee Rd., Thorn. | R13 | 62 |
| Robson Gro. G42 | N16 | 51 |
| Rock Dr. G78 | N 7 | 42 |
| Rock St. G4 | H16 | 21 |
| Rockall Dr. G44 | Q17 | 64 |
| Rockbank Pl. G40 | L19 | 37 |
| *Broad St.* | | |
| Rockbank Pl., Clyde. | C 7 | 5 |
| *Glasgow Rd.* | | |
| Rockbank St. G40 | L19 | 37 |
| Rockburn Dr., Clark. | S14 | 62 |
| Rockcliffe St. G40 | M18 | 52 |
| Rockfield Pl. G21 | G20 | 23 |
| Rockfield Rd. G21 | G20 | 23 |
| Rockmount Av., Barr. | R 8 | 59 |
| Rockmount Av., Thorn. | Q13 | 62 |
| Rockwell Av., Pais. | O 5 | 46 |
| Roden Av. Pais. | O 3 | 45 |
| Roden Rd., Pais. | O 3 | 45 |
| Rodger Dr. G73 | P19 | 65 |
| Rodger Pl., Ruth. | P19 | 65 |
| Rodil Av. G44 | Q17 | 64 |
| Rodney St. G4 | J16 | 35 |
| Roebank Dr., Barr. | R 8 | 59 |
| Roebank St. G31 | K19 | 37 |
| Roffey Park Rd., Pais. | L 8 | 31 |
| Rogart St. G40 | L18 | 36 |
| Rogerfield Rd., Bail. | K26 | 40 |
| Rokeby Ter. G12 | H14 | 20 |
| *Great Western Rd.* | | |
| Roman Av. G15 | E10 | 6 |
| Roman Av., Bear. | C12 | 7 |
| Roman Ct., Bear. | C12 | 7 |
| Roman Dr., Bear. | C12 | 7 |
| Roman Gdns., Bear. | C12 | 7 |
| Roman Rd., Bear. | C12 | 7 |
| Roman Rd., Clyde. | C 7 | 5 |
| Romney Av. G44 | P17 | 64 |
| Rona Ter. G72 | Q21 | 66 |
| Ronaldsay Dr., Bish. | E20 | 11 |
| Ronaldsay Pl., Cumb. | D 1 | 70 |
| Ronaldsay St. G22 | F17 | 22 |
| Ronay St. G22 | F17 | 22 |
| Rooksdell Av., Pais. | N 5 | 46 |
| Rose Cotts. G13 | G12 | 19 |
| *Crow Rd.* | | |
| Rose Dale, Bish. | F19 | 23 |
| Rose Knowe G73 | N18 | 52 |
| Rose St. G3 | K16 | 35 |
| Rosebank Av., Blan. | R27 | 69 |
| Rosebank Dr. G72 | Q23 | 67 |
| Rosebank Ter., Bail. | M27 | 57 |
| Roseberry Pl., Clyde. | E 7 | 5 |
| *Kilbowie Rd.* | | |
| Rosebery Pl., Clyde. | E 7 | 5 |
| *Miller St.* | | |
| Rosebery St. G5 | N18 | 52 |
| Rosedale Av. G78 | O 2 | 44 |
| Rosedale Dr., Bail. | M25 | 56 |
| Rosedale Gdns. G20 | F14 | 20 |
| Rosefield Gdns., Udd. | O27 | 57 |
| Roselea Gdns. G13 | F12 | 19 |
| Roselea Pl., Blan. | R26 | 68 |
| Rosemount Cres. G21 | J19 | 37 |
| Rosemount St. G21 | J18 | 36 |
| Rosemount Ter. G51 | L15 | 35 |
| *Paisley Rd. W.* | | |
| Rosevale Rd., Bear. | D12 | 7 |
| Rosevale St. G11 | J13 | 34 |
| Rosewood Av., Pais. | N 4 | 45 |
| Rosewood St. G13 | F12 | 19 |
| Roslea Dr. G31 | K19 | 37 |
| Roslyn Dr., Bail. | L27 | 41 |
| Ross Av., Renf. | J 7 | 31 |
| Ross Hall Pl., Renf. | H 8 | 17 |
| Ross St. G40 | L17 | 36 |
| Ross St., Pais. | M 7 | 47 |
| Ross St., Pais. | M 7 | 47 |
| Rossendale Rd. G43 | O14 | 50 |
| Rosshall Av., Pais. | M 8 | 47 |
| Rosshill Av. G52 | L 9 | 32 |
| Rosshill Rd. G52 | L 9 | 32 |
| Rossie Cres., Bish. | F20 | 23 |
| Rosslea Dr., Giff. | R14 | 62 |
| Rosslyn Av. G73 | O19 | 53 |
| Rosslyn Rd., Bear. | C10 | 6 |
| Rosslyn Ter. G12 | H14 | 20 |
| *Horslethill Rd.* | | |
| Rostan Rd. G43 | P14 | 62 |
| Rosyth Rd. G5 | N18 | 52 |
| Rosyth St. G5 | N18 | 52 |
| Rotherwick Dr., Pais. | M 9 | 48 |
| Rotherwood Av. G13 | E11 | 7 |
| Rotherwood Av., Pais. | O 3 | 45 |
| Rotherwood La. G13 | E11 | 7 |
| *Rotherwood Av.* | | |
| Rotherwood Pl. G13 | F11 | 19 |
| Rothes Dr. G23 | E14 | 8 |
| Rothes Pl. G23 | E14 | 8 |
| Rothlinn Av., Lenz. | B24 | 13 |
| Rottenrow East G4 | K17 | 36 |
| Roual Ter., Pais. | L 7 | 31 |
| *Greenlaw Av.* | | |
| Rouken Glen Rd., Thorn.& Giff. | R12 | 61 |
| Roukenburn St. G46 | Q12 | 61 |
| Roundhill Dr., John. | M 3 | 45 |
| Rowallan Gdns. G11 | H13 | 20 |
| Rowallan La. E. G11 | H13 | 20 |
| *Churchill Dr.* | | |
| Rowallan La. G11 | H13 | 20 |
| *Churchill Dr.* | | |
| Rowallan Rd., Thorn. | R12 | 61 |
| Rowallan Ter. G33 | H22 | 24 |
| Rowan Av., Renf. | H 8 | 17 |
| Rowan Cres., Lenz. | C23 | 13 |
| Rowan Dr., Dalm. | D 6 | 4 |
| Rowan Gate, Pais. | N 6 | 46 |
| Rowan Gdns. G41 | M13 | 50 |
| Rowan Gdns. G71 | Q28 | 69 |
| Rowan Pl. G72 | P22 | 66 |
| *Allison Dr.* | | |
| Rowan Pl. G72 | P23 | 67 |
| *Caledonian Circuit* | | |
| Rowan Pl., Blan. | S26 | 68 |
| Rowan Rd. G41 | M13 | 50 |
| Rowan Rd., Cumb. | B 4 | 71 |
| Rowan Rd., Linw. | K 1 | 28 |
| Rowan St., Pais. | N 6 | 46 |
| Rowand Av. Giff. | R14 | 62 |
| Rowandale Av., Bail. | M25 | 56 |
| Rowanlea Av. G78 | O 3 | 45 |
| Rowanlea Dr., Giff. | Q14 | 62 |
| Rowanpark Dr., Barr. | P 7 | 59 |
| Rowans Gdns., Both. | Q28 | 69 |
| Rowans, The, Bish. | E18 | 10 |
| Rowantree Av. G73 | P19 | 65 |
| Rowantree Gdns. G73 | P19 | 65 |
| Rowantree Rd., John. | NO9 | 43 |
| Rowchester St. G40 | L19 | 37 |
| Rowena Av. G13 | E11 | 7 |
| Roxburgh Dr., Bear. | B12 | 7 |
| Roxburgh La. G12 | H14 | 20 |
| *Saltoun St.* | | |
| Roxburgh Rd., Pais. | O 2 | 44 |
| Roxburgh St. G12 | H14 | 20 |
| Roy St. G21 | H17 | 22 |
| Royal Bank Pl. G1 | K17 | 36 |
| *Buchanan St.* | | |
| Royal Cres. G3 | J15 | 35 |
| Royal Cres. G42 | N16 | 51 |
| Royal Exchange Bldgs. G1 | K17 | 36 |
| *Royal Exchange Sq.* | | |
| Royal Exchange Ct. G1 | K17 | 36 |
| *Queen St.* | | |
| Royal Exchange Sq. G1 | K17 | 36 |
| *Campbell St.* | | |
| Royal Inch Cres., Renf. | G 8 | 17 |
| Royal Ter. G3 | J15 | 35 |
| Royal Ter. G42 | N16 | 51 |
| *Queens Dr.* | | |
| Royal Terrace La. G3 | J15 | 35 |
| *North Claremont St.* | | |
| Royston Hill, G21 | J18 | 36 |
| Royston Rd. G21 | J18 | 36 |
| Royston Sq. G21 | J18 | 36 |
| Rozelle Av. G15 | D10 | 6 |
| Rubislaw Dr., Bear. | D12 | 7 |
| Ruby St. G40 | M19 | 53 |
| Ruchazie Pl. G33 | K21 | 38 |
| Ruchazie Rd. G32 | L21 | 38 |
| Ruchill Pl. G20 | G15 | 21 |
| Ruchill St. G20 | G15 | 21 |
| Ruel St. G44 | O16 | 51 |
| Rufflees Av., Barr. | Q 8 | 59 |
| Rugby Av. G13 | F10 | 18 |
| Rullion Pl. G33 | K21 | 38 |
| Rumford St. G40 | M18 | 52 |
| Rupert St. G4 | J15 | 35 |
| Rushyhill St. G21 | H19 | 23 |
| *Cockmuir St.* | | |
| Ruskin La. G12 | H15 | 21 |
| Ruskin Pl. G12 | H14 | 20 |
| *Great Western Rd.* | | |
| Ruskin Sq., Bish. | E19 | 11 |
| Ruskin Ter. G12 | H15 | 21 |
| Ruskin Ter. G73 | N19 | 53 |
| Russel Pl., Linw. | L 1 | 28 |
| *Gilmerton Rd.* | | |
| Russell Cres. G81 | B 6 | 4 |
| Russell Cres., Bail. | M26 | 56 |
| Russell Dr., Bear. | C12 | 7 |
| Russell Rd., Clyde. | C 6 | 4 |
| Russell St. G11 | J13 | 34 |
| *Vine St.* | | |
| Russell St., John. | M 1 | 44 |
| Russell St., Pais. | K 5 | 30 |
| Rutaerford Av., Chr. & Waterside | C25 | 14 |
| *Chryston Rd.* | | |
| Rutherford La. G2 | K16 | 35 |
| *Hope St.* | | |
| Rutherglen Rd. G5 | L17 | 36 |
| Ruthven Av., Giff. | R14 | 62 |
| Ruthven La. G12 | H14 | 20 |
| *Downside St.* | | |

| Name | Grid | Page |
|---|---|---|
| Ruthven Pl., Bish. | F20 | 23 |
| Ruthven St. G12 | H14 | 20 |
| Rutland Cres. G51 | L15 | 35 |
| Rutland La. G51 | L15 | 35 |
| *Govan Rd.* | | |
| Rutland Pl. G51 | L15 | 35 |
| Ryan Rd., Bish. | E19 | 11 |
| Ryan Way G73 | Q20 | 65 |
| Rye Cres. G21 | G20 | 23 |
| Rye Rd. G21 | G20 | 23 |
| Rye Way, Pais. | N 3 | 45 |
| Ryebank Rd. G21 | G20 | 23 |
| Ryecroft Dr., Bail. | L25 | 40 |
| Ryedale Pl., G15 | D10 | 6 |
| Ryefield Av., John. | N08 | 43 |
| Ryefield Rd. G21 | G19 | 23 |
| Ryehill Gdns. G21 | G20 | 23 |
| Ryehill Pl. G21 | G20 | 23 |
| Ryehill Rd. G21 | G20 | 23 |
| Ryemount Rd. G21 | G20 | 23 |
| Ryeside Rd. G21 | G19 | 23 |
| Rylands Av. G32 | M24 | 55 |
| Rylands Gdns. G32 | M24 | 55 |
| Rylees Cres. G52 | K 9 | 32 |
| Rylees Pl. G52 | L 9 | 32 |
| Rylees Rd. G52 | L 9 | 32 |
| Ryvra Rd. G13 | G11 | 19 |
| Sackville Av. G13 | G12 | 19 |
| Sackville La. G13 | G12 | 19 |
| *Sackville Av.* | | |
| Saddell Rd. G15 | D10 | 6 |
| St. Abbs Dr., Pais. | N 4 | 45 |
| St. Andrews Av., Bish. | E18 | 10 |
| St. Andrews Av., Both. | R28 | 69 |
| St. Andrews Cres. G41 | M15 | 51 |
| St. Andrews Cres., Pais. | J 5 | 30 |
| St. Andrews Cross G41 | M16 | 51 |
| St. Andrews Drive G41 | N14 | 50 |
| St. Andrews La. G1 | L17 | 36 |
| *Gallowgate* | | |
| St. Andrews Rd. G41 | M15 | 51 |
| St. Andrews Rd., Renf. | J 8 | 31 |
| St. Andrews Sq. G1 | L17 | 36 |
| St. Andrews St. G1 | L17 | 36 |
| St. Anns Dr., Giff. | R14 | 62 |
| St. Blanes Dr. G73 | P18 | 64 |
| St. Bothwells Cres., Pais. | N 4 | 45 |
| St. Brides Av., Udd. | O29 | 57 |
| St. Brides Rd. G43 | O14 | 50 |
| St. Brides Way, Both. | Q28 | 69 |
| St. Catherines Rd., Giff. | R14 | 62 |
| St. Clair Av., Giff. | Q14 | 62 |
| St. Clair St. G20 | J15 | 35 |
| *Woodside Rd.* | | |
| St. Conval Pl. G43 | O13 | 50 |
| *Shawbridge St.* | | |
| St. Cyrus Gdns., Bish. | E20 | 11 |
| St. Cyrus Rd., Bish. | E19 | 11 |
| St. Enoch Sq. G1 | L16 | 35 |
| St. Enoch Wynd G2 | K16 | 35 |
| *Argyle St.* | | |
| St. Fillans Rd. G33 | G23 | 25 |
| St. Georges Cross G3 | J16 | 35 |
| St. Georges Pl. G2 | J16 | 35 |
| *St. Georges Rd.* | | |
| St. Georges Rd. G3 | J16 | 35 |
| St. Germains, Bear. | D12 | 7 |
| St. Helena Cres., Clyde. | C 8 | 5 |
| St. Ives Rd., Chr. | D27 | 15 |
| St. James Av., Pais. | K 4 | 29 |
| St. James Pl., Pais. | L 6 | 30 |
| *Love St.* | | |
| St. James Rd. G4 | K17 | 36 |
| St. James St., Pais. | L 6 | 30 |
| St. Johns Ct. G41 | M15 | 51 |
| St. Johns Quad. G41 | M15 | 51 |
| St. Johns Rd. G41 | M15 | 51 |
| St. Johns Ter. G12 | J15 | 35 |
| *Southpark Av.* | | |
| St. Jospehs Pl. G40 | L18 | 36 |
| *Abercromby St.* | | |
| St. Kenneth Dr. G51 | K12 | 33 |
| St. Kilda Dr. G14 | H12 | 19 |
| St. Leonards Dr., Giff. | Q14 | 62 |
| St. Margarets Pl. G1 | L17 | 36 |
| *Bridgegate* | | |
| St. Mark St. G32 | L21 | 38 |
| St. Marnock St. G40 | L19 | 37 |
| St. Marys La. G2 | K16 | 35 |
| *West Nile St.* | | |
| St. Marys Rd., Bish. | E18 | 10 |
| St. Mirren St., Pais. | M 6 | 46 |
| St. Monance St. G21 | G18 | 22 |
| St. Mungo Av. G4 | K17 | 36 |
| St. Mungo Pl. G4 | K17 | 36 |
| St. Mungo St., Bish. | F18 | 22 |
| St. Mungos Rd. G67 | C 2 | 70 |
| St. Ninian St. G5 | L17 | 36 |
| St. Ninians Cres., Pais. | N 6 | 46 |
| *Rowan St.* | | |
| St. Ninians Rd., Pais. | N 6 | 46 |
| St. Peters La. G2 | K16 | 35 |
| *Blythswood St.* | | |
| St. Peters St. G4 | J16 | 35 |
| St. Ronans Dr. G41 | N14 | 50 |
| St. Ronans Dr. G73 | P20 | 65 |
| St. Stephens Av. G73 | Q20 | 65 |
| St. Stephens Cres. G73 | Q21 | 66 |
| St. Valleyfield St. G21 | H18 | 22 |
| *Ayr St.* | | |
| St. Vincent Cres. G3 | K14 | 34 |
| St. Vincent Cres. La. G3 | K15 | 35 |
| *Corunna St.* | | |
| St. Vincent La. G2 | K16 | 35 |
| *Hope St.* | | |
| St. Vincent Pl. G1 | K17 | 36 |
| St. Vincent St. G2 | K15 | 35 |
| St. Vincent Ter. G3 | K15 | 35 |
| Salamanca St. G31 | L20 | 37 |
| Salen St. G52 | L12 | 33 |
| Salisbury Pl. G12 | H14 | 20 |
| *Great Western Rd.* | | |
| Salisbury Pl., Dalm. | C 6 | 4 |
| Salisbury St. G5 | M16 | 51 |
| Salkeld St. G5 | M16 | 51 |
| Salmona St. G22 | H16 | 21 |
| Saltaire Av., Udd. | P28 | 69 |
| Salterland Rd. G53 | P 9 | 60 |
| Saltmarket G1 | L17 | 36 |
| Saltmarket Pl. G1 | L17 | 36 |
| *King St.* | | |
| Saltoun Gdns. G12 | H14 | 20 |
| *Roxburgh St.* | | |
| Saltoun La. G12 | H14 | 20 |
| *Ruthven St.* | | |
| Saltoun St. G12 | H14 | 20 |
| Salvia St. G72 | P21 | 66 |
| Sanda St. G20 | H15 | 21 |
| Sandaig Rd. G33 | L24 | 39 |
| Sandbank Av. G20 | G14 | 20 |
| Sandbank Dr. G20 | G14 | 20 |
| Sandbank St. G20 | G14 | 20 |
| Sandbank Ter. G20 | F14 | 20 |
| Sandeman St. G11 | J12 | 33 |
| Sandend Rd. G53 | O10 | 48 |
| Sanderling Pl., John. | O08 | 43 |
| Sandfield St. G20 | G15 | 21 |
| *Maryhill Rd.* | | |
| Sandford Gdns., Bail. | L25 | 56 |
| *Scott St.* | | |
| Sandgate Av. G32 | M23 | 55 |
| Sandhaven Rd. G53 | O10 | 48 |
| Sandholes, Pais. | M 5 | 46 |
| Sandholm Pl. G14 | G 9 | 18 |
| Sandholm Ter. G14 | G 9 | 18 |
| Sandiefauld St. G5 | M17 | 52 |
| Sandiefield Rd. G5 | M17 | 52 |
| Sandmill St. G21 | J19 | 37 |
| Sandra Rd., Bish. | E20 | 11 |
| Sandringham Dr., John. | O 1 | 44 |
| *Glamis Av.* | | |
| Sandringham La. G12 | H14 | 20 |
| *Kersland St.* | | |
| Sandwood Cres. G52 | L10 | 32 |
| *Sandwood Rd.* | | |
| Sandwood Path G52 | L10 | 32 |
| Sandwood Rd. G52 | L10 | 32 |
| Sandy Rd. G11 | J13 | 34 |
| Sandy Rd., Renf. | J 8 | 31 |
| Sandyford Pl. G3 | K15 | 35 |
| *Sauchiehall St.* | | |
| Sandyford Place La. G3 | J15 | 35 |
| *Elderslie St.* | | |
| Sandyford Rd., Renf. | K 7 | 31 |
| Sandyford St. G3 | K14 | 34 |
| Sandyhills Cres. G32 | M22 | 54 |
| Sandyhills Dr. G32 | M22 | 54 |
| Sandyhills Gro. G32 | N23 | 55 |
| *Hamilton Rd.* | | |
| Sandyhills Pl. G32 | M22 | 54 |
| Sandyhills Rd. G32 | M22 | 54 |
| Sandyknowes Rd., Cumb. | D 3 | 71 |
| Sanguhar Gdns., Blan. | R25 | 68 |
| Sanilands St. G32 | L22 | 38 |
| *Annick St.* | | |
| Sannox Gdns. G31 | K19 | 37 |
| Saracen Gdns. G22 | G17 | 22 |
| Saracen Head La. G1 | L17 | 36 |
| *Gallowgate* | | |
| Saracen St. G22 | H17 | 22 |
| Sardinia La. G12 | H14 | 20 |
| *Great George St.* | | |
| Sardinia Ter. G12 | H14 | 20 |
| *Cecil St.* | | |
| Saucel Lonend, Pais. | M 6 | 46 |
| Saucel St., Pais. | M 6 | 46 |
| Saucelhill Ter., Pais. | M 6 | 46 |
| Sauchenhall Rd., Chr. | C27 | 15 |
| Sauchiehall St. G3 | K15 | 35 |
| Saughs Av. G33 | G21 | 24 |
| Saughs Dr. G33 | G21 | 24 |
| Saughs Gate G33 | G21 | 24 |
| Saughs Pl. G33 | G21 | 24 |
| Saughs Rd. G33 | G21 | 24 |
| Saughton St. G32 | K21 | 38 |
| Savoy Arcade G40 | M18 | 52 |
| *Main St.* | | |
| Savoy St. G40 | M18 | 52 |
| Sawfield Pl. G4 | J16 | 35 |
| *Garscube Rd.* | | |
| Sawmill Rd. G11 | J12 | 33 |
| Sawmillfield St. G4 | J16 | 35 |
| Saxon Rd. G13 | F11 | 19 |
| Scadlock Rd., Pais. | L 4 | 29 |
| Scalpay Pl. G22 | F17 | 22 |
| Scalpay St. G22 | F17 | 22 |
| Scapa Dr. G23 | F15 | 21 |
| Scapa St. G40 | M19 | 53 |
| *Springfield Rd.* | | |
| Scaraway Dr. G22 | F17 | 22 |
| Scaraway Pl. G22 | F17 | 22 |
| Scaraway St. G22 | F17 | 22 |
| Scaraway Ter. G22 | F17 | 22 |
| Scarba Dr. G43 | P13 | 62 |
| Scarrell Dr. G45 | Q19 | 65 |
| Scarrell Rd. G45 | Q19 | 65 |
| Scarrell Ter. G45 | Q19 | 65 |
| Schaw Rd., Pais. | L 7 | 31 |
| Schipka Pass. G1 | L17 | 36 |
| *Gallowgate* | | |
| School Av. G72 | P22 | 66 |
| School Rd. G33 | G24 | 25 |
| School Rd., Pais. | L 9 | 32 |
| School Wynd, Pais. | L 6 | 30 |
| Schoolfield La., Bish. | E19 | 11 |
| Scioncroft Av. G73 | O20 | 53 |
| Scone St. G21 | H17 | 22 |
| Sconser St. G23 | E15 | 9 |
| Scorton Gdns., Bail. | M24 | 55 |
| Scotland St. G5 | L15 | 35 |
| Scotland St. W. G5 | L14 | 34 |
| Scotsblair Av., Lenz. | C23 | 13 |
| Scotsburn Rd. G21 | H20 | 23 |
| Scotstoun Mill Rd. G11 | J14 | 34 |
| *Patrick Bridge St.* | | |
| Scotstoun Pl. G14 | H11 | 19 |
| *Scotstoun St.* | | |
| Scotstoun St. G14 | H11 | 19 |
| Scott Av., John. | O09 | 43 |
| Scott Dr., Bear. | C11 | 7 |
| Scott Rd. G52 | K 9 | 32 |
| Scott St. G3 | J16 | 35 |
| Scott St., Bail. | M25 | 56 |
| Scott St., Dalm. | D 6 | 4 |
| Scotts Rd., Pais. | M 8 | 47 |
| Sea Path G53 | P 9 | 60 |
| Sea Pl. G53 | P 9 | 60 |
| Seafar Rd., Cumb. | D 2 | 70 |
| Seafield Dr. G73 | Q20 | 65 |
| Seaforth Cres., Barr. | Q 7 | 59 |
| Seaforth La., Chr. | E28 | 15 |
| *Burnbrae Av.* | | |
| Seaforth Rd. G52 | K10 | 32 |
| Seaforth Rd. N. G52 | K10 | 32 |
| Seaforth Rd. S. G52 | K10 | 32 |
| Seaforth Rd., Clyde. | E 7 | 5 |
| Seagrove St. G32 | L20 | 37 |
| Seamill St. G53 | P 9 | 60 |
| Seamore St. G20 | J15 | 35 |
| Searfe Av., Linw. | L 1 | 28 |
| *Killin Dr.* | | |

| | | |
|---|---|---|
| Seath Rd. G73 | N19 | 53 |
| Seath St. G42 | N17 | 52 |
| Seaward La. G41 | L15 | 35 |
| *Seaward St.* | | |
| Seaward St. G41 | L15 | 35 |
| Second Av. G33 | G22 | 24 |
| Second Av. G44 | P16 | 63 |
| Second Av., Bear. | D13 | 8 |
| Second Av., Clyde. | D 7 | 5 |
| Second Av., Lenz. | E23 | 13 |
| Second Av., Renf. | J 8 | 31 |
| Second Av., Udd. | N27 | 57 |
| Second Gdns. G41 | M13 | 50 |
| Second St., Udd. | O27 | 57 |
| Seedhill Rd., Pais. | M 6 | 46 |
| Seggielea La. G13 | G11 | 19 |
| *Helenburgh Dr.* | | |
| Seggielea Rd. G13 | G11 | 19 |
| Seil Dr. G44 | Q17 | 64 |
| Selborne Pl. G13 | G12 | 19 |
| *Selborne Rd.* | | |
| Selborne Place La. G13 | G12 | 19 |
| *Selborne Rd.* | | |
| Selborne Rd. G13 | G12 | 19 |
| Selkirk Av. G52 | M11 | 49 |
| Selkirk Av., Pais. | N 4 | 45 |
| Selkirk Dr. G73 | O20 | 53 |
| Sella Rd., Bish. | E20 | 11 |
| Selvieland Rd. G52 | L 9 | 32 |
| Semple Pl., Linw. | K 1 | 28 |
| Seres Rd., Clark. | S14 | 62 |
| Sergeantlaw Rd., Pais. | P 4 | 45 |
| Seton Ter. G31 | K18 | 36 |
| Settle Gdns., Bail. | M24 | 55 |
| Seven Sisters, Lenz. | C24 | 13 |
| Seventh Av., Udd. | O27 | 57 |
| Seyton Av., Giff. | R14 | 62 |
| Shaftesbury St., Dalm. | E 6 | 4 |
| Shafton Pl. G13 | F12 | 19 |
| Shafton Rd. G13 | F12 | 19 |
| Shaftsbury St. G3 | K15 | 35 |
| *Argyle St.* | | |
| Shaftsbury St. G3 | K15 | 35 |
| Shakespeare Av., Clyde. | D 6 | 4 |
| Shakespeare St. G20 | G15 | 21 |
| Shamrock Cotts. G13 | G12 | 19 |
| *Crow Rd.* | | |
| Shamrock St. G4 | J16 | 35 |
| Shandon St. G51 | K14 | 34 |
| *Govan Rd.* | | |
| Shandwick St. G34 | K25 | 40 |
| Shanks Av., Barr. | R 8 | 59 |
| Shanks Cres., John. | N09 | 43 |
| Shanks St. G20 | G15 | 21 |
| Shannon St. G20 | G15 | 21 |
| Shapinsay St. G22 | F17 | 22 |
| Sharp St. G51 | K13 | 34 |
| Sharrocks St. G51 | L14 | 34 |
| *Clifford St.* | | |
| Shaw Pl., Linw. | L 1 | 28 |
| Shaw St. G51 | K13 | 34 |
| Shawbridge St. G43 | O14 | 50 |
| Shawfield Dr. G5 | N18 | 52 |
| Shawfield Rd. G5 | N18 | 52 |
| Shawhill Rd. G43 | O14 | 50 |
| Shawholm Cres. G43 | O13 | 50 |
| Shawlands Arcade G41 | O15 | 51 |
| Shawlands Sq. G41 | O15 | 51 |
| Shawmoss Rd. G41 | N14 | 50 |
| Shawpark St. G20 | G15 | 21 |
| Shearer La. G5 | L15 | 35 |
| Shearer Pl. G51 | L15 | 35 |
| Sheepburn Rd., Udd. | O27 | 57 |
| Sheila St. G33 | H21 | 24 |
| Sheldrake Pl., John. | O08 | 43 |
| Shelley Ct. G12 | G13 | 20 |
| *Shelley Rd.* | | |
| Shelley Dr., Clyde. | D 7 | 5 |
| Shelley Rd. G12 | G12 | 19 |
| Shelly Dr., Udd. | Q28 | 69 |
| Sheppard St. G21 | H18 | 22 |
| *Cowlairs Rd.* | | |
| Sherbrooke Av. G41 | M14 | 50 |
| Sherbrooke Dr. G41 | M14 | 50 |
| Sherburn Gdns., Bail. | M24 | 55 |
| Sheriff Park Av. G73 | O19 | 53 |
| Sherwood Av., Pais. | L 7 | 31 |
| Sherwood Av., Udd. | P28 | 69 |
| Sherwood Dr. G46 | Q13 | 62 |
| Sherwood Pl. G15 | D10 | 6 |
| Shetland Dr. G44 | Q17 | 64 |
| Shettleston Rd. G31 | L20 | 37 |
| Shettleston Sheddings G31 | L21 | 38 |
| Shiel Ct., Barr. | P 7 | 59 |
| Shiel Rd., Bish. | E19 | 11 |
| Shieldaig Dr. G73 | Q19 | 65 |
| Shieldaig Rd. G22 | F16 | 21 |
| Shieldburn Rd. G51 | K11 | 33 |
| Shieldhall Rd. G51 | K11 | 33 |
| Shields Rd. G41 | L15 | 35 |
| Shilford Av. G13 | F10 | 18 |
| Shillay St. G22 | F18 | 22 |
| Shilton Dr. G53 | P10 | 60 |
| Shinwell Av., Clyde. | E 8 | 5 |
| Shipbank La. G1 | L17 | 36 |
| *Clyde St.* | | |
| Shiskine Dr. G20 | F14 | 20 |
| Shore St. G40 | N18 | 52 |
| Shortbridge St. G20 | G15 | 21 |
| *Shanks St.* | | |
| Shortroods Av., Pais. | K 6 | 30 |
| Shortroods Cres., Pais. | K 6 | 30 |
| Shortroods Rd., Pais. | K 5 | 30 |
| Shotts St. G33 | K23 | 39 |
| Shuna Pl. G20 | G15 | 21 |
| Shuna St. G20 | G15 | 21 |
| Shuttle La. G1 | K17 | 36 |
| *George St.* | | |
| Shuttle St. G1 | K17 | 36 |
| Shuttle St., Kilb. | M07 | 42 |
| Shuttle St., Pais. | M 6 | 46 |
| Sidelaw Av., Barr. | R 8 | 59 |
| *Ochil Dr.* | | |
| Sidland Rd. G21 | G20 | 23 |
| Sidlaw Rd., Bear. | B10 | 6 |
| Sielga Pl. G34 | K25 | 40 |
| Siemens Pl. G21 | J19 | 37 |
| Siemens St. G21 | J19 | 37 |
| Sievewright St. G73 | N20 | 53 |
| *Hunter Rd.* | | |
| Silk St., Pais. | L 6 | 30 |
| Silkin Av., Clyde. | E 8 | 5 |
| Silverburn St. G33 | K21 | 38 |
| Silverdale St. G31 | M20 | 53 |
| Silverfir St. G5 | M17 | 52 |
| Silvergrove St. G40 | L18 | 36 |
| Silverwells Cres., Both. | R28 | 69 |
| Silverwells G71 | R28 | 69 |
| *Old Mill Rd.* | | |
| Silverwells, Both. | R28 | 69 |
| Simons Cres., Renf. | G 8 | 17 |
| Simpson Ct., Udd. | P27 | 69 |
| Simpson St. G20 | H15 | 21 |
| Simshill Rd. G44 | Q16 | 63 |
| Sinclair Av., Bear. | C12 | 7 |
| Sinclair Dr. G42 | O15 | 51 |
| Sinclair St., Clyde. | F 8 | 17 |
| Singer Rd., Dalm. & Clyde. | D 6 | 4 |
| Singer St., Clyde. | D 7 | 5 |
| Sir Michael Pl., Pais. | M 5 | 46 |
| Sixth Av., Renf. | J 8 | 31 |
| Sixth St., Udd. | N27 | 57 |
| Skaethorn Rd. G20 | F13 | 20 |
| Skaterig La. G13 | G12 | 19 |
| Skaterigg Rd. G13 | G12 | 19 |
| *Crow Rd.* | | |
| Skelbo Path G34 | J26 | 40 |
| *Auchengill Rd.* | | |
| Skelbo Pl. G34 | J26 | 40 |
| Skene Rd. G51 | L13 | 34 |
| Skerray Quad. G22 | F17 | 22 |
| Skerray St. G22 | F17 | 22 |
| Skerryvore Pl. G33 | K22 | 38 |
| Skerryvore Rd. G33 | K22 | 38 |
| Skibo Dr. G46 | Q12 | 61 |
| Skibo La. G46 | Q12 | 61 |
| Skipness Dr. G51 | K12 | 33 |
| Skirsa Ct. G23 | F16 | 21 |
| Skirsa Pl. G23 | F15 | 21 |
| Skirsa Sq. G23 | F15 | 21 |
| Skirsa St. G23 | F15 | 21 |
| Skirving St. G41 | O15 | 51 |
| Skye Av. G67 | J 8 | 31 |
| Skye Cres., Pais. | O 5 | 46 |
| Skye Ct., Cumb. | D 1 | 70 |
| Skye Dr., Cumb. | D 1 | 70 |
| Skye Gdns., Bear. | C10 | 6 |
| Skye Pl., Cumb. | D 1 | 70 |
| Skye Rd. G73 | Q20 | 65 |
| Skye Rd., Cumb. | D 1 | 70 |
| Skye St. G20 | F14 | 20 |
| *Bantaskin St.* | | |
| Slakiewood Av., Gart. | F27 | 27 |
| Slatefield St. G31 | L19 | 37 |
| Sleads St. G41 | L15 | 35 |
| Sloy St. G22 | H17 | 22 |
| Smeaton St. G20 | G15 | 21 |
| Smith Cres., Clyde. | C 7 | 5 |
| Smith St. G14 | J12 | 33 |
| Smith Ter. G73 | N19 | 53 |
| Smithhills St., Pais. | L 6 | 30 |
| Smiths La., Pais. | L 6 | 30 |
| Smithy Ends, Cumb. | A 3 | 71 |
| Smithycroft Rd. G33 | J21 | 38 |
| Snaefell Av. G73 | Q20 | 65 |
| Snaefell Cres. G73 | P20 | 65 |
| Society St. G31 | L19 | 37 |
| Soho St. G40 | L19 | 37 |
| Sollas Pl. G13 | F 9 | 18 |
| Solway Pl., Chr. | E26 | 14 |
| Solway Rd., Bish. | E20 | 11 |
| Solway St. G40 | N18 | 52 |
| Somerford Rd., Bear. | E12 | 7 |
| Somerled Av., Renf. | J 7 | 31 |
| Somerset Pl. G3 | J15 | 35 |
| Somerset Place Meuse G3 | J15 | 35 |
| *Elderslie St.* | | |
| Somervell St. G72 | P21 | 66 |
| Somerville Dr. G42 | O16 | 51 |
| Somerville St., Clyde. | E 7 | 5 |
| Sorby St. G31 | L20 | 37 |
| Sorn St. G40 | M19 | 53 |
| Souter La., Clyde. | D 8 | 5 |
| South Annandale St. G42 | N16 | 51 |
| South Av., Clyde. | E 7 | 5 |
| South Av., Pais. | O 6 | 46 |
| South Av., Renf. | H 8 | 17 |
| South Bank St., Clyde. | F 8 | 17 |
| South Brook St., Clyde. | D 6 | 4 |
| South Campbell St., Pais. | M 6 | 46 |
| South Carbrain Rd., Cumb. | D 3 | 71 |
| South Carmyle Av. | O22 | 54 |
| South Chester St. G32 | L22 | 38 |
| South Cotts. G14 | J12 | 33 |
| *Curle St.* | | |
| South Croft St., Pais. | L 6 | 30 |
| *Lawn St.* | | |
| South Crosshill Rd., Bish. | E19 | 11 |
| South Deanpark Av., Udd. | R28 | 69 |
| South Douglas St., Clyde. | F 8 | 17 |
| South Dr., Linw. | L 1 | 28 |
| South Elgin Pl., Clyde. | F 8 | 17 |
| *South Elgin St.* | | |
| South Elgin St., Clyde. | F 8 | 17 |
| South Erskine Pk., Bear. | C11 | 7 |
| South Exchange Ct. G1 | K17 | 36 |
| *Queen St.* | | |
| South Frederick St. G1 | K17 | 36 |
| *Ingram St.* | | |
| South Hill Av. G73 | P20 | 65 |
| South Moraine La. G15 | E11 | 7 |
| *Moraine Av.* | | |
| South Muirhead Rd., Cumb. | B 3 | 71 |
| *Grieve Rd.* | | |
| South Park Dr., Pais. | N 6 | 46 |
| South Portland St. G5 | L16 | 35 |
| South Scott St., Bail. | M25 | 56 |
| South St. G14 | H10 | 18 |
| South Vesalius St. G32 | L22 | 38 |
| South Vw., Blan. | R26 | 68 |
| South Vw., Dalm. | D 6 | 4 |
| South Vw., Lenz. | E23 | 13 |
| *Gadloch Av.* | | |
| South Wardpark Ct., Cumb. | A 4 | 71 |
| *Wardpark Rd.* | | |
| South Wardpark Pl., Cumb. | A 4 | 71 |
| South William St., John. | N09 | 43 |
| *Floors St.* | | |
| South Woodside Rd. G4 | J15 | 35 |
| Southampton Dr. G12 | G13 | 20 |
| Southbank St. G31 | L20 | 37 |
| *Sorby St.* | | |
| Southbar Av. G13 | F10 | 18 |
| Southbrae Dr. G13 | G11 | 19 |

| Street | Grid | Pg |
|---|---|---|
| Thornwood Ter. G11 | J12 | 33 |
| Thornyburn Dr., Bail. | M26 | 56 |
| Thornyburn Pla., Bail. | M26 | 56 |
| Three Ell Rd. G51 | K14 | 34 |
| *Govan Rd.* | | |
| Threestonehill Av. G32 | L22 | 38 |
| Thrums Av., Bish. | E20 | 11 |
| Thrums Gdns., Bish. | E20 | 11 |
| Thrush Pl., John. | OO8 | 43 |
| Thrushcraig Cres., Pais. | N 6 | 46 |
| Thurso St. G11 | J14 | 34 |
| *Dumbarton Rd.* | | |
| Thurston Rd. G52 | L10 | 32 |
| Tibbermore Rd. G11 | H13 | 20 |
| Tillet Oval, Pais. | K 5 | 30 |
| Tillie St. G20 | H15 | 21 |
| Tillycairn Dr. G33 | J23 | 39 |
| Tilt St. G21 | J21 | 38 |
| Tintagel Gdns., Chr. | D27 | 15 |
| Tinto Dr., Barr. | S 8 | 59 |
| Tinto Rd. G43 | P14 | 62 |
| Tinto Rd., Bear. | C10 | 6 |
| Tinto Rd., Bish. | E20 | 11 |
| *Fintry Cres.* | | |
| Tinto Sq., Renf. | J 7 | 31 |
| *Ochil Rd.* | | |
| Tinwald Av. G52 | L 9 | 32 |
| Tinwald Path G52 | L10 | 32 |
| Tiree Av., Pais. | O 5 | 46 |
| Tiree Av., Renf. | J 8 | 31 |
| Tiree Ct., Cumb. | D 1 | 70 |
| Tiree Dr., Cumb. | D 1 | 70 |
| Tiree Gdns., Bear. | C10 | 6 |
| Tiree Rd., Cumb. | D 1 | 70 |
| Tiree St. G21 | J20 | 37 |
| Tirry Way, Renf. | J 9 | 32 |
| *Morriston Cres.* | | |
| Titwood Rd. G41 | N14 | 50 |
| Tiverton Av. G32 | M23 | 55 |
| Tobago Pl. G40 | L18 | 36 |
| Tobago St. G40 | L18 | 36 |
| Tobermory Rd. G73 | R20 | 65 |
| Todburn Dr., Pais. | O 6 | 46 |
| Todd St. G31 | K20 | 37 |
| Todholm Rd., Pais. | N 7 | 47 |
| Todholm Ter., Pais. | N 7 | 47 |
| Toll La. G51 | L14 | 34 |
| *Paisley Rd. W.* | | |
| Tollcross Rd. G31 | L20 | 37 |
| Tolsta St. G23 | E15 | 9 |
| Tontine La. G1 | L17 | 36 |
| *Bell St.* | | |
| Tontine Pl. G73 | Q21 | 66 |
| Toppersfield, John. | OO8 | 43 |
| Torbreck St. G52 | L12 | 33 |
| Torbrex Rd., Cumb. | C 3 | 71 |
| Torburn Av., Giff. | Q13 | 62 |
| Tordene Path, Cumb. | B 1 | 70 |
| *Binniehill Rd.* | | |
| Torgyle St. G23 | E14 | 8 |
| Tormore St. G51 | L11 | 33 |
| Tormusk Dr. G45 | Q19 | 65 |
| Tormusk Rd. G45 | Q19 | 65 |
| Torness St. G11 | J14 | 34 |
| Torogay Pl. G22 | F18 | 22 |
| Torogay St. G22 | F17 | 22 |
| Torogay Ter. G22 | F17 | 22 |
| Toronto Wk. G32 | O23 | 55 |
| Torphin Cres. G32 | L22 | 38 |
| Torphin Wk. G32 | L22 | 38 |
| Torr Rd., Bish. | E20 | 11 |
| Torr St. G22 | H17 | 22 |
| Torran Rd. G33 | K24 | 39 |
| Torrance Rd., Bish. | C20 | 11 |
| Torrance St. G21 | H18 | 22 |
| Torridon Av. G41 | M13 | 50 |
| Torrin Rd. G23 | E14 | 8 |
| Torrington Av., Giff. | S13 | 62 |
| Torrington Cres. G32 | M23 | 55 |
| Torrisdale St. G42 | N15 | 51 |
| Torryburn Rd. G21 | H20 | 23 |
| Torwood La., Chr. | E28 | 15 |
| *Burnbrae Av.* | | |
| Toryglen Rd. G73 | O18 | 52 |
| Toryglen St. G5 | N17 | 52 |
| Toward Rd. G33 | K23 | 39 |
| Tower Av., Barr. | Q 8 | 59 |
| Tower Cres., Renf. | J 7 | 31 |
| Tower Dr., Renf. | J 7 | 31 |
| Tower Pl., John. | N 1 | 44 |
| Tower Rd., John. | NO9 | 43 |
| Tower St. G41 | L15 | 35 |
| Tower Ter., Pais. | M 5 | 46 |
| Towerhill Rd. G13 | E11 | 7 |
| Towerhill Ter. G21 | H19 | 23 |
| *Broomfield Rd.* | | |
| Towerside Cres. G53 | N10 | 48 |
| Towerside Rd. G53 | N10 | 48 |
| Towie Pl., Udd. | P27 | 69 |
| Townhead Rd., Gart. | J28 | 41 |
| Townhead Ter., Pais. | M 5 | 46 |
| Townmill Rd. G31 | K18 | 36 |
| Townsend St. G4 | J17 | 36 |
| Tracy St. G43 | O14 | 50 |
| Tradeston St. G5 | L16 | 35 |
| Trafalgar St. G40 | M18 | 52 |
| Trafalgar St., Dalm. | D 6 | 4 |
| Trainard Av. G32 | M21 | 54 |
| Tranent Pl. G33 | K21 | 38 |
| Traquair Av. G78 | O 3 | 45 |
| Traquair Dr. G52 | M10 | 48 |
| Treeburn Av., Giff. | Q13 | 62 |
| Trees Park Av., Barr. | Q 7 | 59 |
| Trefoil Av. G41 | O14 | 50 |
| Tresta Rd. G23 | F16 | 21 |
| Trident Way, Renf. | J 8 | 31 |
| *Newmains Rd.* | | |
| Trinity Av. G52 | M11 | 49 |
| Trinity Dr. G72 | Q23 | 67 |
| Trinley Brae G13 | E11 | 7 |
| Trinley Rd. G13 | E11 | 7 |
| Tronda Pl. G33 | K24 | 39 |
| Tronda Rd. G33 | K24 | 39 |
| Trondra Path G33 | K24 | 39 |
| Trongate G1 | L17 | 36 |
| Troon St. G40 | M19 | 53 |
| Trossachs Rd. G73 | R20 | 65 |
| Trossachs St. G20 | H16 | 21 |
| Troubridge Av., John. | OO7 | 42 |
| Troubridge Cres. G78 | NO7 | 42 |
| Troubridge Cres., John. | OO7 | 42 |
| Truce Rd. G13 | F10 | 18 |
| Truro Rd., Chr. | D27 | 15 |
| Tryst Rd. G67 | C 2 | 70 |
| Tudor La. S. G14 | H11 | 19 |
| *Orleans Av.* | | |
| Tudor Rd. G14 | H12 | 19 |
| Tudor St., Bail. | M24 | 55 |
| Tufthill Av., Bish. | E18 | 10 |
| Tufthill Gdns., Bish. | E18 | 10 |
| Tullis Ct. G40 | M18 | 52 |
| Tullis St. G40 | M18 | 52 |
| Tulloch St. G44 | P16 | 63 |
| Tullochard Pl. G73 | Q20 | 65 |
| Tummel St. G33 | J21 | 38 |
| Tummel Way, Pais. | N 3 | 45 |
| Tunnel St. G3 | K15 | 35 |
| Turnberry Av. G11 | H13 | 20 |
| Turnberry Dr. G72 | P18 | 64 |
| Turnberry Gdns., Cumb. | A 2 | 71 |
| *Eastfield Rd.* | | |
| Turnberry Pl. G73 | P18 | 64 |
| Turnberry Rd., G11 | H13 | 20 |
| Turnbull St. G1 | L17 | 36 |
| Turnlaw Rd. G72 | R22 | 66 |
| Turnlaw St. G5 | M17 | 52 |
| Turret Cres. G13 | F11 | 19 |
| Turret Rd. G13 | F11 | 19 |
| Turriff St. G5 | M16 | 51 |
| Tweed Av., Pais. | N 3 | 45 |
| Tweed Cres. G33 | J21 | 38 |
| Tweed Cres., Renf. | H 9 | 18 |
| Tweed Dr., Bear. | D11 | 7 |
| Tweed Pl., John. | OO8 | 43 |
| Tweedsmuir Cres., Bear. | B12 | 7 |
| Tweedsmuir Rd. G52 | M10 | 48 |
| Tweedsmuir, Bish. | E20 | 11 |
| Tweedvale Av. G14 | G 9 | 18 |
| Tweedvale Pl. G14 | G 9 | 18 |
| Twinlaw St. G34 | J26 | 40 |
| Tylnley Rd., Pais. | L 8 | 31 |
| Tyndrum Rd., Bear. | C13 | 8 |
| Tyndrum St. G4 | J17 | 36 |
| Tyne St. G14 | J11 | 33 |
| Tynecastle Cres. G32 | K22 | 38 |
| Tynecastle Pl. G32 | K22 | 38 |
| Tynecastle St. G32 | K22 | 38 |
| Tynwald Av. G73 | Q20 | 65 |
| Uddingston Rd., Both. | Q28 | 69 |
| Uig Pl. G33 | L24 | 39 |
| Uist St. G51 | K12 | 33 |
| Ulundi Rd., John. | NO9 | 43 |
| Ulva St. G52 | L12 | 33 |
| Unden Pl. G13 | F12 | 19 |
| Underwood La., Pais. | L 5 | 30 |
| Underwood Rd. G41 | O15 | 51 |
| *Tantallon Rd.* | | |
| Underwood Rd. G73 | P20 | 65 |
| Underwood Rd., Pais. | L 5 | 30 |
| Union Pl. G1 | K16 | 35 |
| *Gordon St.* | | |
| Union St. G1 | K16 | 35 |
| Union St., Clyde. | F 8 | 17 |
| Unity Pl. G4 | J16 | 35 |
| *St. Peters St.* | | |
| University Av. G12 | J14 | 34 |
| University Gdns. G12 | J14 | 34 |
| University Pl. G12 | J14 | 34 |
| Unsted Pl., Pais. | M 7 | 47 |
| Uphall Pl. G33 | K21 | 38 |
| Upland Rd. G14 | H11 | 19 |
| Upper Bourtree Ct. G73 | Q20 | 65 |
| *Upper Bourtree Dr.* | | |
| Upper Bourtree Dr. G73 | Q19 | 65 |
| Upper Glenburn Rd., | C11 | 7 |
| Bear. | | |
| Ure Pl. G4 | K17 | 36 |
| *Montrose St.* | | |
| Urquhart Cres., Renf. | J 8 | 31 |
| Urrdale Rd. G41 | L13 | 34 |
| Usmore Pl. G33 | L24 | 39 |
| Vaila Pl. G23 | F15 | 21 |
| *Vaila St.* | | |
| Vaila St. G23 | F15 | 21 |
| Vale Wk., Bish. | F20 | 23 |
| Valetta Pl., Dalm. | D 5 | 4 |
| Valeview Ter. G42 | O16 | 51 |
| Vallay St. G22 | F17 | 22 |
| Valley Vw. G72 | P23 | 67 |
| *Caledonian Circuit* | | |
| Valleyfield St. G21 | H18 | 22 |
| Van St. G31 | L20 | 37 |
| Vancouver Pl., Dalm. | D 5 | 4 |
| Vancouver Rd. G14 | H11 | 19 |
| Vanguard St., Clyde. | E 8 | 5 |
| Vanguard Way, Renf. | J 8 | 31 |
| Varna La. G14 | H12 | 19 |
| Varna Rd. G14 | H12 | 19 |
| Veitchs Ct., Clyde. | C 6 | 4 |
| *Dumbarton Rd.* | | |
| Vennacher Rd., Renf. | H 7 | 17 |
| Vennard Gdns. G41 | N15 | 51 |
| Vere St. G22 | H17 | 22 |
| Vermont Av. G73 | O19 | 53 |
| Vermont St. G41 | L15 | 35 |
| Vernon Dr., Linw. | L 1 | 28 |
| Verona Av. G14 | H11 | 19 |
| Vesalius St. G32 | L22 | 38 |
| Vicarfield Pl. G51 | K13 | 34 |
| *Vicarfield St.* | | |
| Vicarfield St. G51 | K13 | 34 |
| Vicarland Pl. G72 | Q22 | 66 |
| Vicarland Rd. G72 | P22 | 66 |
| Vicars Wk. G72 | P22 | 66 |
| Victoria Circus G12 | H14 | 20 |
| Victoria Cres. G12 | H14 | 20 |
| *Dowanside Rd.* | | |
| Victoria Cres. La. G12 | H14 | 20 |
| *Victoria Crescent Rd.* | | |
| Victoria Cres. Rd. G12 | H14 | 20 |
| Victoria Cross G42 | N16 | 51 |
| *Victoria Rd.* | | |
| Victoria Dr. E., Renf. | J 8 | 31 |
| Victoria Dr., Renf. | H 7 | 17 |
| Victoria Park Corner | H11 | 19 |
| G14 | | |
| Victoria Park Dr. N. G14 | H12 | 19 |
| Victoria Park Dr. S. G11 | H11 | 19 |
| Victoria Park Gdns. N. | H12 | 19 |
| G11 | | |
| Victoria Park Gdns. S. | H12 | 19 |
| G11 | | |
| Victoria Park La. N. G14 | H11 | 19 |
| *Westland Dr.* | | |
| Victoria Park La. S. G14 | H11 | 19 |
| *Westland Dr.* | | |
| Victoria Park St. G14 | H11 | 19 |
| Victoria Rd. G33 | G23 | 25 |
| Victoria Rd. G42 | N16 | 51 |
| Victoria Rd. G73 | P19 | 65 |
| Victoria Rd., Barr. | Q 7 | 59 |
| Victoria Rd., Lenz. | D23 | 13 |
| Victoria Rd., Pais. | N 5 | 46 |
| Victoria St. G73 | O19 | 53 |

# Personal Information

| Name | Address | Tel. No. | Notes |
|------|---------|----------|-------|
| | Post Code | | |
| | Post Code | | |
| | Post Code | | |
| | Post Code | | |
| | Post Code | | |
| | Post Code | | |
| | Post Code | | |
| | Post Code | | |
| | Post Code | | |
| | Post Code | | |

# Personal Information

| Name | Address | Tel. No. | Notes |
|------|---------|----------|-------|
|      | Post Code |        |       |
|      | Post Code |        |       |
|      | Post Code |        |       |
|      | Post Code |        |       |
|      | Post Code |        |       |
|      | Post Code |        |       |
|      | Post Code |        |       |
|      | Post Code |        |       |
|      | Post Code |        |       |
|      | Post Code |        |       |

# Personal Information

| Name | Address | Tel. No. | Notes |
|------|---------|----------|-------|
| | Post Code | | |
| | Post Code | | |
| | Post Code | | |
| | Post Code | | |
| | Post Code | | |
| | Post Code | | |
| | Post Code | | |
| | Post Code | | |
| | Post Code | | |
| | Post Code | | |

# Personal Information

| Name | Address | Tel. No. | Notes |
|------|---------|----------|-------|
| | Post Code | | |
| | Post Code | | |
| | Post Code | | |
| | Post Code | | |
| | Post Code | | |
| | Post Code | | |
| | Post Code | | |
| | Post Code | | |
| | Post Code | | |
| | Post Code | | |

# Personal Information

| Name | Address | Tel. No. | Notes |
|---|---|---|---|
| | Post Code | | |
| | Post Code | | |
| | Post Code | | |
| | Post Code | | |
| | Post Code | | |
| | Post Code | | |
| | Post Code | | |
| | Post Code | | |
| | Post Code | | |
| | Post Code | | |

# Personal Information

| Name | Address | Tel. No. | Notes |
|------|---------|----------|-------|
| Brian & Wendy Fidler, Broompark, Liberton Drive, Edinburgh Post Code EH16 6HT | | 031-666-1346 | Through un-made road of park) garden centre/holiday place). About 1 mile off main road. |
| Post Code | | | |
| Post Code | | | |
| GLASGOW Post Code | | | |
| Kelt Hatcho, Food & Beverdge Hospitality Inn, Post Code | | Manager, | |
| IRVINE, Post Code | | | |
| Post Code | | | |
| Post Code | | | |
| Post Code | | | |
| Post Code | | | |